DATE			

CHARLES M. RUSSELL

PAINTINGS OF THE

Old American West

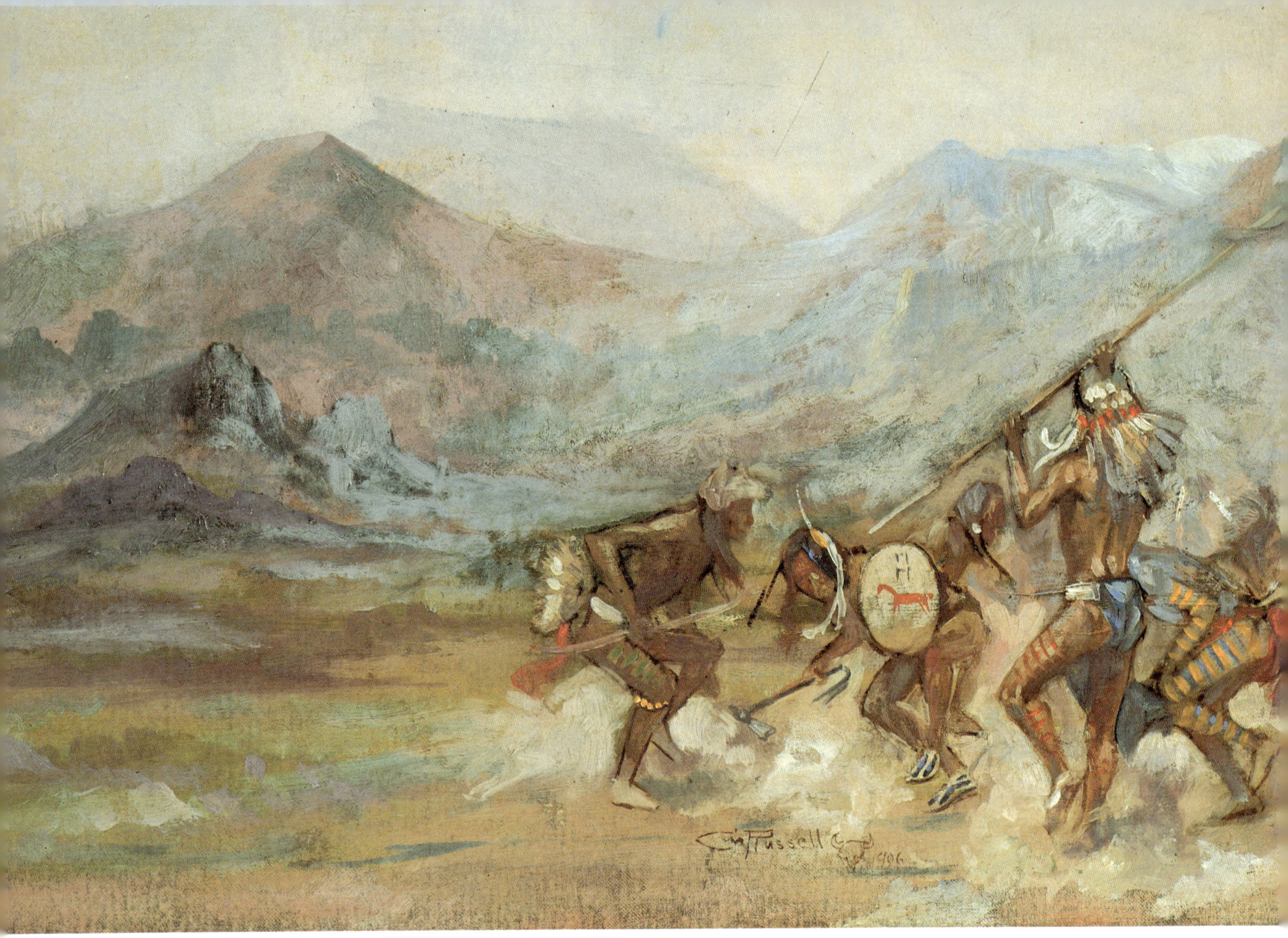

CHARLES

Paintings of the

INTRODUCTION AND COMMENTARIES BY

LOUIS CHAPIN

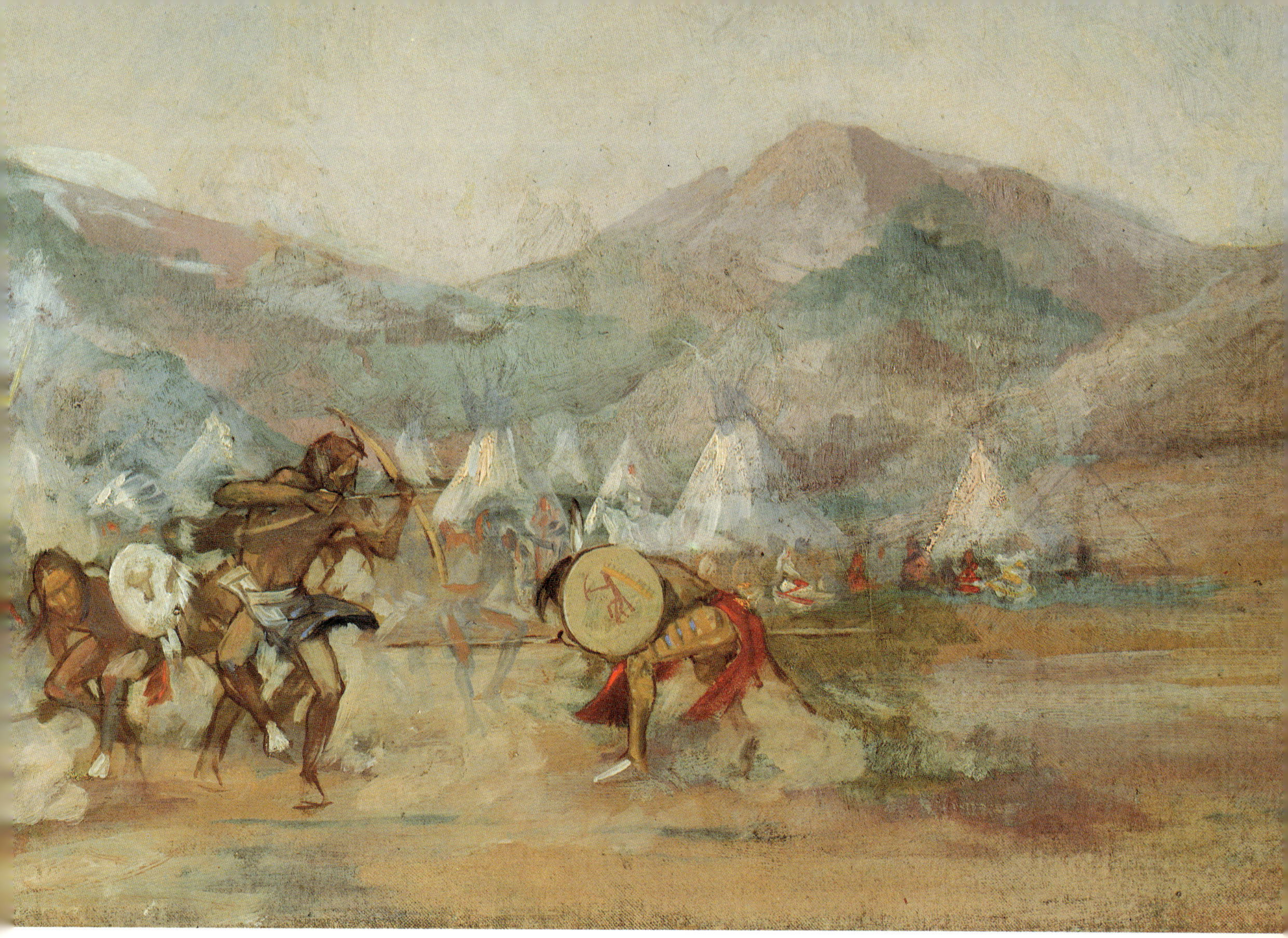

M. RUSSELL

Old American West

AN Artabras BOOK

CROWN PUBLISHERS, INC. NEW YORK, N.Y.

On the JACKET:
Indians Attacking
Commentary on page 138

On the TITLE PAGE:
Detail of *The Indian War Dance,*
Commentary on pages 134-135

Library of Congress Cataloging in Publication Data

Russell, Charles Marion, 1864-1926.
Charles M. Russell paintings of the old American West.
"An Artabras book."
1. Russell, Charles Marion, 1864-1926. 2. The West in art. 3. The West—History. I. Chapin, Louis. II. Title.
ND237.R75A4 1978a 759.13 78-16730
ISBN 0-517-53546-7

 Printed and bound in Japan

CONTENTS

INTRODUCTION

by LOUIS CHAPIN

"CHARLIE RUSSELL? OH YES," we remember conveniently, "He was the cowboy artist." So he was —as well, for instance, as being a raconteur of such prodigious gifts that when he and his friend Will Rogers were in the same room, it was hoped that Russell would tell the stories. But why "the" cowboy artist? Do we mean he was the only one? Of course not. We could use the term for any number of people ranging from Frederic Remington to Harry Jackson, and still with the definite article. Yet to anyone who has moved among and meditated among these oils and watercolors from the Amon Carter Museum, Russell seems to invite the definite article with special naturalness and authenticity. This may be, in part, because the other two words in the designation seem so admirably integrated in his life. He was no more simply an artist who found the Old West a saleable subject than he was simply a cowboy who found he could draw, paint, and model. As artist and cowboy, he was one wise man, bound together by his love for both. But not, of course, instantly. He grew that way.

Charles Marion Russell was born on March 19, 1864, near St. Louis, to a family of some prominence in business and public affairs. His father's family-owned firm was a major manufacturer of firebrick. A great-grandfather, Silas Bent, had been in charge of surveying the Louisiana Territory and was later an eminent justice; and four remarkable great-uncles, Charles (appointed the first American governor of New Mexico), William (who married happily into the Cheyennes), George, and Robert Bent, had been fur traders on the upper Missouri and builders of Bent's Fort on the Arkansas in 1828. So young Charlie had deep ties with, and an insatiable interest in, the West, which did nothing for his formal education. His lively enjoyment of drawing and modeling did little more, though it was prompted from infancy by characters in the Bible his mother read aloud.

Other parental contributions included a beloved pony, a sizable amount of patience, and the eventual decision to send their restless sixteen-year-old out to Montana Territory under the assumption (magnificently unfounded) that the privations of the life there would hurry him home wiser and more tractable, ready to step into the family business.

His first job in the Judith Basin was herding sheep for a friend of his father's, and it was as disastrous as it was meant to be. But Charlie soon found a providentially understanding friend and mentor in a solitary hunter, trapper, and ex-prospector called Jake Hoover, who kept him and his art going until Charlie's first ranch job as "nighthawk," watching the cowboys' horses while their owners slept.

None of the jobs that followed, including night-herding cattle, measured up to his idyllic anticipations as a St. Louis teenager. Montana was still rough country and the work was hard; the last big Indian wars were fresh in memory, outlaws and hostile Indians were in the land, not to mention bears and wolves. But "Kid" Russell seemed to belong, as an allegedly inept cowpoke who made friends everywhere and regaled them with the stories he'd learned from Hoover, and with his own. He belonged even then as recorder of a vanishing world—many of the images and incidents being stashed away in his extraordinary memory to be taken out and painted years later, when the colors were brighter, rangier, and more fluently applied. He looked and acted like a somewhat frowzy drifter, but still as though there were a kind of plan behind his drifting, drawing and drawling his way from job to job, cowtown to cowtown, selling his art for a pittance if at all, mostly giving it away.

The plan came into sharper focus during the savage winter of 1887, when his quick sketch of an emaciated frozen steer dramatized the cattlemen's losses, found him an instant patron in Utica saloon-keeper James R. Shelton and gave him a sudden new notoriety; and it shifted into a different focus a year later during his months with the Blackfeet in Canada, storing Indian images and Indian ideas that would nourish his work from then on.

The most decisive sharpening of plan, however, resulted from his marriage in 1896 to Nancy Cooper, scarcely more than half his age but destined to be a powerful influence in ordering and systematizing his career. Charlie was selling more widely than before, but mostly at prices in the ten to twenty-five dollar range. Nancy, recognizing his gifts *and* the market for them, soon recognized (under pressure of their new household expenses in Cascade, Montana, and later in Great Falls) her own gifts at negotiating sales. Prices began rising, reaching in the course of time into the thousands and tens of thousands of dollars. On a first foray into New York in 1903 they sold few paintings but did receive magazine and book assignments for Russell the illustrator—who was also, under Nancy's firm encouragement, starting to become Russell the author. It took all of Nancy's considerable determination to keep Charlie working regular hours in his log-cabin studio on the Great Falls property, to keep his barroom sessions with old cronies down to a minimum, and to keep fancier fees flowing back through those doors that Charlie's work and her insistence were opening up.

But she succeeded, and during these turn-of-the-century years Charlie was producing as he perhaps never would have otherwise, out of his own fully articulated memories of the West long gone. Later Nancy was to find and develop new customers from the Hollywood film colony such as Will Rogers and Douglas Fairbanks. Meanwhile she was cultivating an international clientele. In 1914 came two shows in London, where the artist himself, his boots and red sash, his knowledgeable, drawled commentaries, were as much of an exhibit —and as well liked—as the art.

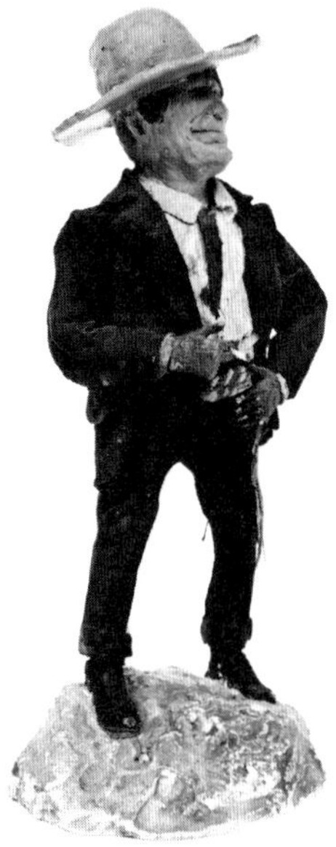

CHARLIE HIMSELF
Wax on Cloth
11¾ × 5¼"

Recognition grew steadily, even back in Montana, which in 1911 had commissioned a big mural for the State Capitol. The "Rawhide Rawlins" stories sold well, as a vehicle for Charlie's own yarns in the insistently misspelled, misgrammared jargon without which the author apparently didn't recognize his own voice, though he was quite capable of "correct usage." This style was not just part of a public image; he used it also in those letters to his closest friends which he so often graced with humorous but finely finished watercolors.

After 1919, part of each winter was spent in California, and shortly before Charlie's death in 1926 a big new house had been built by Nancy's initiative on the outskirts of Pasadena. Charlie never lived there. It would have been hard to imagine the big part of him that still made its spiritual home out on the free range ever settling into a suburban, pueblo-style house of stucco.

Is this to say that Charlie Russell lived mainly in his earliest cowboy past when, in his own words and spelling, "baring the Indians an a few scattered whites the country belonged to God?" Yes, to an extent. He went on in that letter to lament that "now the real estate man an nester have got moste of it grass side down . . . but thank God I was here first." And in another, to fellow Western artist Edward Borein, he mused, "Lonesumniss makes strong friends of Shy strangers," and wrote of "this big camp where the lodges hide the Sun and its people rube shoulders but do not speek."

He lived in the past to the extent that a historian must live in the past. His work as artist-historian was there, done with the relish of an unregenerate cowboy and with an incredible grasp of his visual language. A critic can look at these paintings without condescension, finding an artist who taught himself to paint with color, to excavate space with line, to compose action with irrepressible rhythm. In a more-distant age and world Giotto painted out of the past as well, and told stories: Like Russell he staged complete dramas with scene, plot, actors; and he, also, rejoiced in humanity. The comparison seems to me not wholly far-fetched; nor, if we were to include some of the line drawings and those modelings of grinning Indians into which Russell spilled his marvelous sense of irony, would be a reference to Daumier.

Furthermore, in his capacious way, Russell also lived and loved in the present. When he died, the humorist Irvin S. Cobb paid ardent tribute to "the spirit of the man, the essence of him . . . a keen but gentle philosophy, a gorgeous darting wit which tickled but never stung; a lover of natural things and of genuine things; a lover of friendships and of children, and of horses and dogs—yes, and underdogs; a genius whose culture came not out of books but out of the heart of a born gentleman."

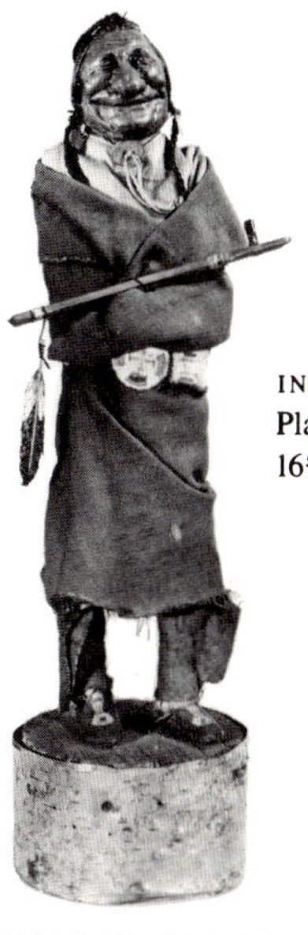

INDIAN BRAVE
Plaster, Wood and Cloth
16⅝ × 4⅝″

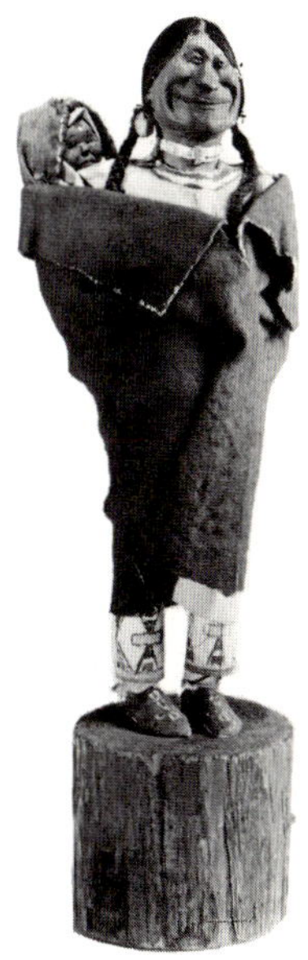

INDIAN SQUAW AND PAPOOSE
Plaster, Wood and Cloth
16¼ × 3⅞″

In at least one way, too, he was a man of not only the present but the future. For most of Russell's contemporaries, the American Indian—however he might be sentimentalized at a safe distance—was a lesser specimen of humanity, usefully and logically replaced on this continent by the white immigrant. Charlie Russell knew him and showed him as a deeply skilled and perceptive human being, with certain unique environmental gifts and a unique dignity. It may be that this artist's strongest meaning for the future has to do with his grasp of the Indian past.

If one is inclined to shrink Charles M. Russell conveniently into one stereotype or another—heart-of-gold type, clever-cowboy type, mere-illustrator type: go and look again at the build and range and language of the painting itself. *Loops and Swift Horses Are Surer than Lead,* maybe. Or *Wild Horse Hunters.* Or pick your own. You may find yourself thinking with an echo of Charlie: "Thank God he was there first."

CHARLES M. RUSSELL

PAINTINGS OF THE

Old American West

Indians Hailing Immigrants

c. 1890 • 16⅜ × 23⅜ in. • Watercolor on paper.

As an artist whose love of the Northwest warmly embraced its original inhabitants, Charles Russell gave as much attention to the friendliness and magnanimity of Indians as he did to their ferocity when aroused to battle. The scenes of the latter, generally showing intertribal war, are naturally at a high pitch of excitement. Yet the more peaceful moments are no less alive with interest.

In the foreground here is a cluster of Assiniboin Indians. They are members of a Siouan buffalo-hunting tribe, which during the middle years of the century had migrated west toward the Saskatchewan prairies, just over the border from Montana Territory.

They are apparently returning from a trading expedition to Hudson's Bay, wearing the brilliantly colored "capotes," or blanket coats, which they have received there in exchange for furs. The distant party, as Frederic G. Renner points out in his monograph on the artist, was probably mistaken for immigrants by someone who needed to come up with a title for the painting; most likely they were half-breeds, using typical Red River carts that had been introduced early in the century by the Hudson's Bay Company. In any case, it is the kind of encounter that carried great appeal for Russell, warming an otherwise lonely land with hospitality and humanity. He gives articulacy to the communication through his characteristically tight, brisk rhythm of horses and riders.

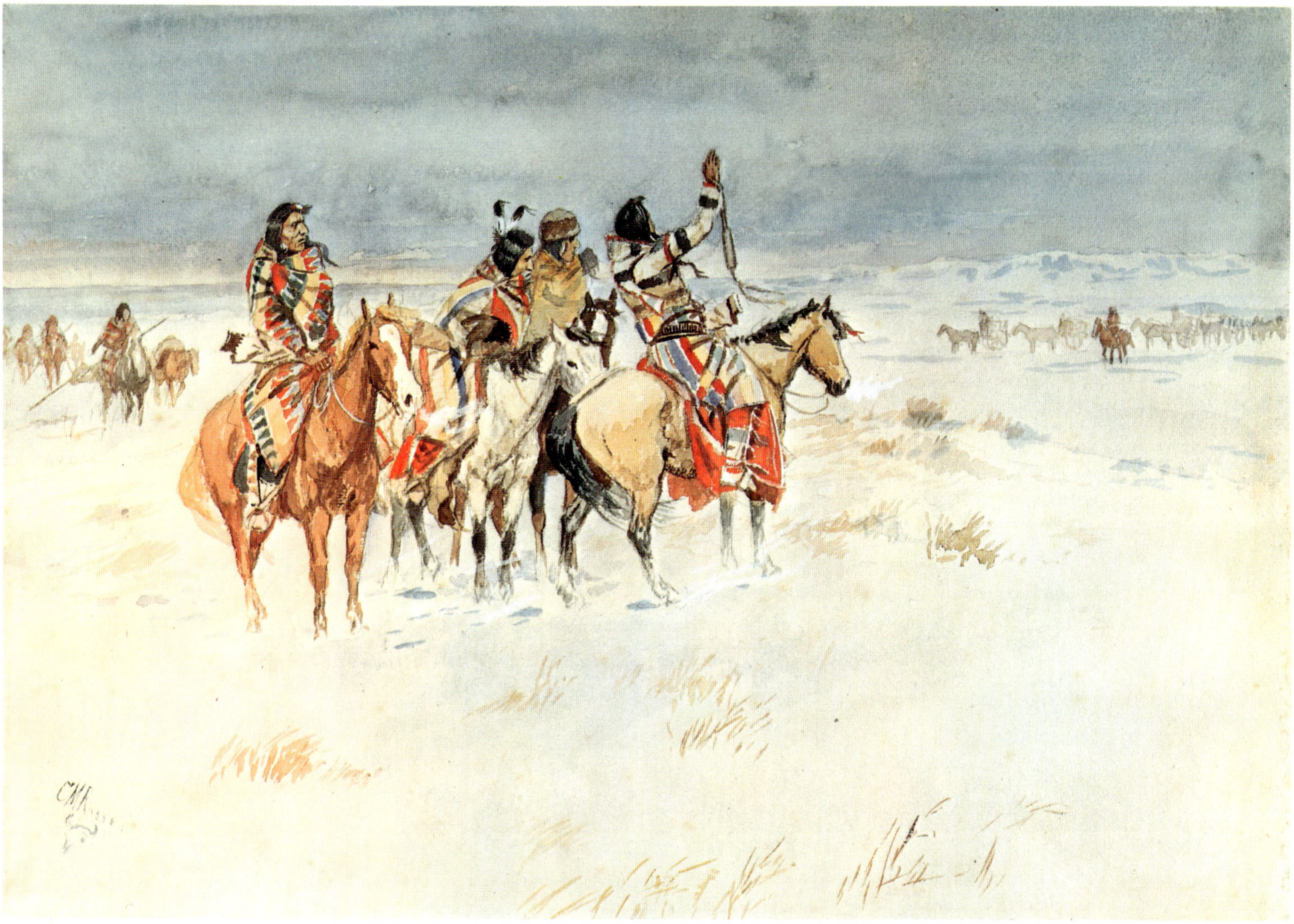

Shooting a Spy

c. 1888 • 29⅜ × 48 in. • Oil on canvas.

RUSSELL WAS ABOVE ALL a painter of human events. While he gave close, expert, and sometimes quite laborious attention to particulars of landscape, the natural surroundings rarely became the entire subject. Even in their hugeness and wildness they simply fed into the human drama.

This painting, for a time, was an exception. It was begun as a dark, forbidding expanse of Montana Badlands, a kind of stage set against which Russell planned to paint his complete moment of drama in the form of these fatally opposed Indians.

But before completing the painting, he was obliging his friend Mrs. Nat Collins, "The Cattle Queen of Montana," with a set of three illustrations for her autobiography, and he had already painted two. One day Mrs. Collins saw the unpopulated landscape and decided that it would be ideal for the third painting. Russell objected that it was unfinished and that he had other ideas for it. But the lady was not to be put off, and he reluctantly allowed her to publish the picture under the title, "A View of the Badlands," before completing it with his three Indians.

As for the Badlands themselves, Red Bird, an old chief of the Mandan tribe, told a newspaper reporter in 1884 that the then-barren countryside of jagged, rocky buttes and tree-covered ridges had once been a high tableland spread with rich pastures and forests, abounding in game—the peaceful hunting grounds of many tribes. But a fierce mountain tribe had taken possession, keeping all others away, and at last the Great Spirit had shaken the earth in his wrath, scorching and upheaving the land and wreaking desolation on the haughty tribe, of which not one member was left alive.

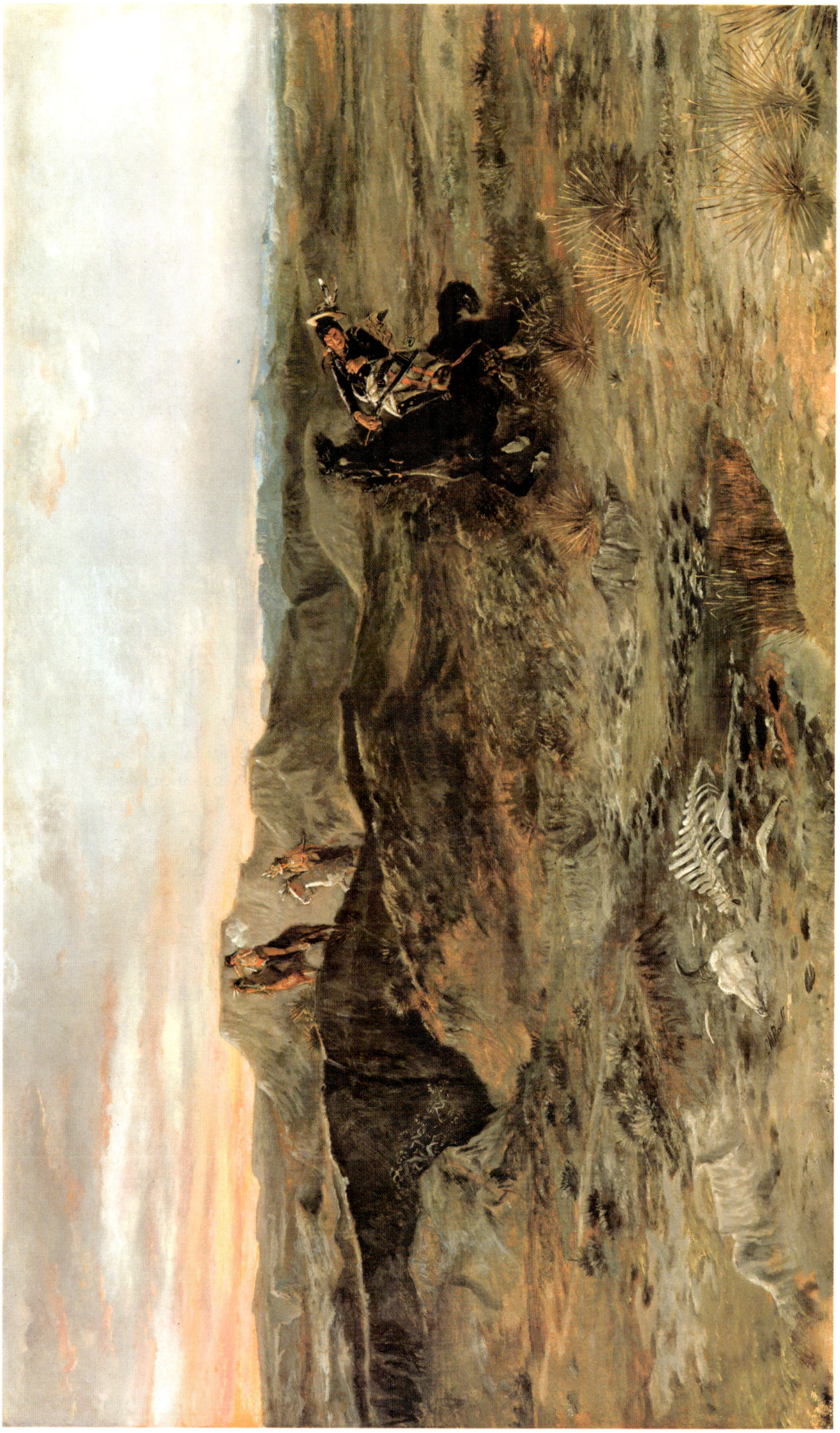

Smoke Signal

1896 • 14¼ × 21 in. • Watercolor on paper.

As a means of communication, smoke signals worked for the Indian over far greater distances than voices or waving arms. (And they were quicker, sometimes, than telegraph: Pawnee Indians far distant from Little Bighorn told their agent about Custer's total defeat ten days before he heard of it through any other means.) Through the controlling of rising puffs with a blanket, a variety of messages could be sent and received by prearrangement, and even with some secrecy if a combustible was used that produced pale smoke. One puff was translated "An enemy is near"—useful in emergencies for its quickness, though when the danger was great two groups of three puffs were used. Two single puffs, meaning "We are camping here," had to be answered with caution, for they might be luring the unwary into an enemy ambush.

Smoke signals served usefully both in the hunt and in war; the low profile of men and horses here indicates the latter situation. Whatever the case, the distance between the central height and the answering signal near the right margin has provided Russell with a spaciously communicative subject, and one of which he could take full advantage.

The sender and his message are backed up compositionally by three groupings: the gentle huddle of horses to the left; the more active trio of Indians nearer the center; and the culminating sequence of three big rocks. These last, in their more abstract form, start a kind of rhythmic impulsion that climbs up to the main rock and helps lift the message into space.

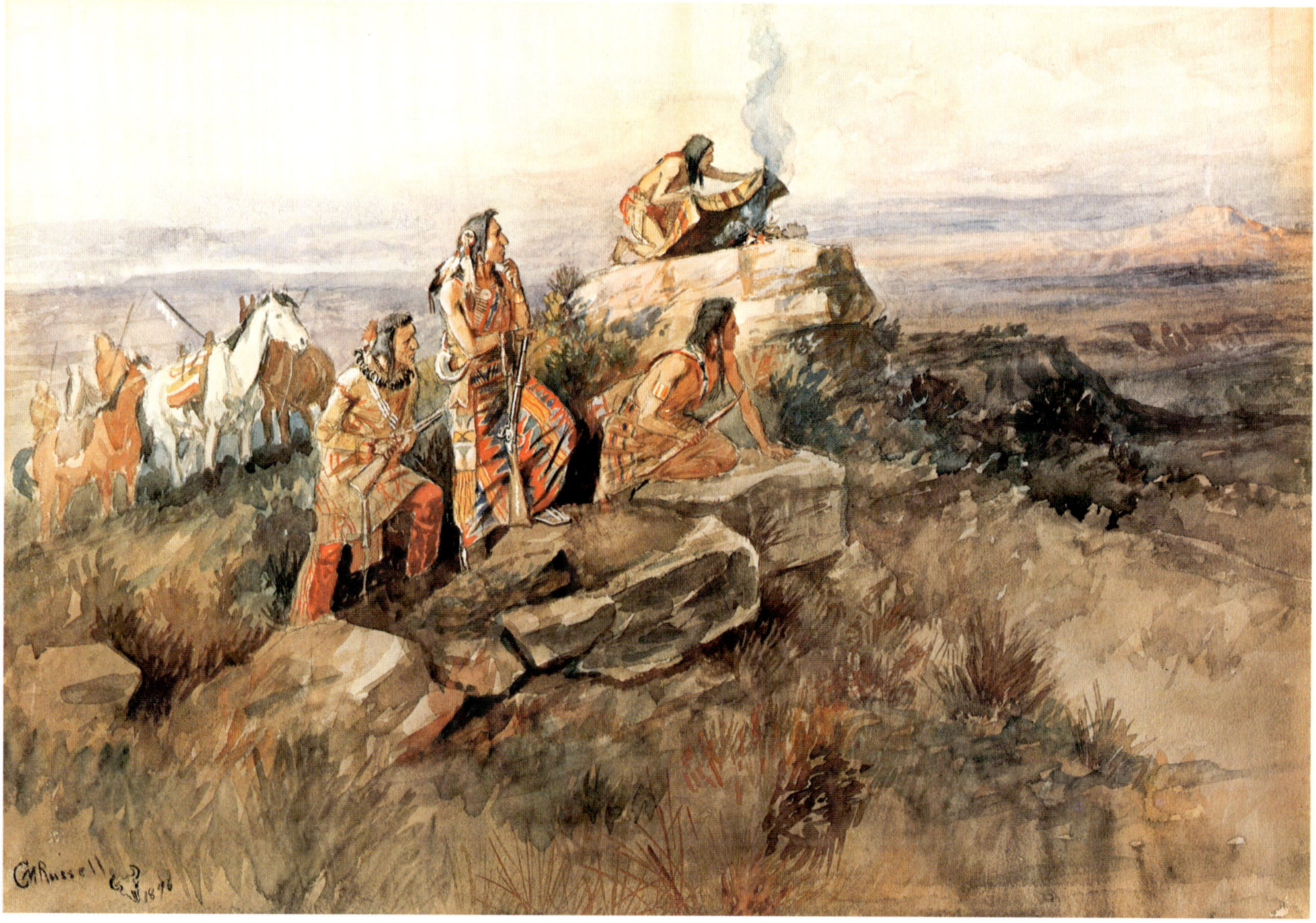
CMRussell
1896

Watching for the Smoke Signal

1907 • 21⅞ × 32 in. • Watercolor on paper.

HERE WE ARE on the receiving end of a signaling operation, one that evidently does not require two-way communication. But the watching is so intent that these Indians—and even two of their animals—seem to be listening as well.

This time we are given only a hint of the height and space involved, through a small patch of far hills to the left. Yet the feeling of distance behind us is expansive, and Russell has brought it off again through not only the gazing of his Indians but also his intuitive gift for composition. The outline of the figures is concave, from the forward-thrust head of the standing brave to the outstretched leg of the one seated to the left. The group's compact shape as a receiver—almost like a cup lying on its side—is lent intensity by the sharp diagonal of the lance. So full of meaning is the left-hand area of his painting that Russell decided to put his signature, against his usual practice, to the right. It might otherwise have been an intrusion.

The horse nearest to us, by the way, is an Appaloosa, a breed generally associated with the Nez Percé Indians across the Rockies, and so perhaps in this instance stolen from them. The other horses are Montana's more customary pintos.

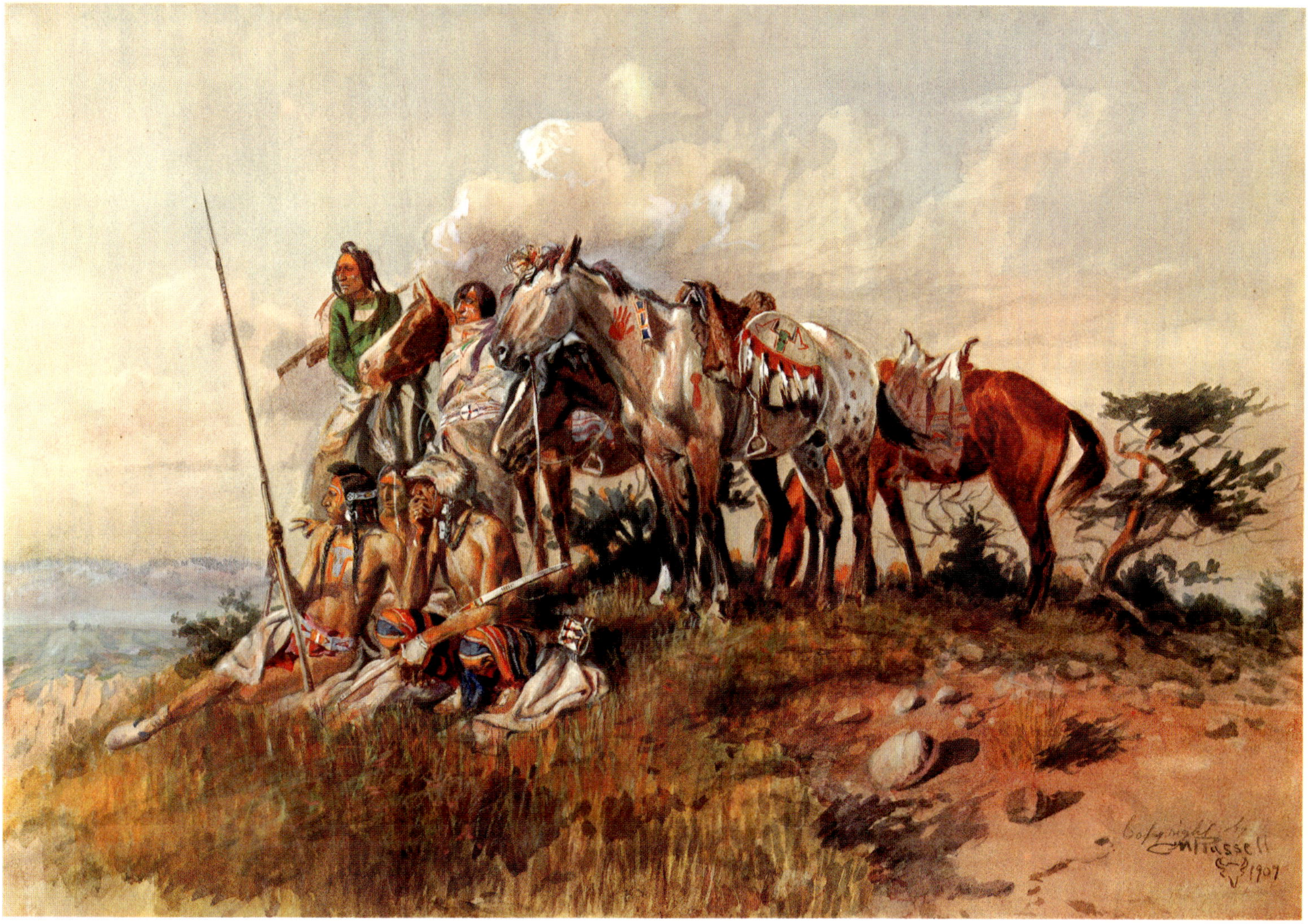
Copyright by
CM Russell
1907

Indian Signalling

1901 • 10⅛ × 14⅛ in. • Watercolor on paper.

Russell's paintings are consistent above all in their convincing, deft realism and in their sense of the Montana scene expansively surrounding some human event. And quite often the event itself, even though it may involve (as here) only one visible participant, will take in reaches of Northwest country far beyond the picture frame.

Because this Indian is a scout, he immediately implies the existence of fellow tribesmen at war. And because he is signalling to them, his message very likely has to do with the whereabouts and movements of that other tribe they are fighting.

The artist encourages our imagination to fill out the full range of the larger picture, first of all through the explicit vitality and implicit resourcefulness of this muscular brave and his vivid, mettlesome horse. Then, after partly encircling him with tightly repeated accents of brush and stone, the artist gets out of the way, so to speak, with a landscape whose character and extent are hinted at only in the most subtle terms. So there is nothing to distract us in our own communication with and concerning those invisible tribes.

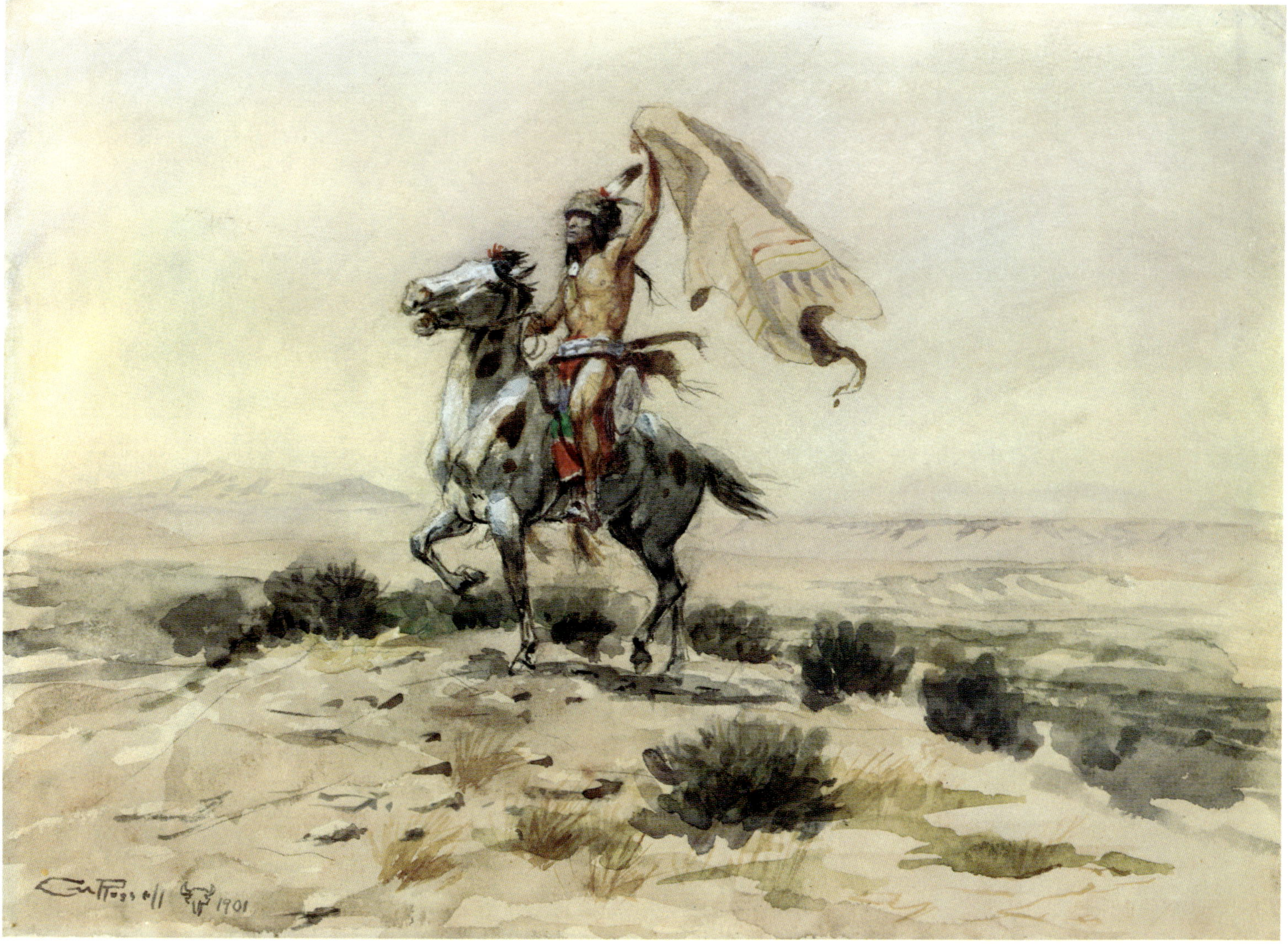
CMRussell 1901

Approach of the White Men

1897 • 17¾ × 23⅝ in. • Oil on canvas.

To VISUALIZE, as a native American, the first appearance of white foreigners on one's own homeland, requires of a non-Indian a conscious and careful act of the imagination. In a time still close to the "Indian troubles," this had to mean stripping away the stereotyped view of the "Red man" as either servile or hostile, either nobly or brutally "savage." It meant knowing him, instead, as a human being who was often forced to fit such stereotypes by the ignorant behavior of the white man himself.

Russell had discovered this at first hand, during his months of life with the Blackfoot Indians of Alberta. So he shows his subjects here as not particularly fearing or hating the strangers who have come into sight just over our right shoulder. On the contrary, these men will be glad, we are led to assume, to look over the white strangers' wonderful hardware and dry goods, and to trade them for furs. In their individual ways, the Indians are understandably curious, speculative, amazed yet noncommittal, watchful for any cue as to their next move. They are ready to be the traders, helpers, providers, and guides that so many became.

The artist, through the respect and affection that speaks so naturally here, seems to invite the white viewer to experience freshly his or her own "approach to the Indians."

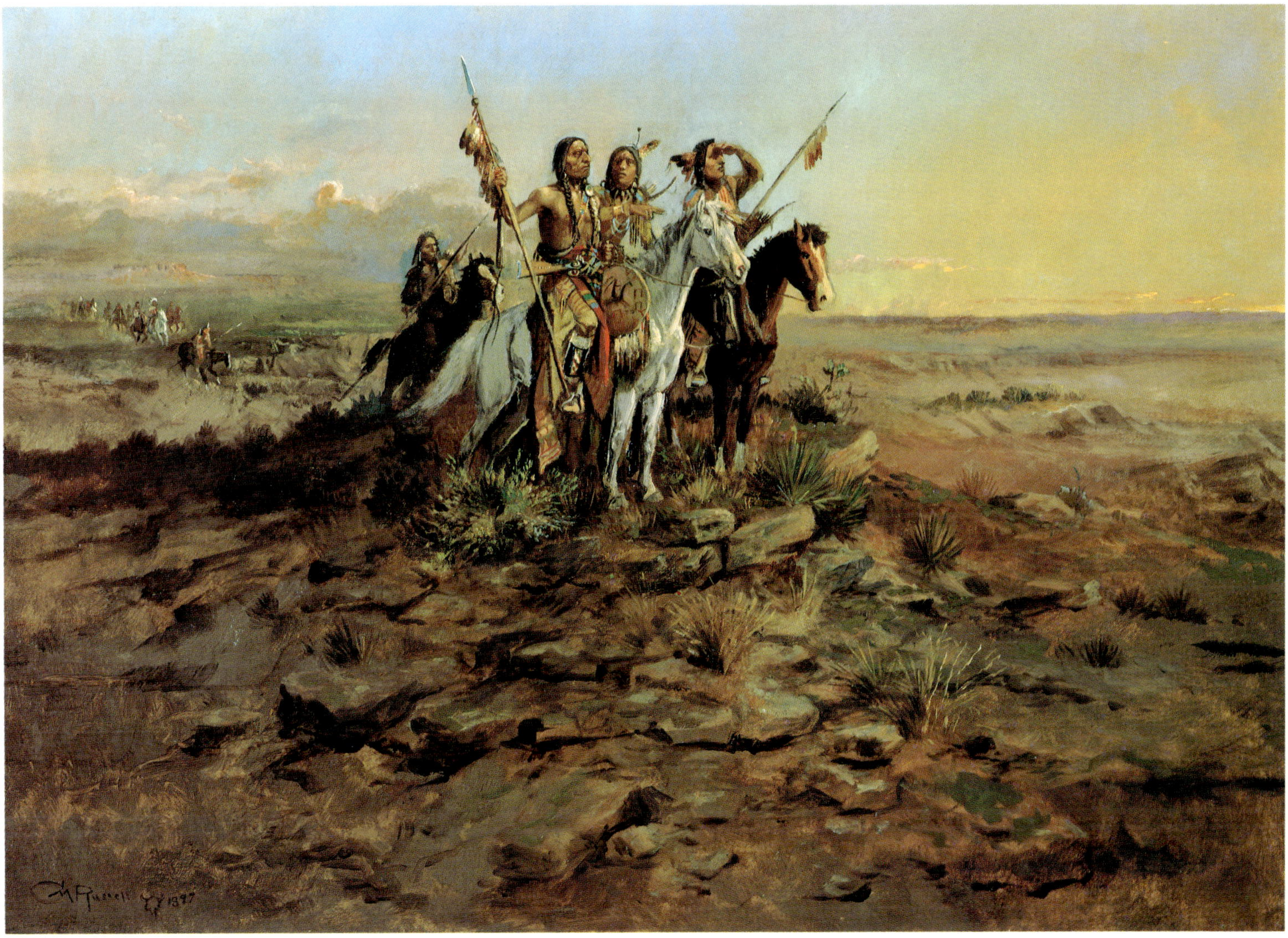

Approach of the White Men

1897 • $17\frac{3}{4} \times 23\frac{5}{8}$ in. • Watercolor on paper.

PAINTED IN THE SAME YEAR and under the same title as the preceding oil, this watercolor might have been expected to take its place as an approximate duplicate, allowing only for technical accommodations to the change of medium. But whichever one was executed first, a new painting offered a new way of thinking about the subject, and of composing it.

The oil is simpler in its sense of direction, its forward thrust. The near group of braves is heading a procession of others that we see in the lefthand distance. And all those in the vanguard—including horses—seem to be concentrating their attention on some point behind our right shoulder.

In the watercolor, however, the foreground Indians are on their own, with less evidence of having come from anywhere and less inclination to go on. They focus rather more toward each other than toward approaching whites; the brave on the right, a study of profound puzzlement, is balanced by the oppositely turned figure on the white horse to the left. The result is a scene more static than mobile, pulling more into itself in the face of tremendous exchanges to come.

Even the cracked, more precipitous land in the right foreground underlines this difference. And both paintings suggest the land's age, long antedating the time when the Indians—perhaps coming across dry ground from northern Asia—made their own gentle approach.

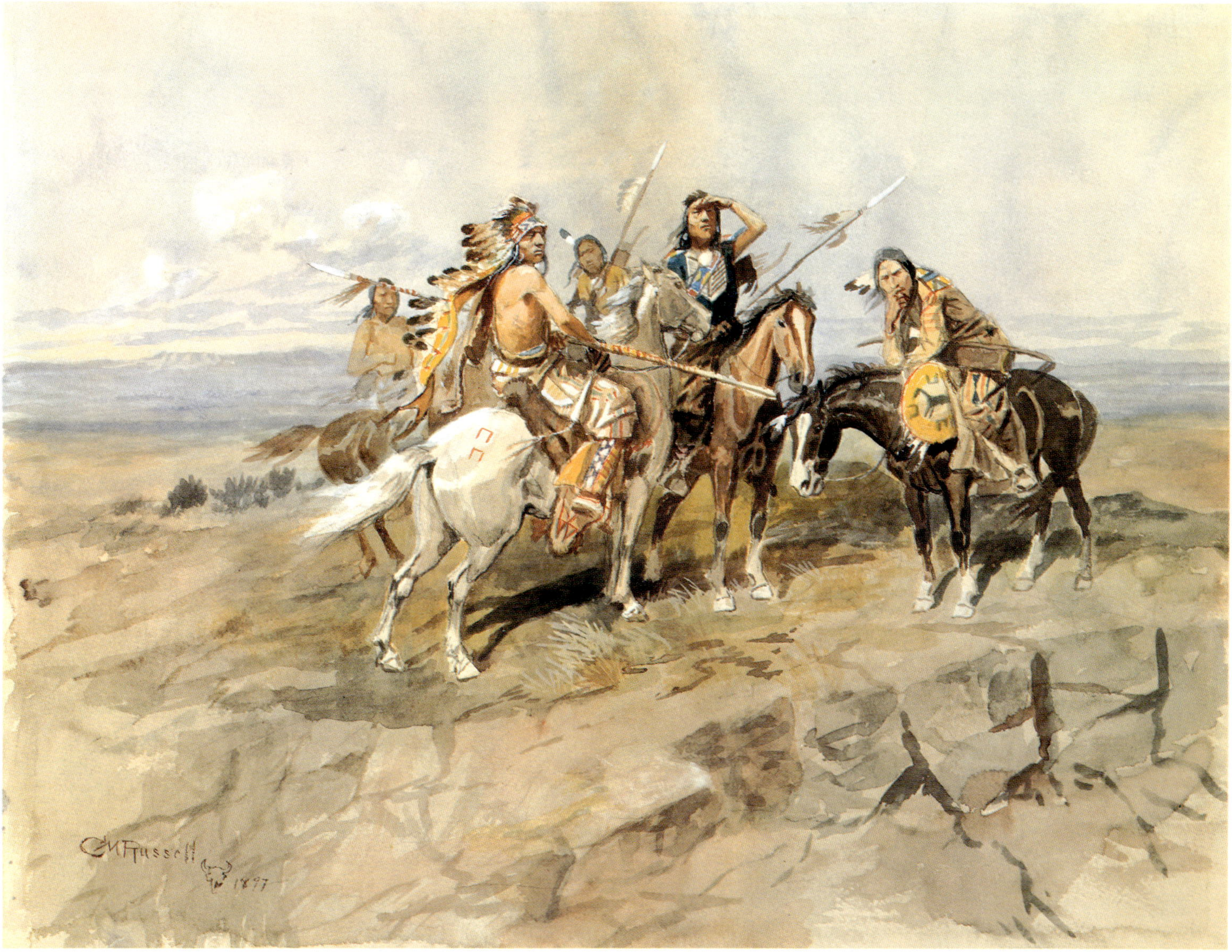
CMRussell
1897

Lewis and Clark on the Lower Columbia

1896 • 18½ × 22⅝ in. • Watercolor on paper.

THE LEWIS AND CLARK EXPEDITION, arranged by President Jefferson in 1803, was important to early United States history not only as wide-ranging exploration but as a signal, a gesture of authority to be read most particularly by the Indians. Russell was intrigued by this strongly dramatic aspect of the expedition, with its encounters and dialogues between representatives of the new republic and these original Americans of the Northwest, along thousands of miles of their own remote territory. Several paintings resulted.

The dialogues had to bridge deep differences of culture, perspective, language. Invaluable in the attempt to do so was the seventeen-year old Indian girl Sacagawea, shown here standing beside Captain Meriwether Lewis in one of the expedition's three boats. (Captain William Clark is sitting with his back to us, wearing a cocked hat.) She is signaling to the Chinook Indians in the approaching boat, perhaps concerning the robe of sea-otter skins that Captain Lewis told of buying in his journal.

Sacagawea, born a Shoshone, had been kidnapped as a youngster and taken east—probably by the Hidatsa—and had become the squaw of a French-Canadian fur trapper. Lewis, discussing routes with this man while encamped nearby during his first winter, found Sacagawea herself—ideally qualified to guide them in the Rockies and to interpret among the Indians, though she insisted that her husband and newborn infant join the party as well.

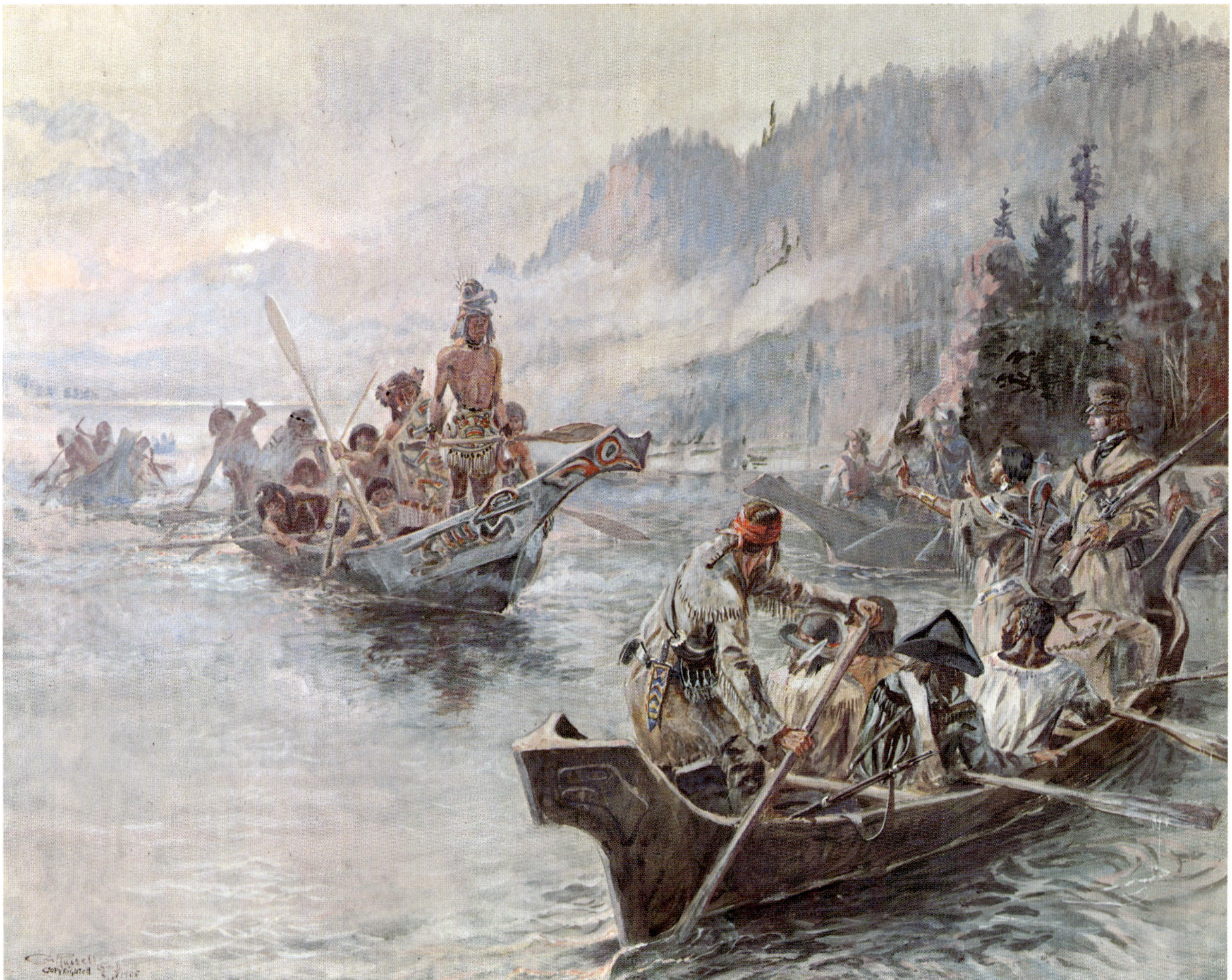
Russell
Copyrighted

A Doubtful Guest

1896 • 18½ × 22⅝ in. • Watercolor on paper.

One reason for the sharp reality in a typical Russell painting is that, like any good storyteller, the artist drew on scenes and details of scenes he had lived close to. Sometimes, as in this case, the scene came directly out of his life. The young man here, though not exactly a self-portrait, is a stand-in for Russell; the older one would be Jake Hoover, who took young Charlie under his wing during his first two years in Montana.

The two men have been startled by the arrival of a pair of Indians, foragers returning inconspicuously to their former homeland. These "guests" seldom ventured into white settlements—the possibility of war still being very real in 1882—but knew that they could depend on a cordial (if cautious) reception at Jake Hoover's camp on the high, narrow trail along South Fork. By the time they leave they'll probably have acquired a free meal (and by Russell's later account no food from the best hotels in Europe and America "could touch that which came from Jake's frying pan"), as well as some tobacco, a pouch of salt, or a handful of .44 cartridges.

Russell painted this watercolor fourteen years later, but remembered fresh particulars of a hunter's life against an idyllic autumn setting: the traps and the saddles, the heavy blankets, and the beaver skin staked out to dry. He also remembered the first sting of tension on both sides of any such encounter—even as friendly a one as this.

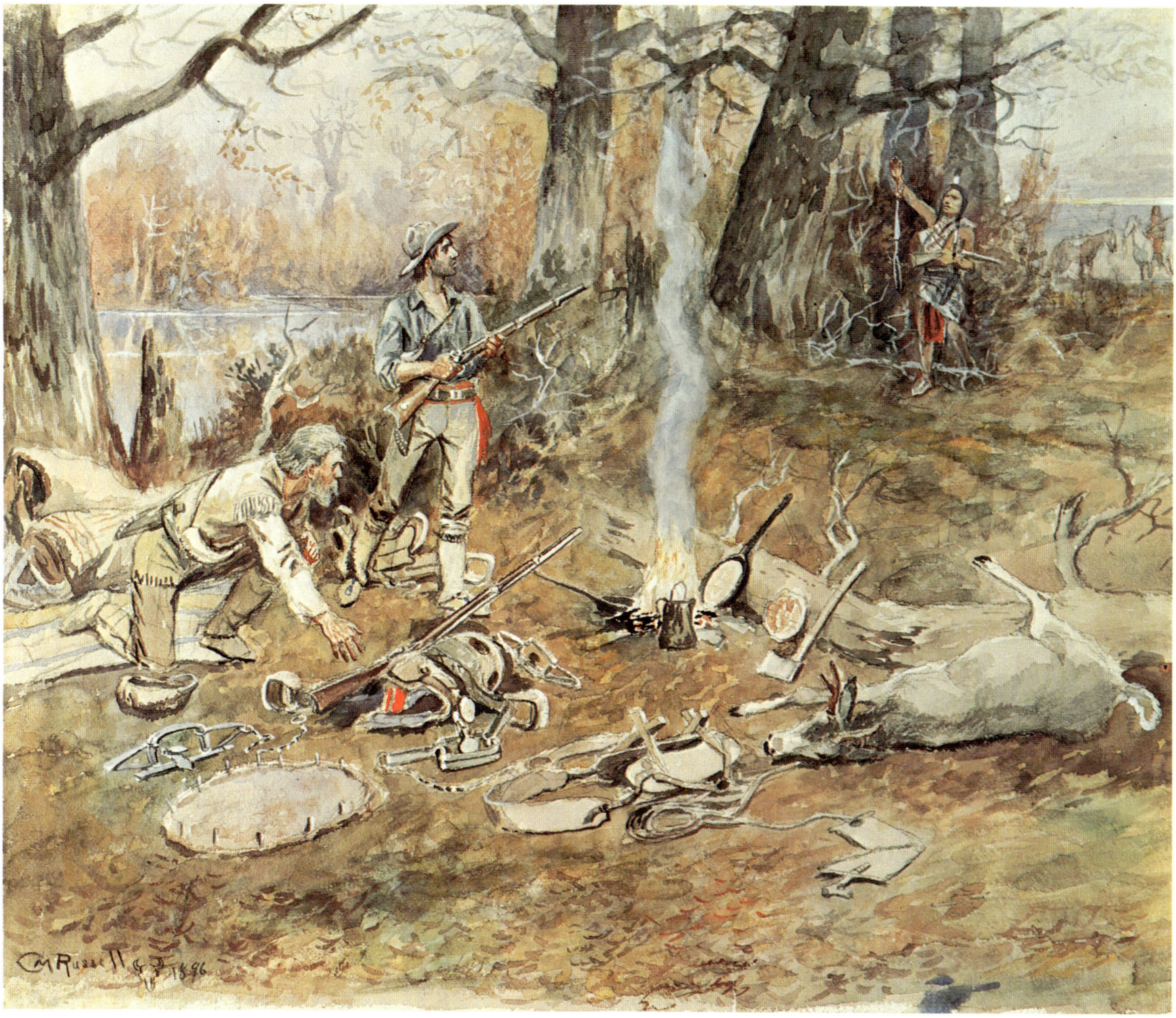

Intercepted Wagon Train

1898 • 19⅝ × 27¾ in. • Watercolor on paper.

THE COMMON OWNERSHIP of land was a basic assumption of Indian society. An individual could own such items as a horse, bows and arrows, or the buffalo hides to make a tepee. But the land, quite simply, belonged like the sea and the air to everyone—or rather it was held and cherished by everyone, equally. Real estate was a phenomenon quite foreign to the Indian.

The first and many subsequent government treaties had recognized and respected this, at least in writing. It was possible, however, for an agreement that might mean eventual ownership or control to a white leader to be read by the Indian as merely allowing temporary rights of passage, hunting, or grazing to the transient visitor. Russell here shows a band of Indians exercising such illusory and vanishing rights.

In 1841 the first train of covered wagons moved westward. It was followed, for a time, by a migration of perhaps five hundred people a year. Some of the early, lightly armed wagon trains were lost to Indians who felt fiercely possessive of their land. So the trains were enlarged and their members equipped with long-range guns. The Indians then became willing, by the force of the guns and the treaties, to take their toll in fairly nominal gifts of oxen, tobacco, and other goods, instead of in human lives.

Russell again gives us the Indian view of such an encounter, with an emissary on his way down to conduct negotiations. But the distant line of wagons also prefigures the inexorable movement of an entire country's history.

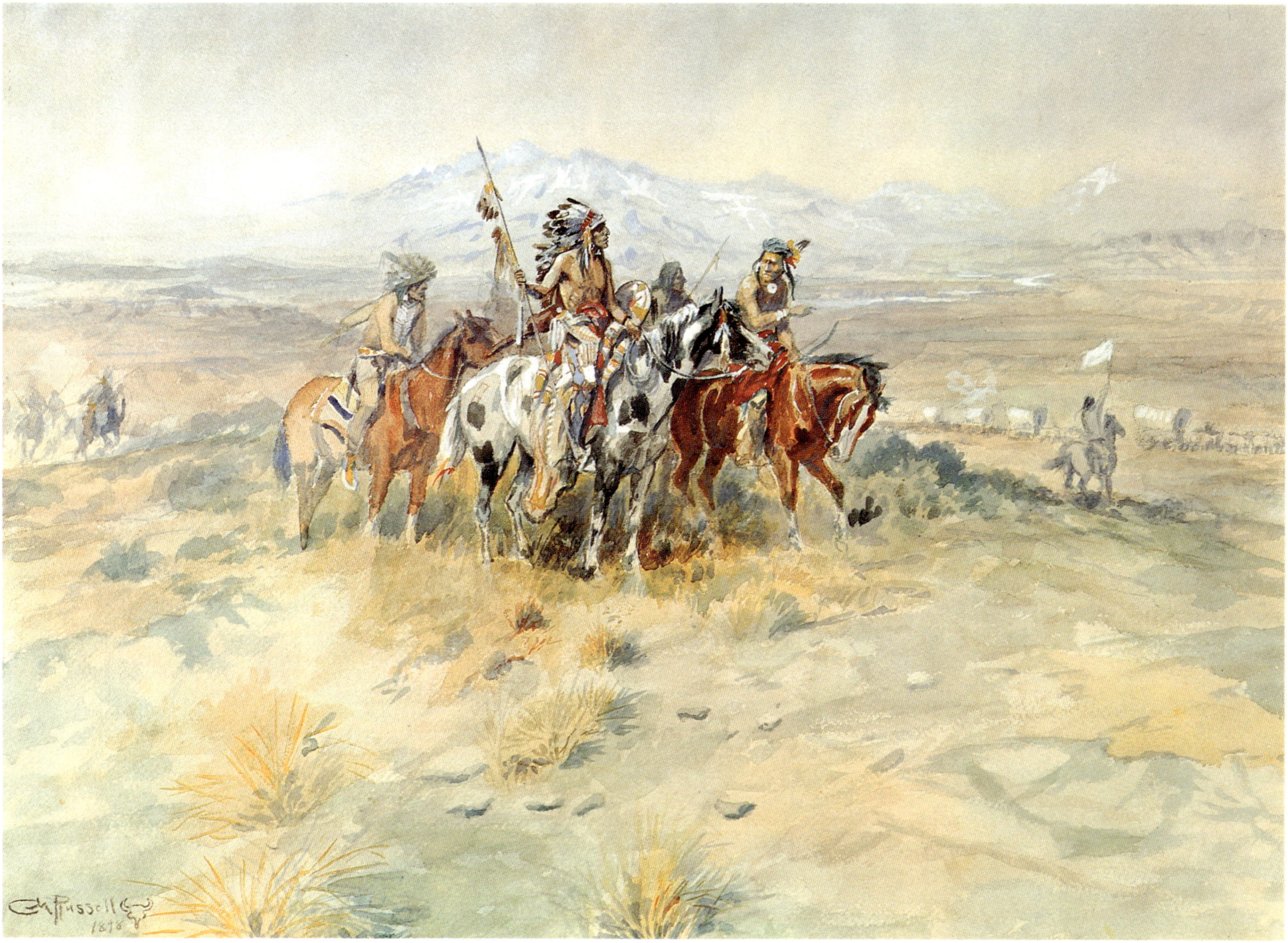
CM Russell

Indian Fight

1898 • 12½ × 19 in. • Watercolor on paper.

ALTHOUGH, AS WE HAVE SEEN, the Indians encountered on the westward trail learned for a time to be restrained, if not often cordial, to their white visitors, the new wave of migration following the Civil War was less welcome than ever. For the most part, again, these emigrants were in transit, on their way to eventual settlement further west, very likely in Oregon. But they were crossing the Indian hunting grounds, and game was being depleted and scattered along the trails.

In this watercolor Russell has envisioned one of the countless attacks by Sioux Indians that occurred after an 1866 treaty opened the Bozeman (Montana) Trail to the settlers. The United States Army undertook to enforce the treaty, and then Chief Red Cloud, who had refused to sign, went into action. By 1868, new and more humanitarian treaties had been negotiated, the trail was officially closed, and the government had agreed to withdraw its forces.

From then on, however uneven the success of the new policy, more stress was placed on education and assimilation, less on mere force of arms.

Russell, this time, has put the viewer directly in the line of Indian fire. We experience the scene not simply as observers but as members of a threatened wagon train, wondering how likely we are to reach that Montana mining country or the long-sought home further west.

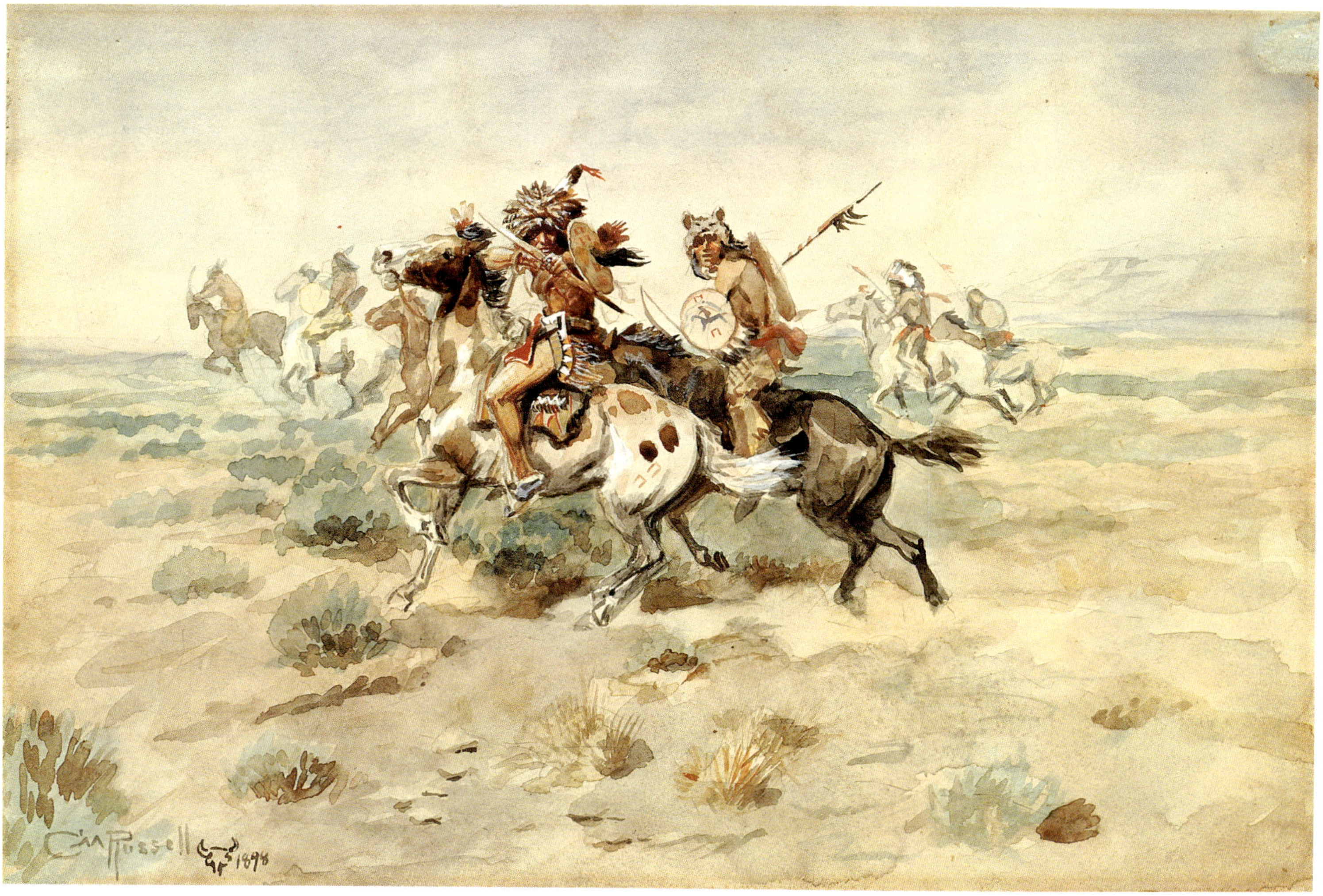
CMRussell
1898

Jumped

1914 • 30⅛ × 48¼ in. • Oil on canvas.

FORT BENTON was a trading center at the head of Missouri River navigation, where the upper arm of the river reaches across northern Montana. During the gold-filled sixties, it came fully alive as the meeting place of steamboat traffic and three overland trails. The most notorious of these three was the Whoop-up Trail, leading north to Canada and giving Russell the scene of his wide and energetic painting.

The sale of whiskey to Indians had been outlawed by the government; accordingly Fort Benton traders circumvented the law by setting up a branch office across the Canadian border, and the Whoop-up Trail was the way there—carrying not only the whiskey customers but also, in the course of time, millions of dollars worth of general supplies. It was named, reportedly, when a merchant was asked about the state of his business and replied, "Oh, they're damn well whoopin' it up."

Piegan Indians decided, at first, to share in the "whoop-up" spirit, and so staged surprise attacks like this one on the wagon trains. But Russell shows them receiving more devastating fire than they could return with their bows and arrows and more primitive guns, and as a result they gave up the practice of "jumping."

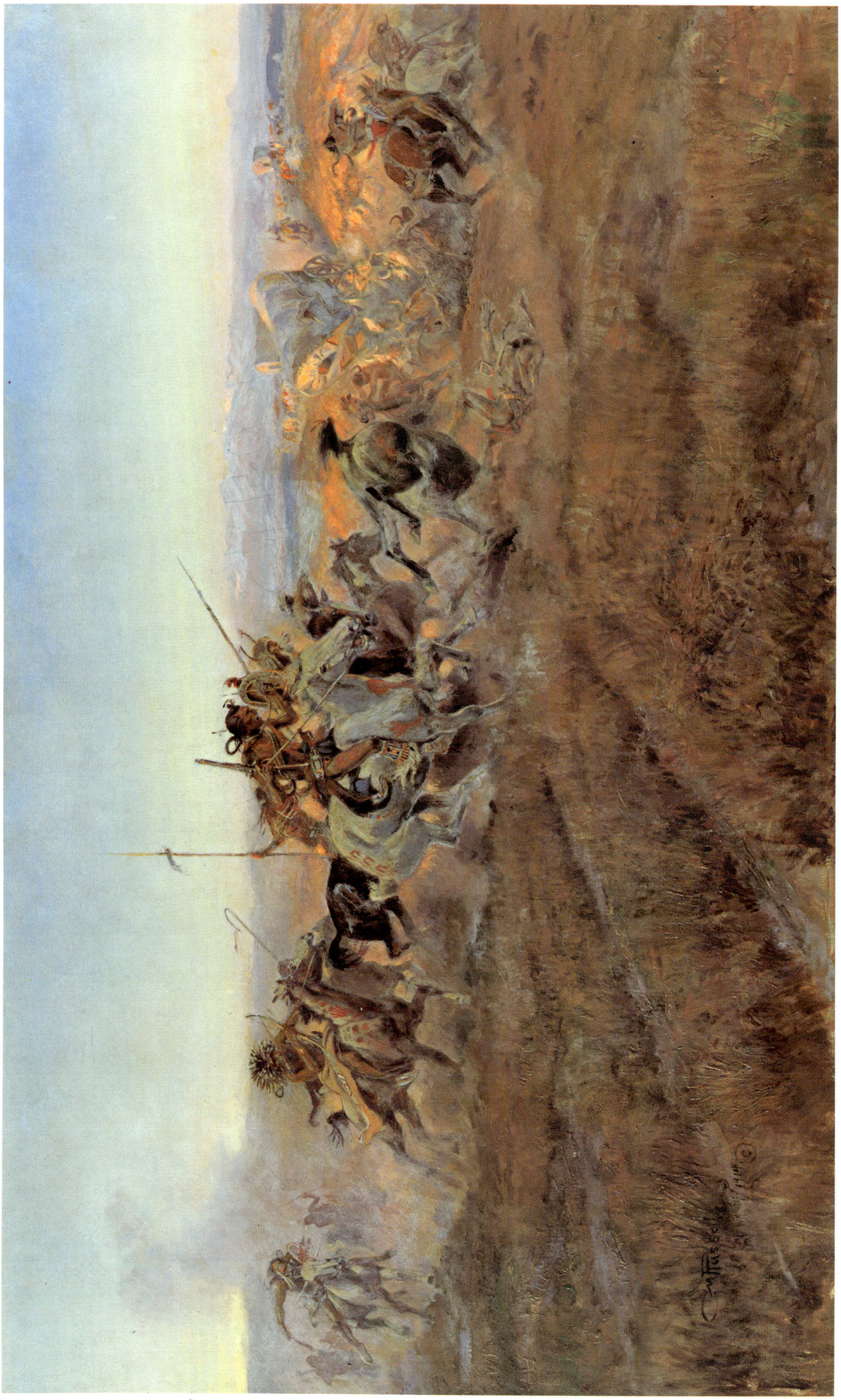

The Attack

1900 • 18½ × 24⅜ in. • Oil on panel.

"FIRST SETTLERS ALONG the Missouri," writes Joseph Kinsey Howard in *Montana, High, Wide and Handsome,* "were the half-breed trappers, who feared nothing on earth. Wolves, bobcats, mountain lions and coyotes swarmed there. . . . But there were compensations. It was the best game region in Montana, and fur bearing animals were reasonably plentiful."

Mr. Howard forgot one more threat to the free trapper, half-breed or not: the Indian. This was Blackfoot country, and its original occupants disliked seeing their beavers disturbed. Most trappers, therefore, preferred to move around at night, either as loners or in pairs, and to keep the lowest possible profile by day. On the other hand, some banded together and trusted their guns and numbers to hold Indians at a distance during daytime travel.

Russell shows such a group here, experiencing considerable difficulty across an open stretch, having to defend themselves at high speed against members of an Indian war party to left and right. They are racing toward the hoped-for shelter of timberland. But Russell has again held the movement in place—most conspicuously by the rearguard rider who turns and fires behind him and the figure who has just been hit and leans back sharply; his position is echoed and emphasized by the accented butte in the middle distance.

As so often, we are left with an unanswered question: will any of these men survive to enjoy "compensations," or is the gamble lost? That's Russell's way: he throws the viewer into the middle of action, and says, in effect, "Swim your way out!"

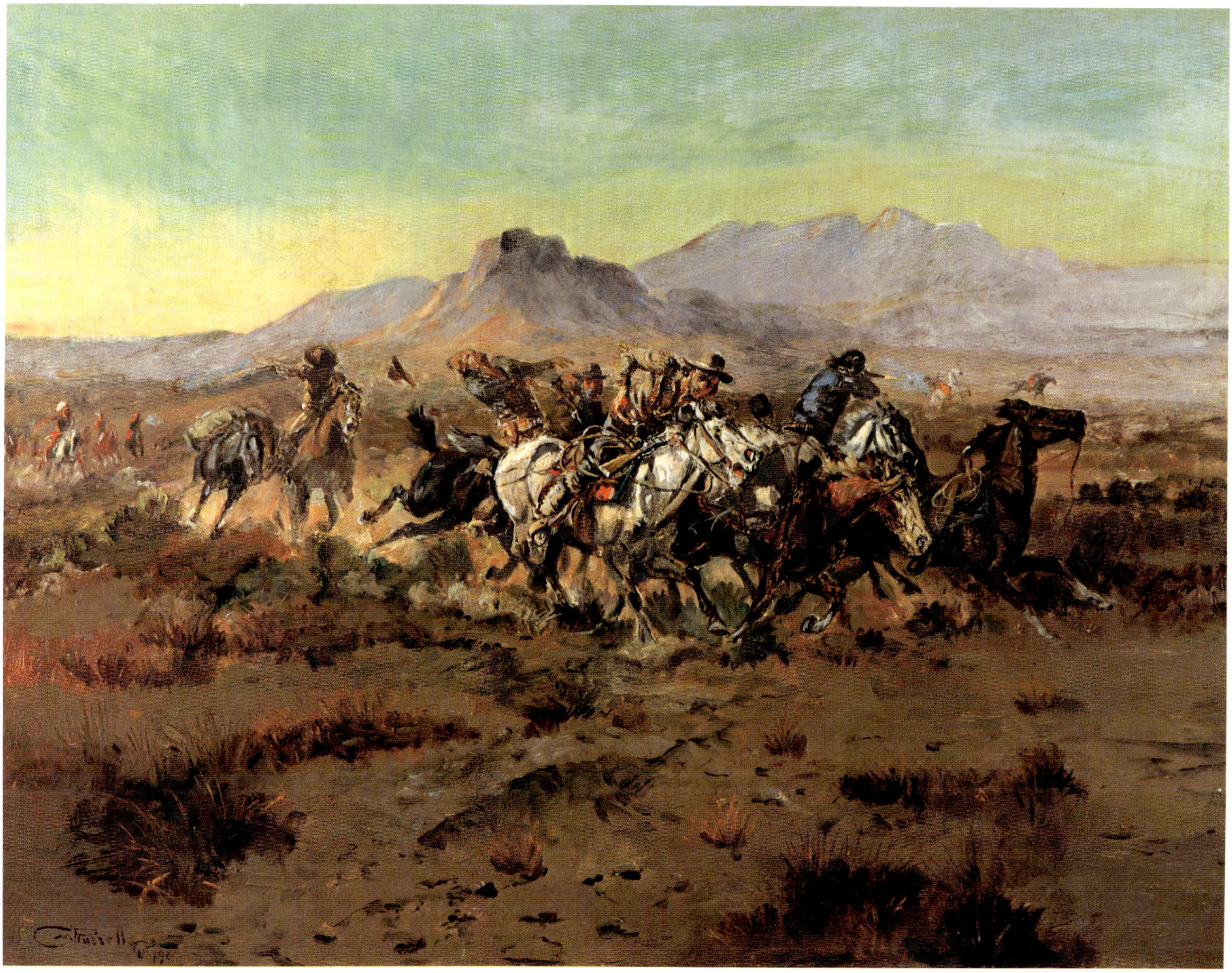

A Desperate Stand

1898 • 24⅛ × 36⅛ in. • Oil on canvas.

THE PHRASE "A Desperate Stand" is as terse and telling an invitation to dramatic action as the best of the old silent movie titles. The words arouse anticipations which the scene itself, at least in this case, admirably fulfills.

As viewers, we are most immediately conscious of the stand—being taken here by a small and dwindling band of frontiersmen, probably again fur trappers. At the same time Russell makes us aware of their desperation, underlining the realism of it by the tight, quivering arrangement of the men and the horses over which they are shooting in every direction.

We find them obviously surrounded; and in another second or two the surrounding forces, which we may already have noticed galloping from right to left in the distance, are identified for us by the Blackfoot brave who has just fallen in the left foreground. So we feel the danger, and in a way are part of it. Charlie Russell, who never leaves his viewers far out of the action, has put us in a position where we are almost Indians.

His consistently sympathetic portrayal of them helps to make that at least imaginable. Even so, our own immediate sympathies are more likely to be with the far outnumbered men at the center of this hostile ring. Therefore we resist the impulse to keep moving with the other Indians, and stay watching where we are, hoping that somehow these pioneers, like the racing ones in the last picture, can hold their own.

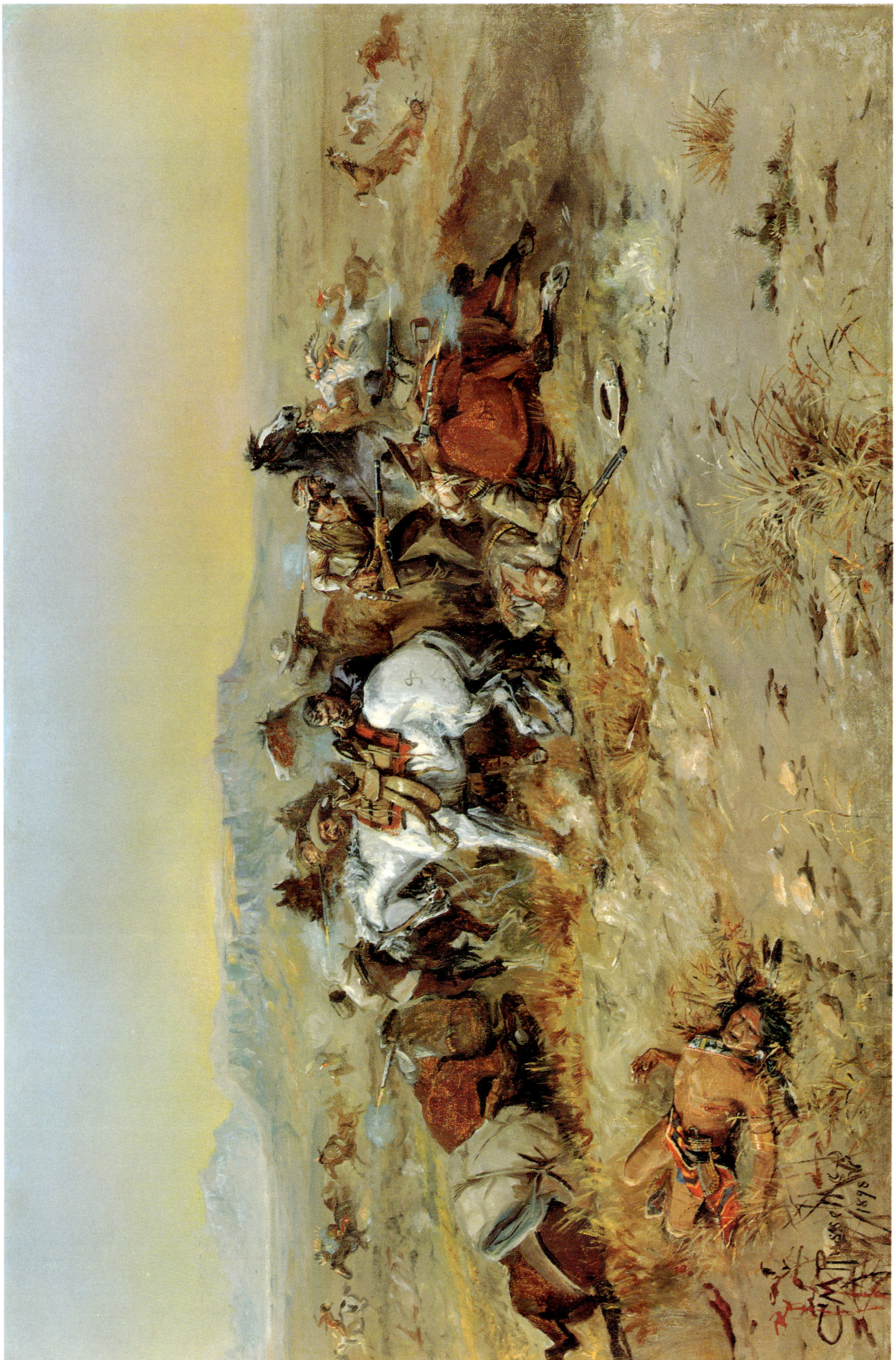

Close Quarters

c. 1889 • 20⅛ × 30⅛ in. • Oil on canvas.

CHARLES RUSSELL'S PRECOCITY as a young, untrained painter in oils burst through his early technical limitations in a variety of ways. Sometimes it helped him to seize the sheer verve of the cowboy in springtime (see page 67); or at other times, to treat a snow scene with notable sophistication (see page 53).

Here, however, his raw talent emerges in a still more striking way. The subject—cowboys under attack by Indians—is one which he would be returning to later with much more realistic success. He would show men and horses who have fallen on hard ground instead of floating slightly above it as these seem to. And he would color them more convincingly.

But never would he surpass the nightmarish excitement of these Indians circling the rise of land beyond, firing as they go. The side view of them, along the plane of the ridge, has been relatively easy to handle, and Russell has described them there with startlingly dramatic staging and lighting. In contrast to the dark, static foreground, the figures flicker past in a glow that somehow manages to be both murky and creamy. As far as the viewer is concerned, the unfortunate cowboys are not only gone but virtually forgotten.

Their story was pictured in Russell's first book, a portfolio of twelve plates, published without text under the title, *Studies of Western Life*. A second printing included comments by the artist's rancher friend Granville Stuart, who observed in this case that the cowboys might have survived if they'd killed both their horses right away and gotten between them.

It was another old friend who apparently promoted the idea of the book. The copyright was taken out in the name of Ben R. Roberts, Helena saddlemaker and buyer of Russell's famous 1886 watercolor of the frozen steer, *Waiting for a Chinook* (a thawing wind).

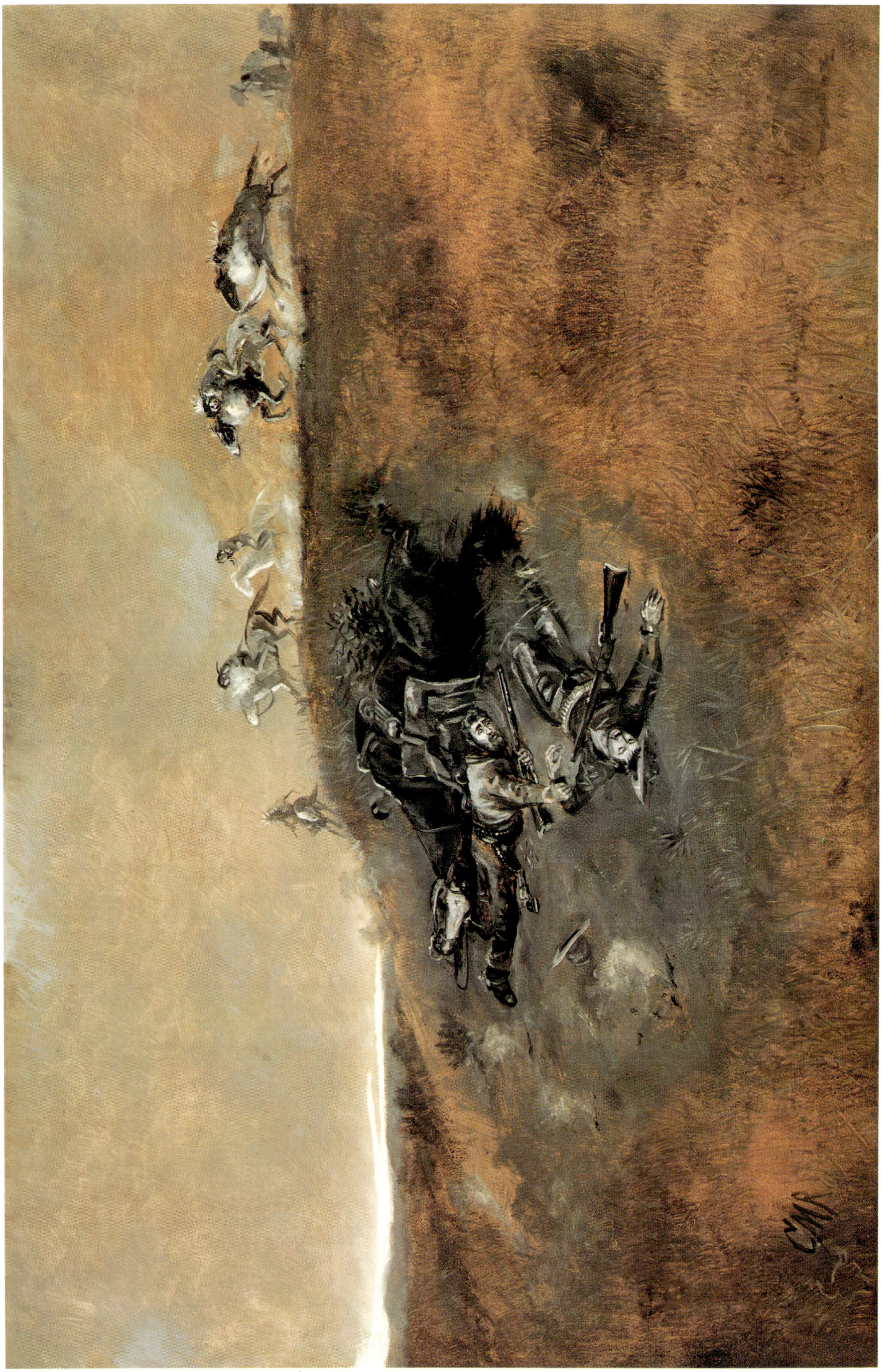

At the Spring

c. 1896 • 15 × 21⅛ in. • Watercolor on paper.

THE CHOICE OF A marriage partner was not likely, among the Indians, to be the emotion-charged, compulsive decision that it has so often become elsewhere. Young girls were trained in a tradition of great reticence and encouraged to take only the most indirect initiative during courtship—which in itself could be an elusive process. As a Cheyenne girl was warned by her aunt, after receiving attentions from her first suitor, "It is silly to exchange too many glances and smiles with this young man, especially in the presence of people. He will think you are too easy and immoral."

Among the Blackfeet, courtship was reduced almost to the vanishing point by the practice of arranged marriages. Yet a young man might initiate or encourage an arrangement through his father, who would then bring gifts with his offer to the girl's father. From then until the marriage itself, contact between the young people would be largely confined to the kind of "chance" encounter described in Russell's painting.

Even this brief meeting would be a rarity, since a young girl seldom left her tepee except with an older woman; and however deep the interest, there probably would be no words exchanged. But Russell, through his sensitive grasp of gesture, has portrayed the distinct exchange that *is* occurring between these almost completely averted figures: the girl moving slowly, lingeringly, the waterpot held against her hip with easy grace; and the young man sitting with almost military formality, glancing sideways with the intense detachment we sometimes give to reading our neighbor's newspaper on the bus.

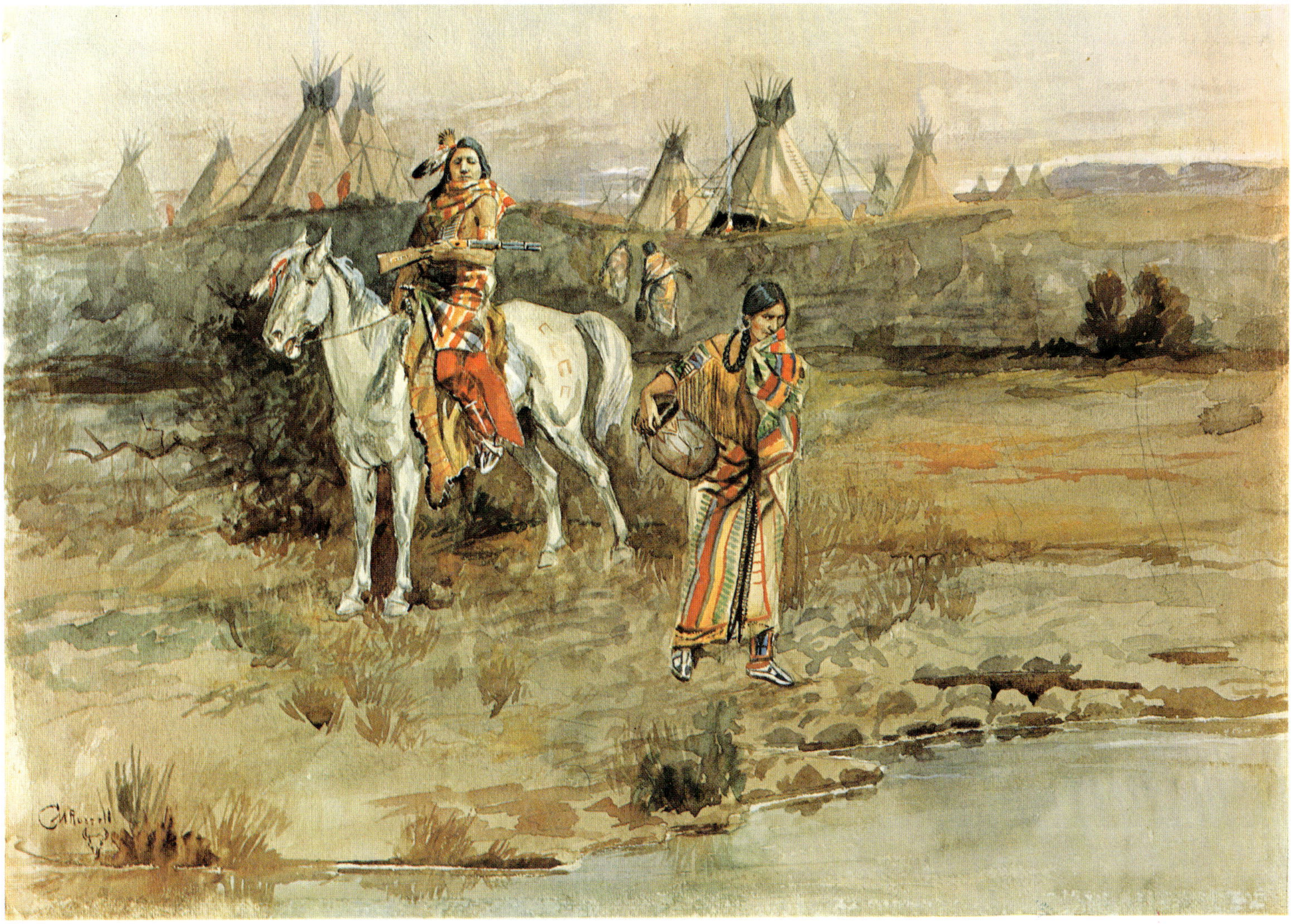

Powder Face

1903 • 12 × 9 in. • Watercolor on paper.

POWDER FACE WAS A NORTHERN ARAPAHO warrior whose headpiece tells that he was a member of the Ravens, a tribal secret society. During the latter part of his life he moved from Indian Territory to Montana. Russell portrays him here as a man of considerable command, in full battle regalia, and in a superb equilibrium of rest and readiness, of alert ease.

As an equestrian watercolor, focussed in the sharp, aquiline profile of its subject, the work touches back to the best equestrian sculpture, remembered also in profile: Donatello's *Gattamelata*, for instance, or Verrocchio's *Colleoni*. War paint is naturally suggested, but only to mark a human face, and suggest a decisive mind.

Russell's attention to the humanity of all subjects, white or Indian, is attested to by the impartial dignity of this finished head. He ignored the tendency of those within any cultural era to secure their place by assuming superiority to some "less civilized" phase—as happened, even without a racial difference, during the Renaissance in regard to the Gothic, during the neoclassic age in regard to the Baroque, and so forth. Though the Indians were sometimes complimented (supposedly) as "noble savages," they also happened to be in the way, an inconvenience to settlement. Yet as the abolitionist Wendell Phillips said in 1868, advocating a more humane Indian policy, "We shall never be able to be just to other races, or reap the full benefit of their neighborhood till we 'unlearn contempt.' "

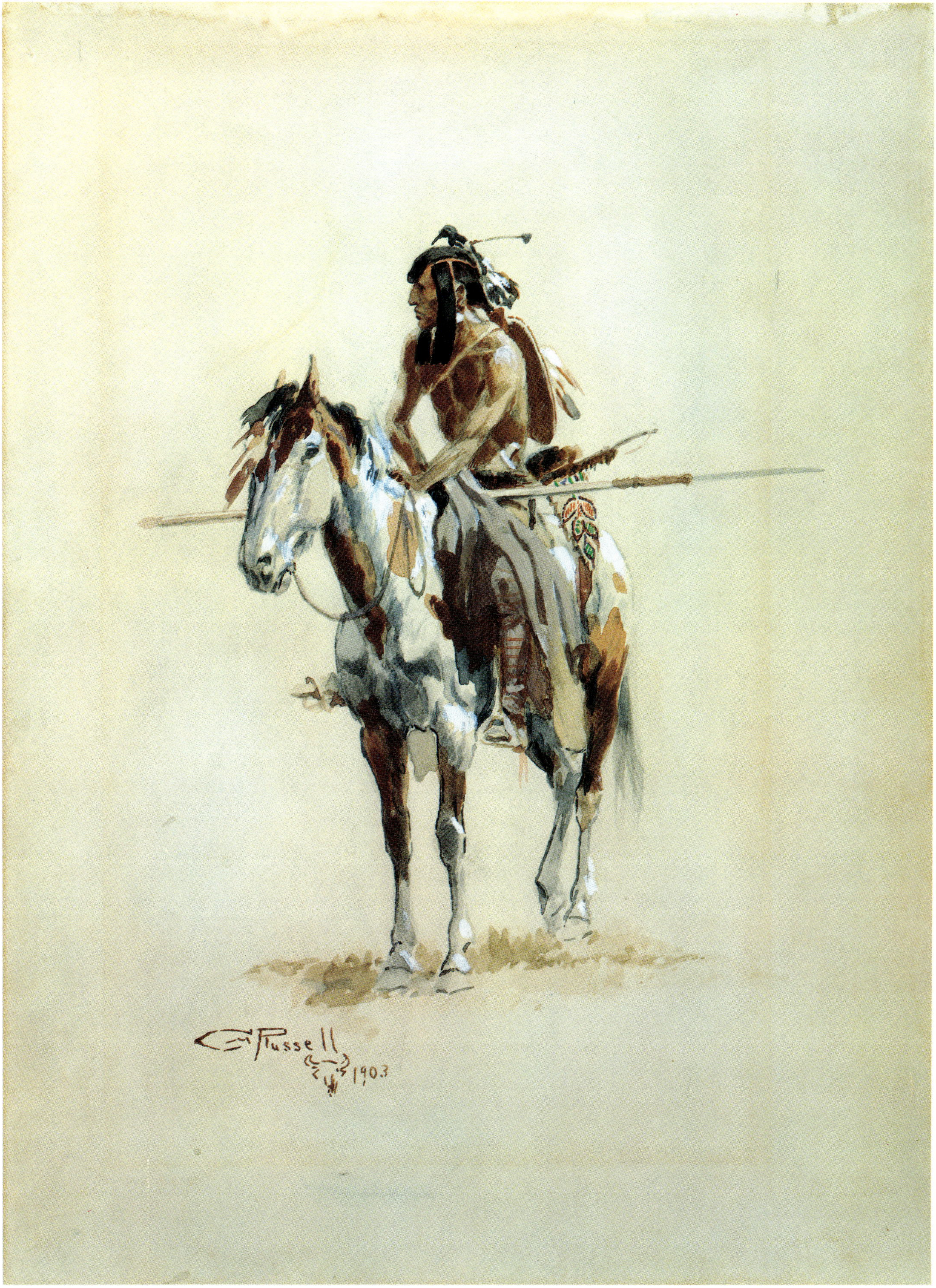
CM Russell
1903

Duel to the Death

c. 1891 • 21 × 17 in. • Watercolor on paper.

ALTHOUGH NEIGHBORING TRIBES of traditionally hostile Indians were in the rather frequent habit of raiding each other's territory, the usual result was a thundering good chase and a few stolen horses. Occasionally, however, these encounters did get out of control, or perhaps one side or the other found itself in such a position that to stand and fight was the only honorable recourse. Then would occur such a hand-to-hand duel as this one (though perhaps "spear-to-spear" is the more exact phrase), between what are probably a Piegan and a Crow.

Showing the decisive moment of victory, Russell with his gift for telling a complete story has included in that moment the full fury of approach and attack preceding it, as well as the falling of the slain form that must have followed it. And he holds it all together compositionally in a near-parallelogram of movement.

The bodies of the two horses provide a sloping base, from which rise the forward and backward leaning figures of the braves. At the top, the shape is completed by the sharp focus of encounter: the two lances are almost identical in quick thrust from head to head, though one has been deflected by a shield and the other, to put it mildly, has not.

On one level Russell was illustrating the realism of a single instant of action. But the stupendous energy of such a painting as this stays with us because he knew as a composer how to build that action to last.

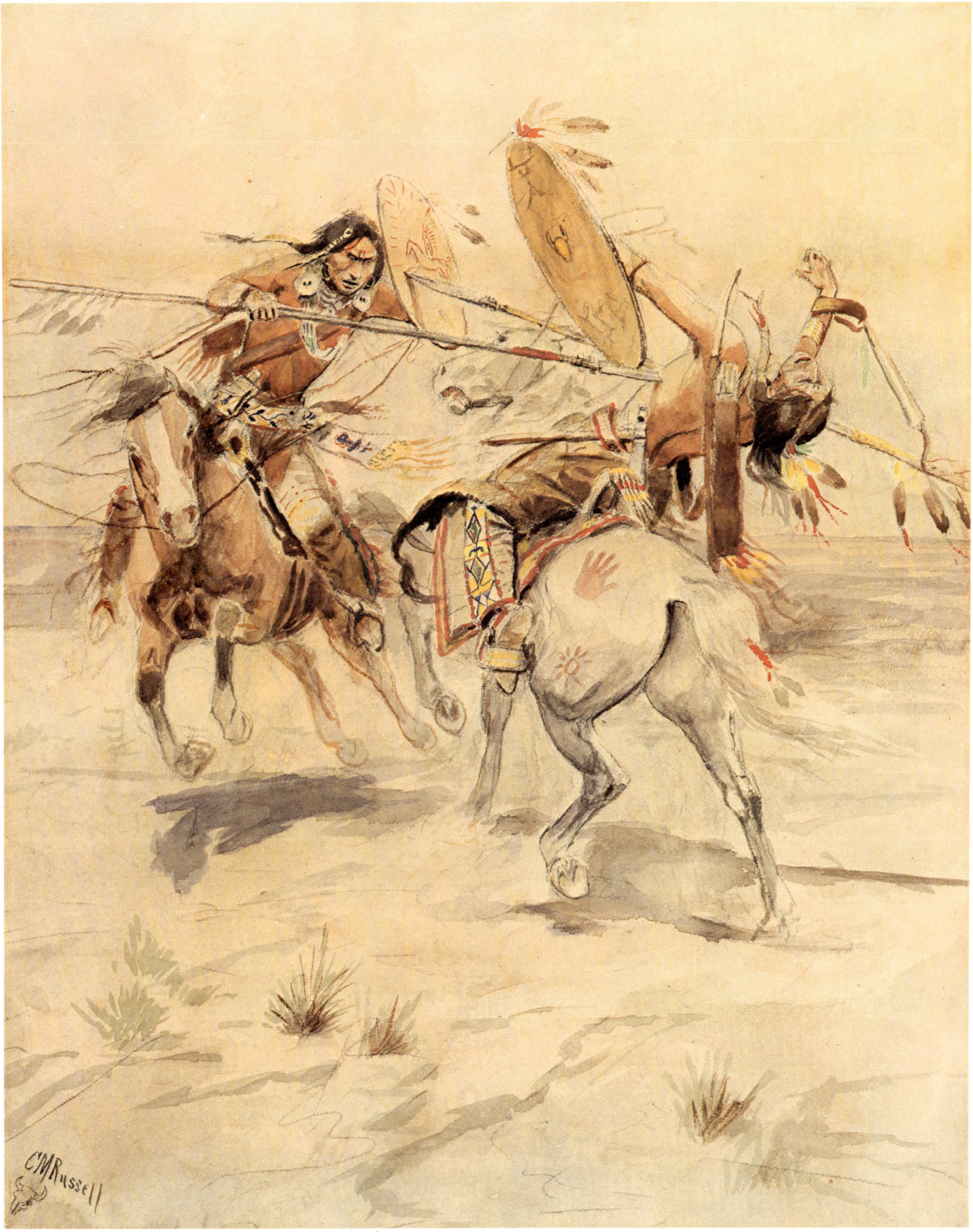
CMRussell

Joy of Life

No date • $14\frac{1}{8} \times 20$ in. • Gouache on artist's board.

A MASTERPIECE? Probably not. But the zesty—some would have said outrageous—humanity that informed the durable liveliness of Russell's best paintings covered a wide range of the cowboy's experience, much of it lonely and away from "respectable" women. This is one of a number of paintings that come from his own close identification with that experience, and were designed for the amusement of his convivial bachelor friends in the barroom.

On the original surface of the painting, behind the left-hand flap of the tepee, is an explicit portrayal of an assignation between a cowboy and an Indian woman. The flap is a separate piece of board, latched on one side and hinged on the other. It was installed for years in a private room at Sid Willis's Great Falls saloon and gallery, The Mint, so that insertion of a coin would open the flap.

But all censoriousness aside, the painting makes a more interesting comment with the flap closed, with a kind of imaginative quietness to replace mere voyeurism. The West was then a world permeated by loneliness, which is reflected in all the separated and somehow solitary figures here; and with Charlie Russell's honesty, and in the irony of the title, his painting becomes a perhaps inadvertent comment on the lonely margins of that world.

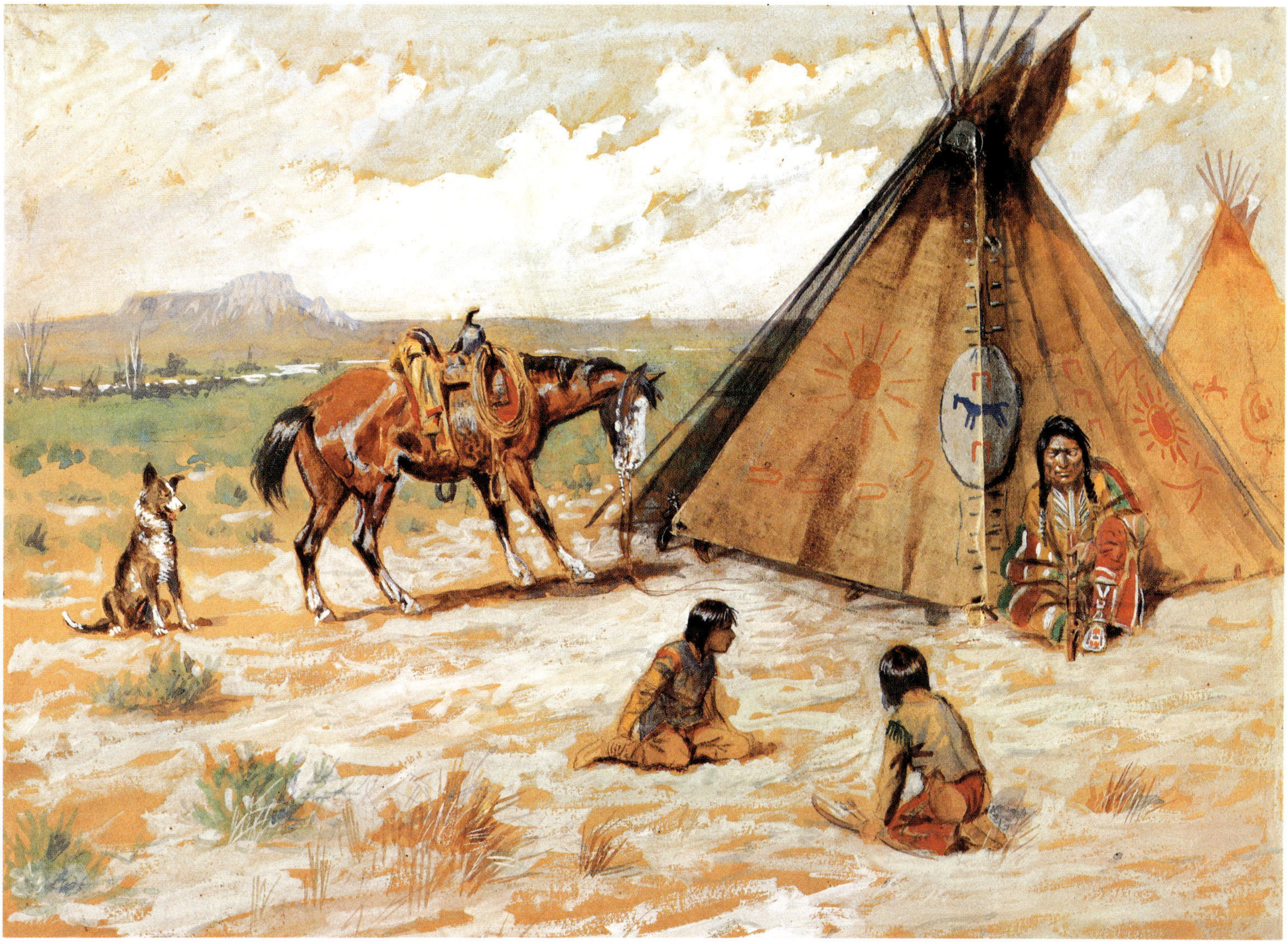

Keeoma

1896 • 18½ × 24½ in. • Oil on panel.

A GOOD NUMBER OF RUSSELL'S paintings may be classified technically as illustrations, whether or not they were intended for publication as such. He evidently had an eye and a descriptive flair for the unfolding action of a story. But to call him an illustrator in any limiting sense is to overlook so much else in his motivation as an artist and in his approach to a subject.

In the July, 1897 issue of *Western Field and Stream* William Blaisdell Cameron published a story called "Keeoma's Wooing," and Russell's sumptuous painting provided the story's illustration. The romantic languor of his picture was later to encourage eager speculation: was this the girl whom he knew and allegedly almost married during his stay among the Blackfeet in 1888? Not likely. Frederic Renner shows in his monograph a photo of Nancy Russell toying with the peace pipe as she poses. Though it would be hard to argue for this painting as her portrait, it would be still harder to link it with anyone else in Russell's life.

What is more probable here is the conscious transplanting of a voluptuous Ingres *odalisque* or a Goya *maja* from either a Turkish harem or a Spanish bedchamber into the rather different ambience of an Indian tepee. Russell has draped her and her surroundings with much more than is visible in the photo of Nancy. Then he's perfumed the space with a wisp of woodsmoke and bathed it with light from somewhere over Keeoma's head.

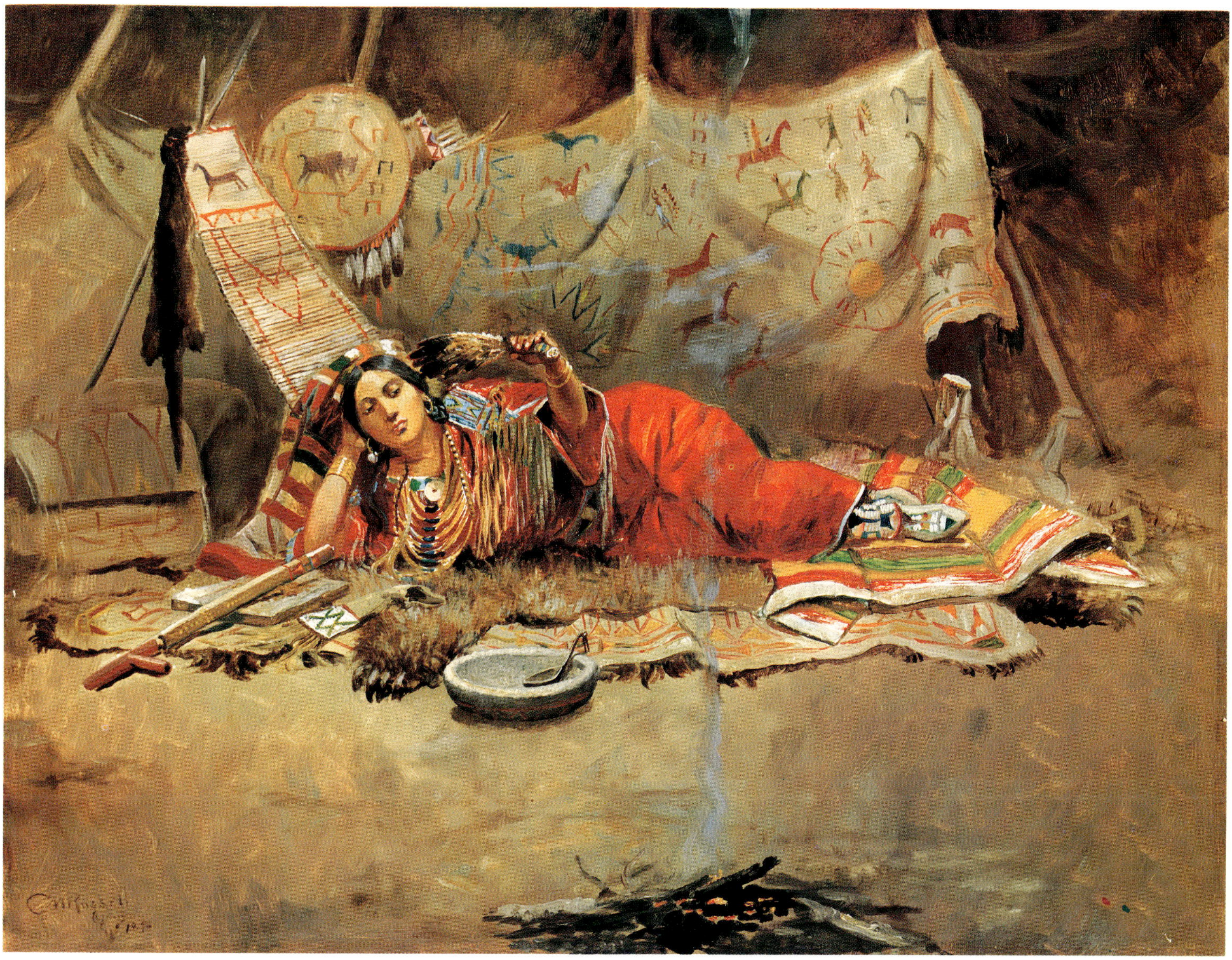

Crow Indians Hunting Elk

c. 1887 • 18⅛ × 24 in. • Oil on canvas.

DURING RUSSELL'S EARLY YEARS as "cowboy artist" he showed little outward intention to paint for a living. This remarkably professional-looking work from 1887, for instance, was done as a wedding present for his friend Johnny Sellers—and then apparently forgotten. When Sellers reintroduced it to the artist nearly thirty years later, Russell was as surprised as many critics have been at its expertness. He seems to have jumped into a maturity of rendition and composition more typical of his later work, when the paintings *were* finding a market.

What was there about this subject that might have prompted Russell to outdo himself? The wintriness, perhaps—an incitement to any oil painter, who must make its whitened colors look crisply cold and not just bleached. Russell obviously found a flair for snowy landscape, as evidenced a year later in simpler terms (*Lost in a Snowstorm—We are Friends;* see page 157).

Yet the two Indians themselves are of course the central subject, and no doubt the main stimulus to the artist. Even before his actual encounter with Indian life in 1888, Russell was responding to the full humanity of those he already knew. He would have agreed with young Lieutenant Scott, who after visiting a Crow encampment in 1877 described its inhabitants as "rich in everything an Indian required to make him happy," whose "wonderful dresses" were of "buckskin ornamented with beads, porcupine quills, and ermine. . . ."

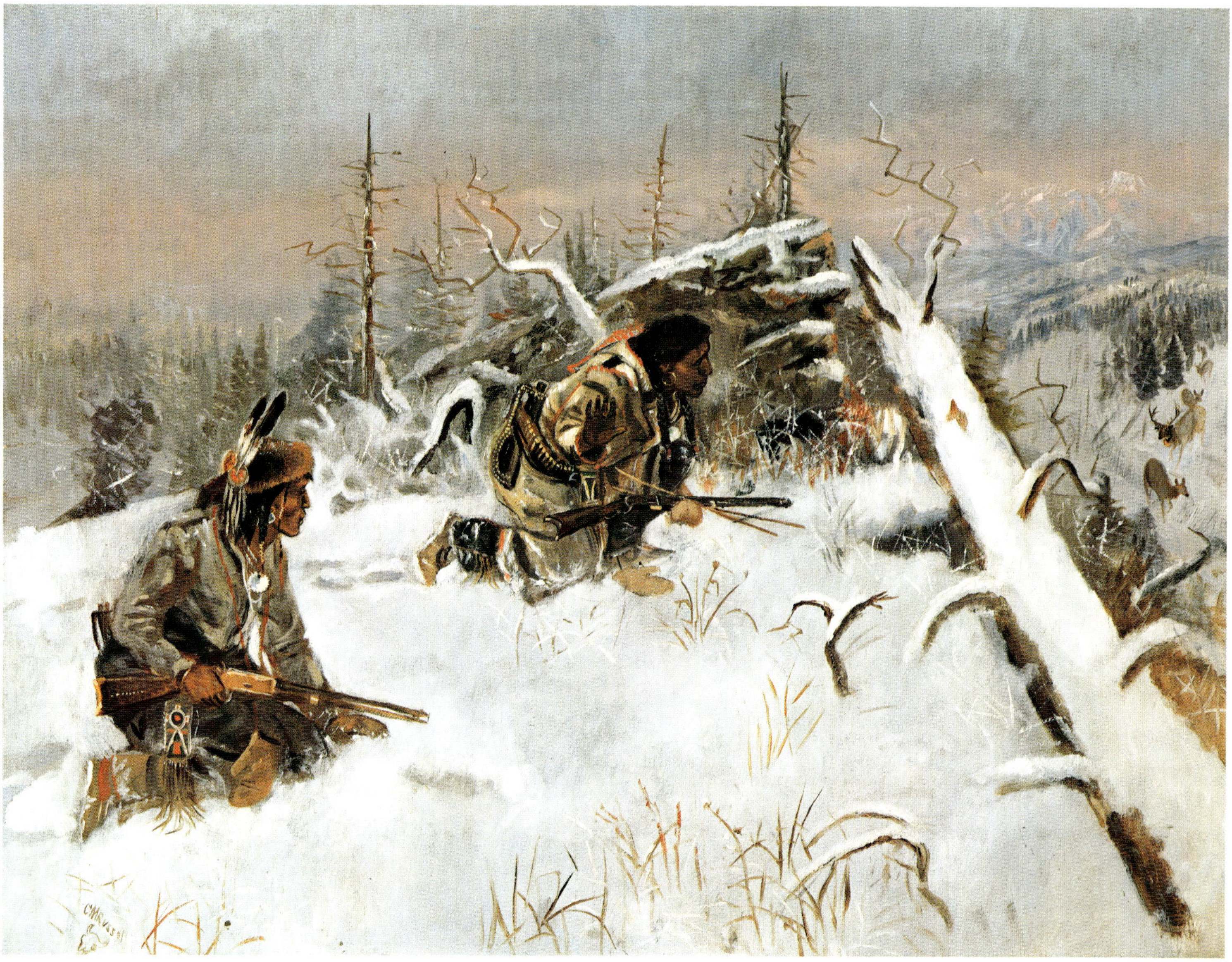

The Prize Shot

1905 • 16 × $22\frac{3}{4}$ in. • Watercolor on paper.

It could be argued that one of Charles Russell's favorite subjects was distance. Not just the distant object itself, though the snowy slopes and far peaks in this watercolor are affectionately warmed by that sunset light. But his feeling for distances was a comparative one, establishing space and the passage through space by means of successive measuring points, from the nearest twig to the farthest haze.

Certainly there's much in this painting to support such an argument—and most notably the careful emergence of the pack-horses out of their windy shroud of snow. The trail itself is only visible as it rounds this near bend to where the moose has been dropped; but we feel it all the way back to the far huntsman, because of those stages of emergence.

Yet no matter how careful and skillful this strategy, Russell's picture is not primarily a picture of space, or even of objects in space. Everything he has put into his painting is in service to the men and the animals it contains, and so our argument becomes as relative as the distances themselves.

Space, in other words, is *serving* his favorite subjects. It is helping us to take in the late fall, late-in-the-day experience of these men, their aloneness with nature and their success in the hunt, apparently realized over a considerable distance.

Russell, we are told, had no liking for the hunt as an excuse for killing. But the coordination which it required between one hunter and another, and between both of them and the many distances of their countryside, was a subject of which he was clearly fond.

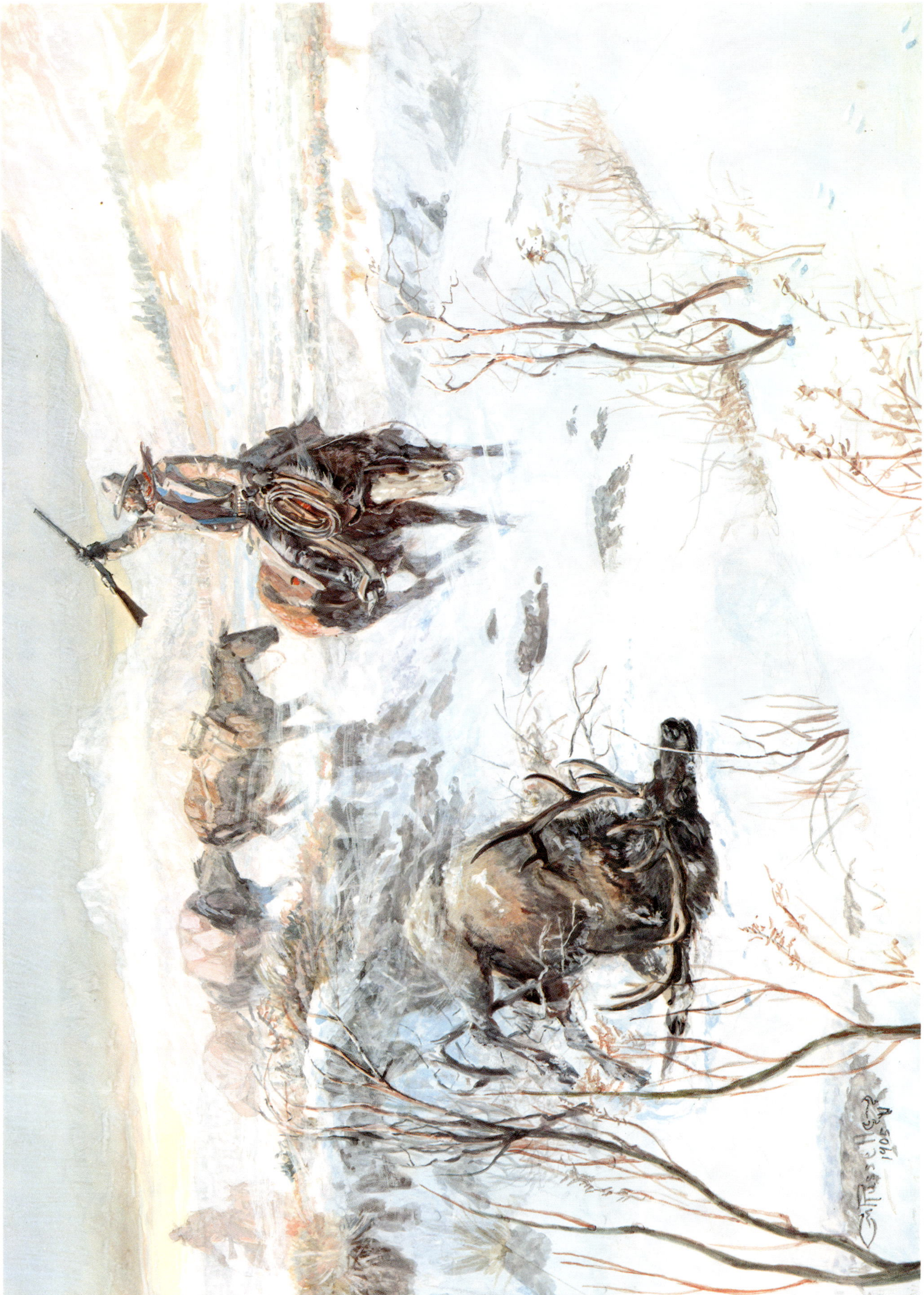

Breaking Camp

c. 1885 • 18½ × 36½ in. • Oil on canvas.

YOUNG CHARLIE RUSSELL'S first plunge into oil painting, completed in 1885, was described in the Helena, Montana *Weekly Independent* of May 5, 1887, in an infectious and quite objective sample of Old West art criticism: "On the Wall in Huntley and Pruitt's store hangs a painting with a strange history. It is on canvas, about two by two and a half feet [actual measurements are 18½ by 36½ inches], and if slightly inartistic in some of its details, is of fine conception and, in the main, finely colored and executed. It was painted in the seclusion of a cow camp on the Judith Range, and by a cowboy. It represents a roundup camp, scattered out on the range after early breakfast—the boys saddling their unruly cayuses, the vicious beasts bucking in every conceivable shape or flying away towards the herds. . ."

"Altogether it is a wonderfully faithful picture and one that bears much study. . . ."

Shortly thereafter a more fulsome article in the Helena *Weekly Herald* came round to commenting that "Mr. Russell's forte lies in depicting animated scenes . . . and their faithfulness is surprising."

Although this journalist happened to have another painting in mind, "animated" is certainly the word for *Breaking Camp;* and even after some acquaintance with the work the sheer whoop-and-holler exuberance of the cowboys, near and far, keeps catching the viewer by surprise.

Russell himself, who rounded up all twenty-five of the Utica crew at one place or another in his painting, was so delighted with the picture that he sent it off to be shown at the St. Louis Art Exposition, before it came home to the ownership of Jesse Phelps of Huntley and Pruitt's store, one of the artist's earliest advocates.

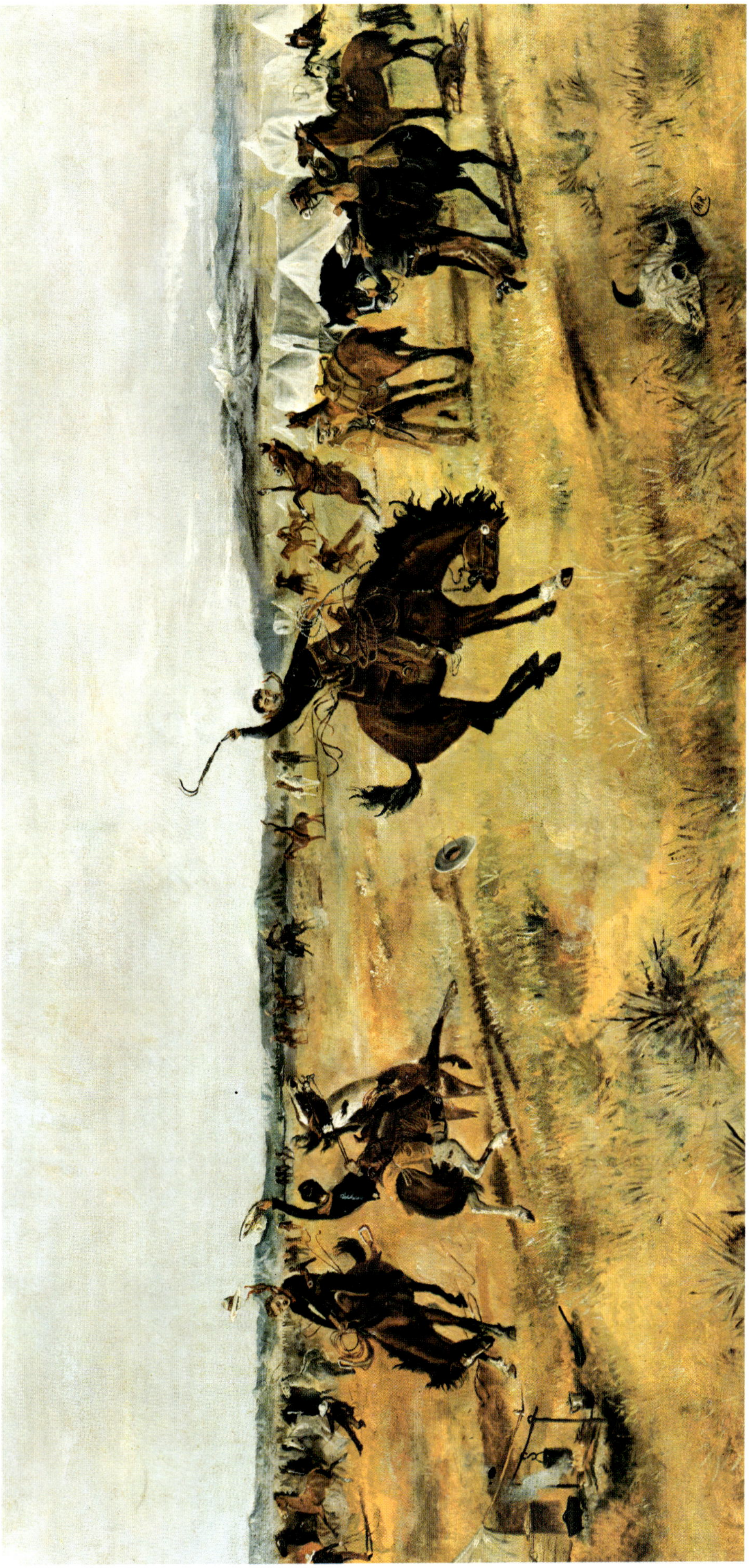

Bronco Busting

1895 • 14⅛ × 20⅛ in. • Watercolor on paper.

THE SEASONED COWBOY and bronc rider (in this case, Bob Thoroughman) was a ruler of the plains—at least of *his* plains; and like any successful ruler he preferred to stay on top. The challenge to this came not so much from rival rulers (two or three of whom we see cheering him on) as from those half-broken, half-wild, independent creatures known as broncos, from a Spanish word meaning "rough," or "rude."

Other cowboys might outdistance and out-rope him in the roundup, out-cook him, out-eat-or-drink him, or out-climb the tallness of his stories around the campfire. But only a horse could unhorse him—and then certainly not for long. Bronco-busting was and is one of the zestiest and most picturesque of skills; and it had to do in very practical ways, of course, with contingencies on the range which could require any cowboy to stay glued to his horse.

Much of the picturesqueness, for Charlie Russell, came from the effect of a cowboy's coming unglued without actually doing so, as that four-legged firecracker under him bucked and pitched, jackknifed and "came apart" every way at once.

Russell uses arms and legs and twisting bodies, then, as border skirmishes surrounding an inward encounter with space, which at a given moment is either mastered or—as in the wry watercolor sketch topping a letter—is not. The mastery may be encouraged by what an experienced cowboy has been known to tell a greenhorn rider: "Keep a leg on each side and your mind in the middle. And don't make your ride till you're on."

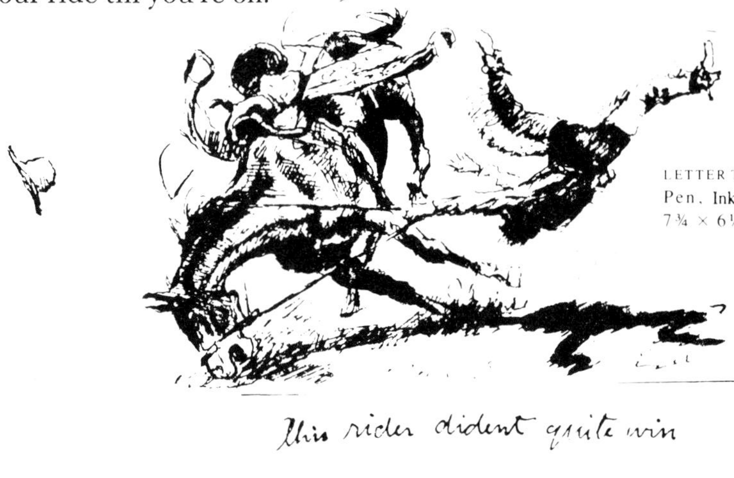

LETTER TO FRIEND GUY
Pen, Ink Watercolor
7¾ × 6½"

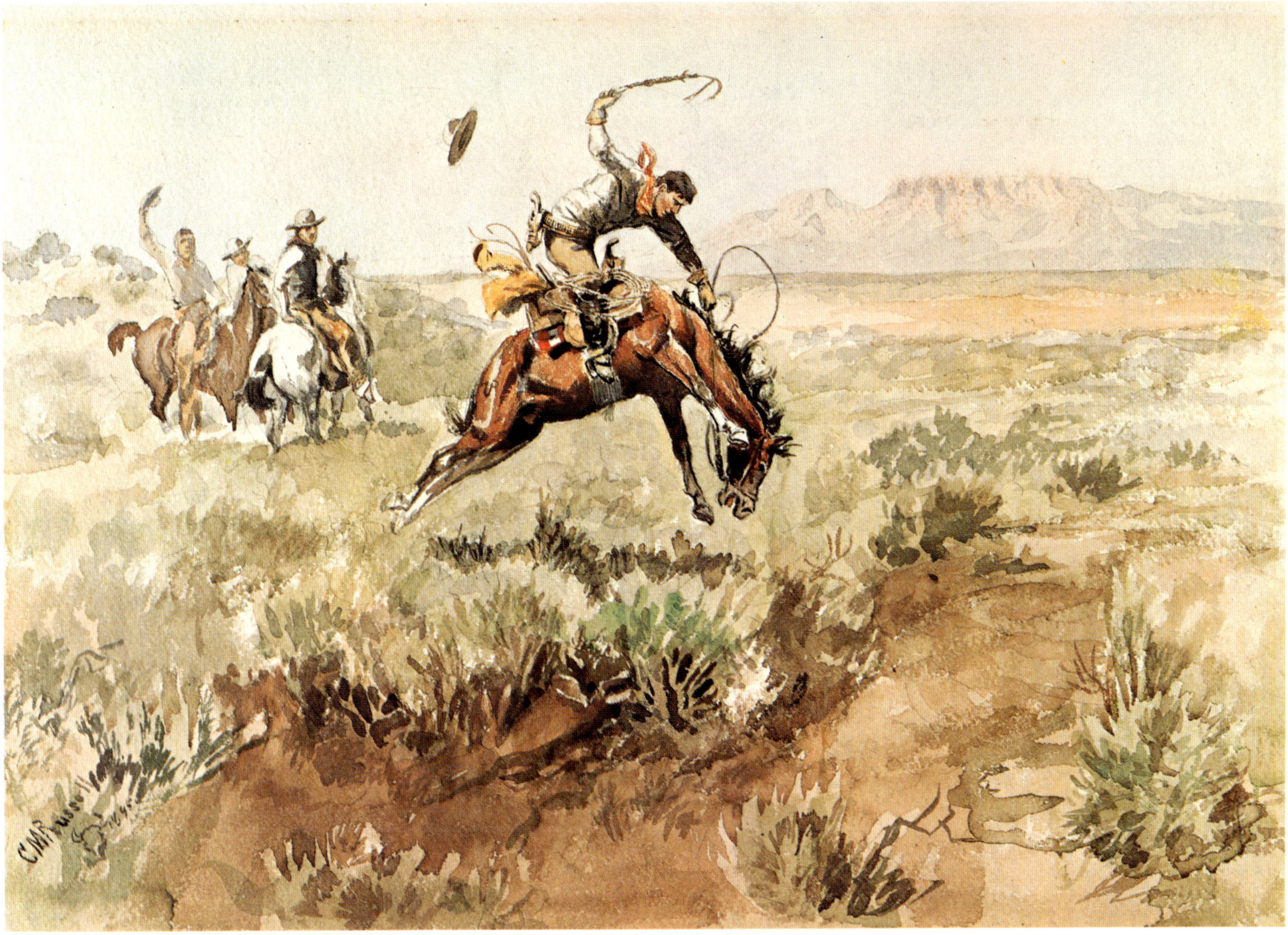

Bronco Busting. Driving In. Cow Puncher.

c. 1889-1890 • 20⅛ × 30⅛ in. • Oil on canvas.

THE GENESIS FOR THIS composite painting was again the book, *Studies of Western Life*, which Russell's staunch friend, Ben Roberts, published for him in 1890 (see page 41). The artist was evidently reluctant to waste space in the twelve-picture portfolio, and so brought into this one canvas three distinct phases—three movements, you might say—of cowboy life.

The first and main one is, as in most symphonies, a steady *allegro*—the cowboy in action, at his basic job of riding herd, in this case (presumably) as part of a spring roundup. The "slow movement," to the right, is one of complete stillness, a man temporarily apart from his horse (though remembering it in the shape of his legs), and contemplative in the way that this lonely life made easy, and necessary. The final *allegro vivace* is the cowboy astride the shuddering arch of a "half-broke" horse.

The relationship between Russell and his self-appointed promoter was an important and productive one. Harold McCracken, in his *Charles M. Russell Book*, reports a long conversation in which Robert's daughter, Mrs. Charles L. Sheridan, reminisced about the encouragements her father gave his friend: setting him up, for instance, in the stone barn in Helena, Montana, that became his first studio.

She told McCracken of the two men's first meeting. "One day Russell rode up to our barn, on his beautiful pinto pony Monte. 'Hello, Ben,' said Russell. 'How in blankety blank did you know I was Ben and who in blankety blank are you?' chuckled Dad. 'Well—my name's Charlie Russell,' he drawled, 'an' I was told if I found a fellow that was homelier than I am, it would be Ben Roberts.' They were the best of friends from that time on."

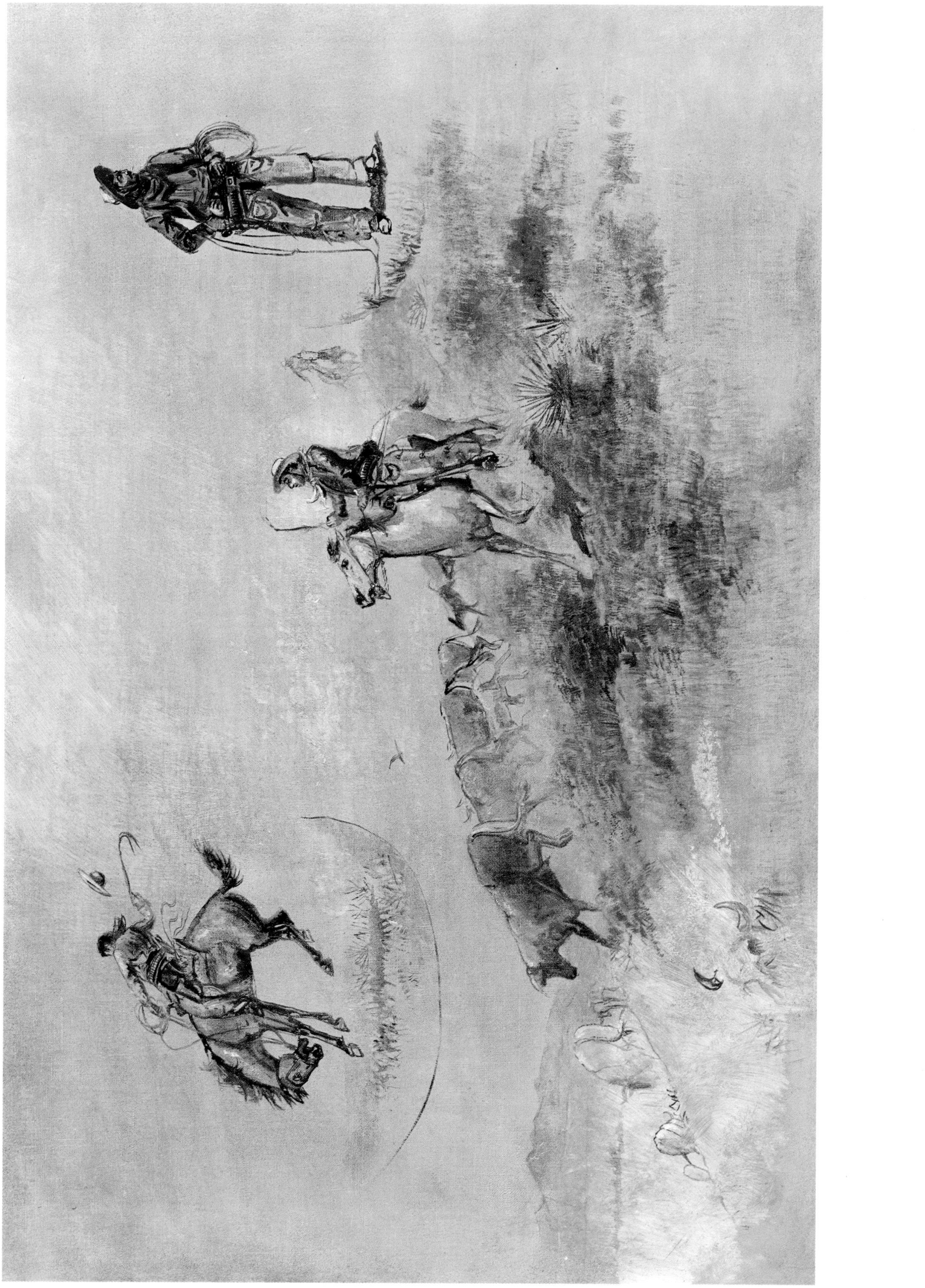

Bucking Horse and Cowgirl

c. 1925 • 13⅜ × 11¼ in. • Watercolor on paper.

In view of the rugged, outdoors virility of his typical subjects, Russell it not really thought of as a painter of femininity; it might even be suspected that he had no knack for it. Most of his squaws, after all, were fairly formidable.

In fact, he showed a flair in this direction that might, if he had wished, have rivaled that of Charles Dana Gibson. Evidence for this appears not only in his not-so-formidable *Keeoma* (see page 51) but in a diaphanously veiled wood nymph from about 1896 and in a shapely pair of Egyptian dancing girls—to name just a few from the Amon Carter collection.

Yet this cowgirl may be the most convincing evidence of all, since she brings a credible femininity to one of the toughest tests of any cowperson's stamina: bronc riding. Whether or not Russell had ever *seen* a girl (or even a man) stay glued with such aplomb, he certainly makes it seem possible.

The painting was one of a his-and-hers pair which he produced as a personal favor for Guy Weadick, organizer of the Calgary Stampede. Though they were meant to go on the program cover, they apparently never found their way there.

It is perhaps typical of Russell that, with all the closeness of subject and function within the pair, this watercolor shows a distinct difference of technique from its companion piece. Paint was laid on the cowboy as a simple watercolor wash; but there is pen-and-ink hatching over most of the girl and her horse. Perhaps this shading underlines her vigorous qualifications for a "man's" job.

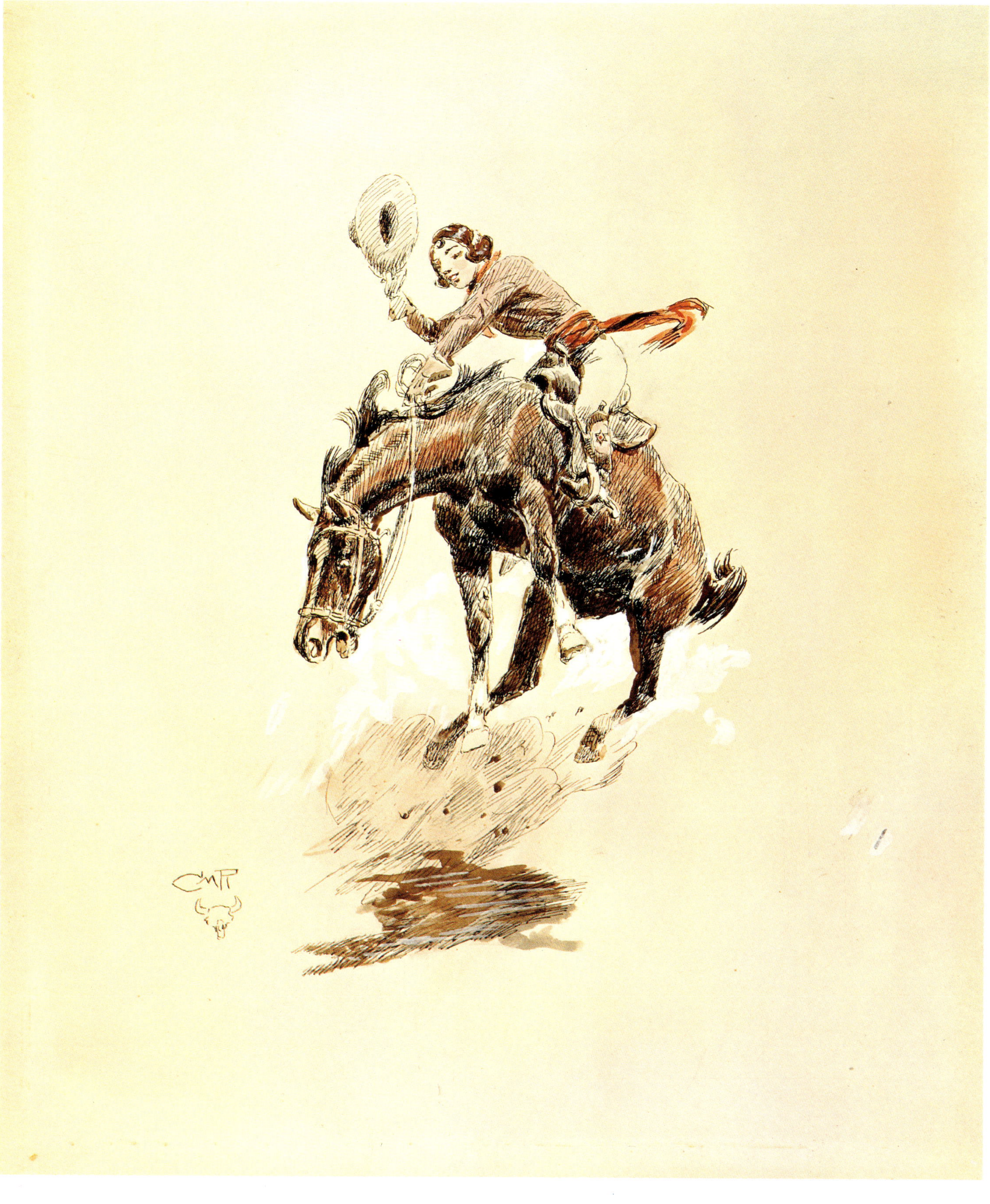

Bronc in Cow Camp

1897 • 20⅛ × 31¼ in. • Oil on canvas.

To compare this obstreperous scene with the earlier oils of cowboy life such as *Breaking Camp* (page 57) from twelve years before, is to find Russell in firmer control of the medium, using a wider and subtler range of color, and with an easier sense of movement in space. And though he still had problems in achieving naturalness and proportion—particularly here with the startled figure to the right—his people are now more convincingly worked into the scene and give less of the effect of being cut out and pasted on. As they move into the distance, too, their forms are softened and corroded by a surrounding atmosphere.

What he was rapidly learning through observation and his artist's intuition was, in a way, what had to be learned about portraying human reality at the start of the Italian Renaissance (for one big instance)—and notably in the evolving realism of the painter Giotto.

In each case the most important thing was to tell a story believably, with fullest appreciation of the subject. And Russell has had a marvelous time telling this one, with its stageful of entertaining characters: the intensely preoccupied bronc-riding of the expert Bob Thoroughman (Russell's close friend) as his outlaw horse "Pinto" crashes through the campfire like a bucking tornado; the outraged cook, whose gut response seems unlikely to calm the situation; and the onlookers, either amused or confounded, depending upon where they are vis-à-vis the tornado's path.

It was one of the many kinds of encounters depicted by Russell's storytelling gifts—visual or verbal—and he painted its comedy in many variations.

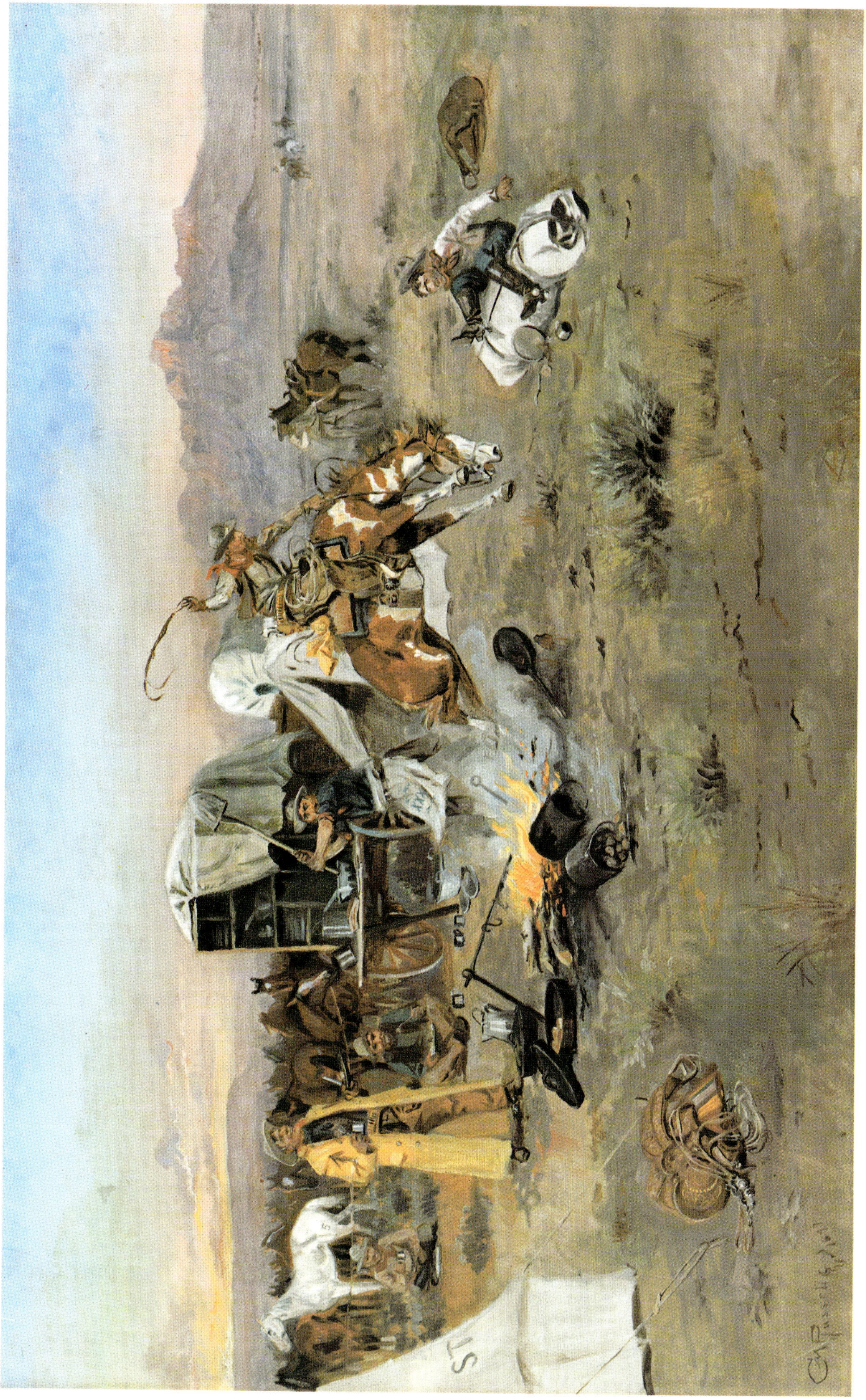

Cowboy Camp During the Roundup

c. 1887 • 23½ × 47¼ in. • Oil on canvas.

THROUGHOUT THE LONG WINTERS here in the Judith Basin the cattle roamed at will, foraging for themselves over the free expanses of still-unfenced grassland. Belonging to large and small herds of many owners, by springtime they were bound to be scattered and intermixed, with new and unbranded calves.

So the owners would bring themselves and their cowboys together to organize and carry out a spring roundup: 1882 in the Judith Basin was the time and place for an especially important and thorough one. And it gave Russell his second experience as "nighthawk," tending horses through the night while the other cowboys slept.

To judge from this exuberant painting of a few years later, commissioned by James R. Shelton, none of these first, rather menial jobs dampened Russell's enthusiasm for life among the "rawhide" fraternity. Taking a wide sweep of the Judith, he has spilled and sprinkled over a large canvas the energetic makings of his chosen world, centering here on the little settlement of Utica—in which, by the way, the painting was first hung on the wall of art patron Shelton's saloon.

That area is just one of several "movements," as they might be called in such a musically organized work. They include also the lively party of identifiable cowboys in the foreground, the almost equally animated though quite geometric gathering of tents and wagons on the middle plane just behind them, and the procession of horses to the right—specifically connecting the life of this scene to the further distances of hill and sky.

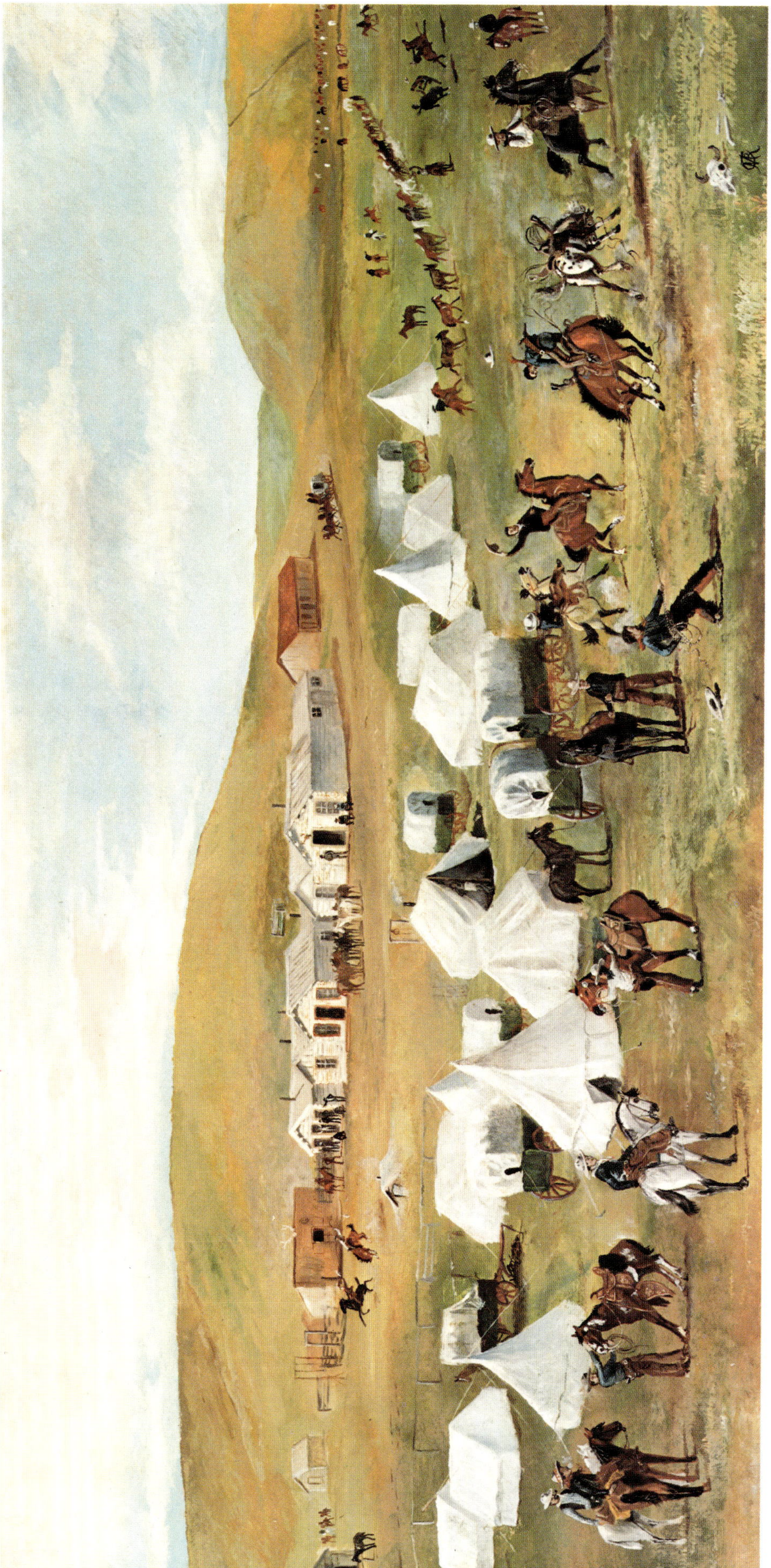

Loops and Swift Horses Are Surer Than Lead

1916 • 30¼ × 48⅛ in. • Oil on canvas.

RUSSELL HERE TELLS THE STORY of an actual bear-roping incident near Saco, Montana, in 1904. The skills and the mounts of these cowboys (Charlie Shufelt, Frank Howe, and Joe Reynolds) had to be surer than lead, since on that occasion none of them carried a gun (even though Russell felt duty-bound to put one in Howe's holster). The artist heard the tale from his cowboy-poet friend, Wallace Coburn, of the Circle C outfit, and his picture leaves very little to be told—except how it started, and how it ended:

One early morning after a rain (look at the clear, rinsed light and shadow), about forty horses had been reported missing. Suddenly they were seen hightailing for home, and in pursuit was a big brown bear. The three cowboys moved in. Shufelt's horse, to the left here, got too close, and the bear swiped a piece of its tail (thereby keeping Shufelt busy during the rest of the action).

After several loops have been thrown off by the bear, Reynolds has finally caught her by the hind feet, so that Howe can drop a loop over her head that will stay. Then, while the horses hold the ropes taut, the men will kill her with rocks.

Russell has added immense depth to the sunny-and-shadowed freshness of this scene through the classic device of the spiral line. Beginning with Shufelt's turning horse, to the left, our eye swings over the foreground, is turned by Reynolds towards the two distant cowboys, and then back and forth along the shadowed ridges beyond.

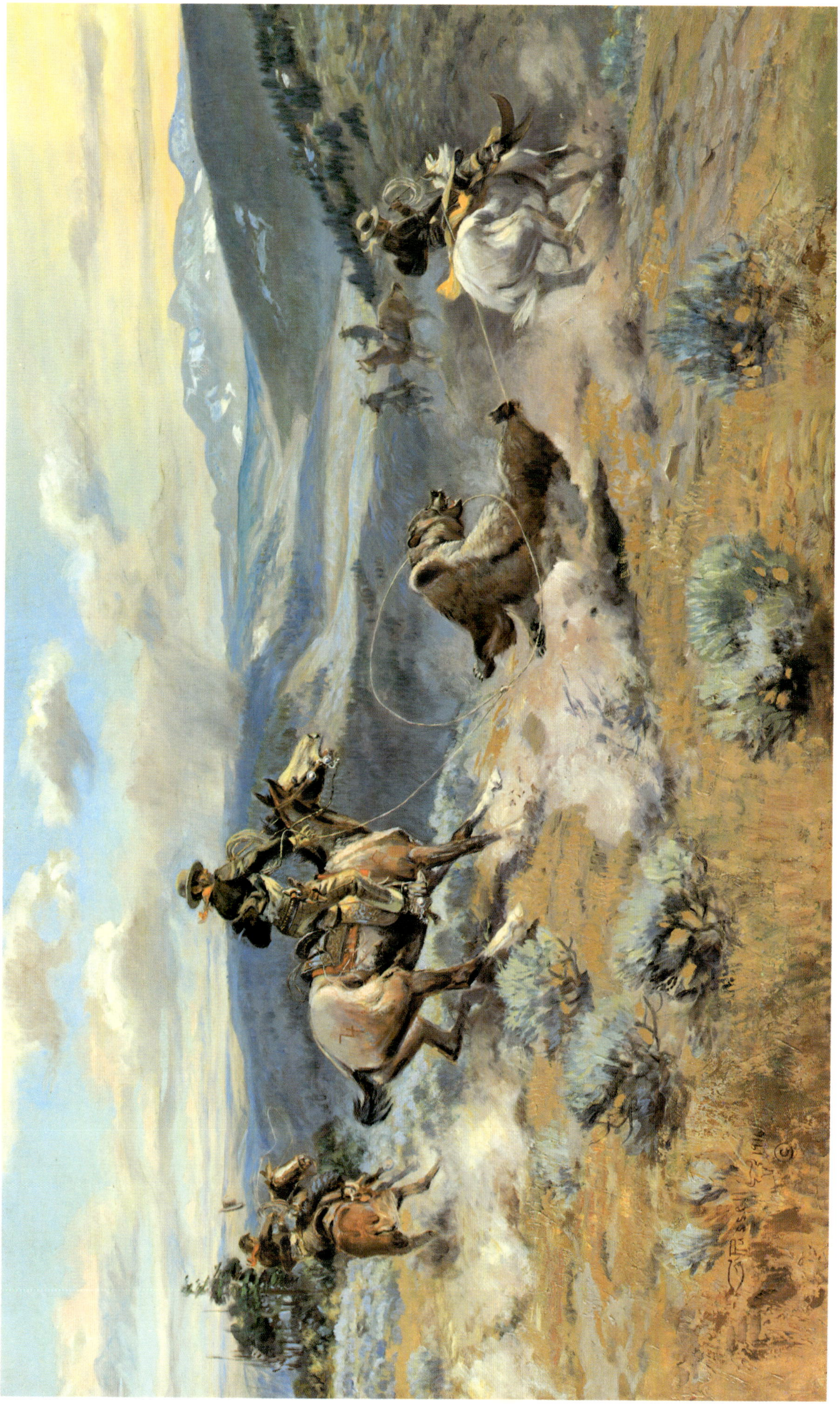

A Moment of Great Peril in a Cowboy's Career

c. 1904 • 24 × 16 in. • Watercolor on paper.

RUSSELL KNEW PERILS of this kind first-hand, and even though his long title has a melodramatic tinge to it, there's much more truth than melodrama to the encounter itself. It's a truth that could take in this mean-tempered, ring-tailed bull's career as well as the cowboy's: both, after all, are subject to some peril. And the bull's career has an even deeper tradition, having been paid the respects of the prehistoric cave-painters and then of the followers of Moses and their golden calf.

But by the time he pictured this precarious situation, it would appear that in Russell's own deepest concern the peril of either the cowboy or the bull was incidental to what he saw as a broader calamity: the whole Western change from the free land on which cowboy, cattle, Indian, and buffalo had for a while coexisted, to the parceling out that came with the land's settlement; and that domestication worked against the buffalo, the Indian, and the cowboy, in that order. It was well underway when Russell arrived, and it continued, making most of his paintings into a reminder of the past and a protest against a more "civilized" present.

The pen drawing below instances another medium of protest functioning pungently—not as a careful, affectionate record of the past, but as a casually ironic comment on the present.

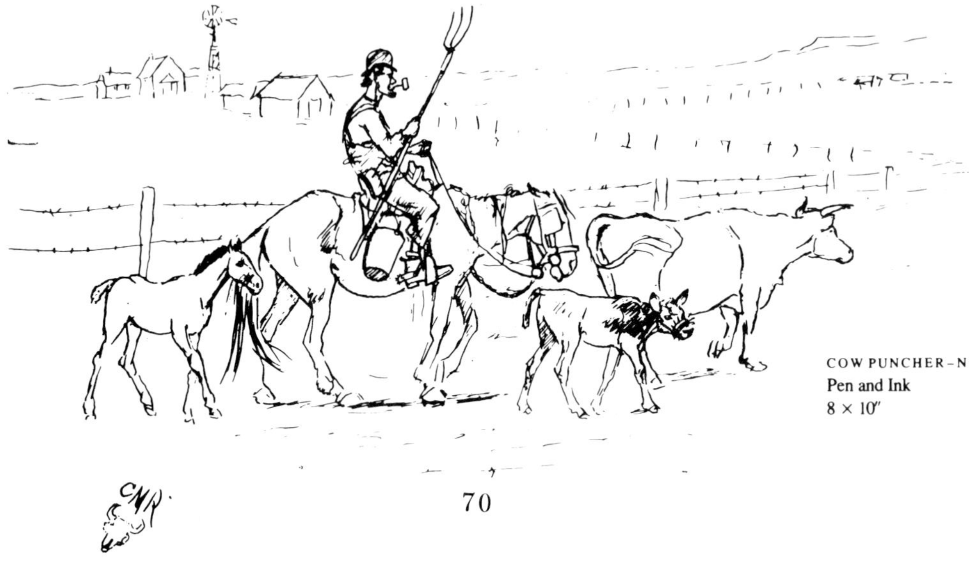

COW PUNCHER–NEW STYLE
Pen and Ink
8 × 10″

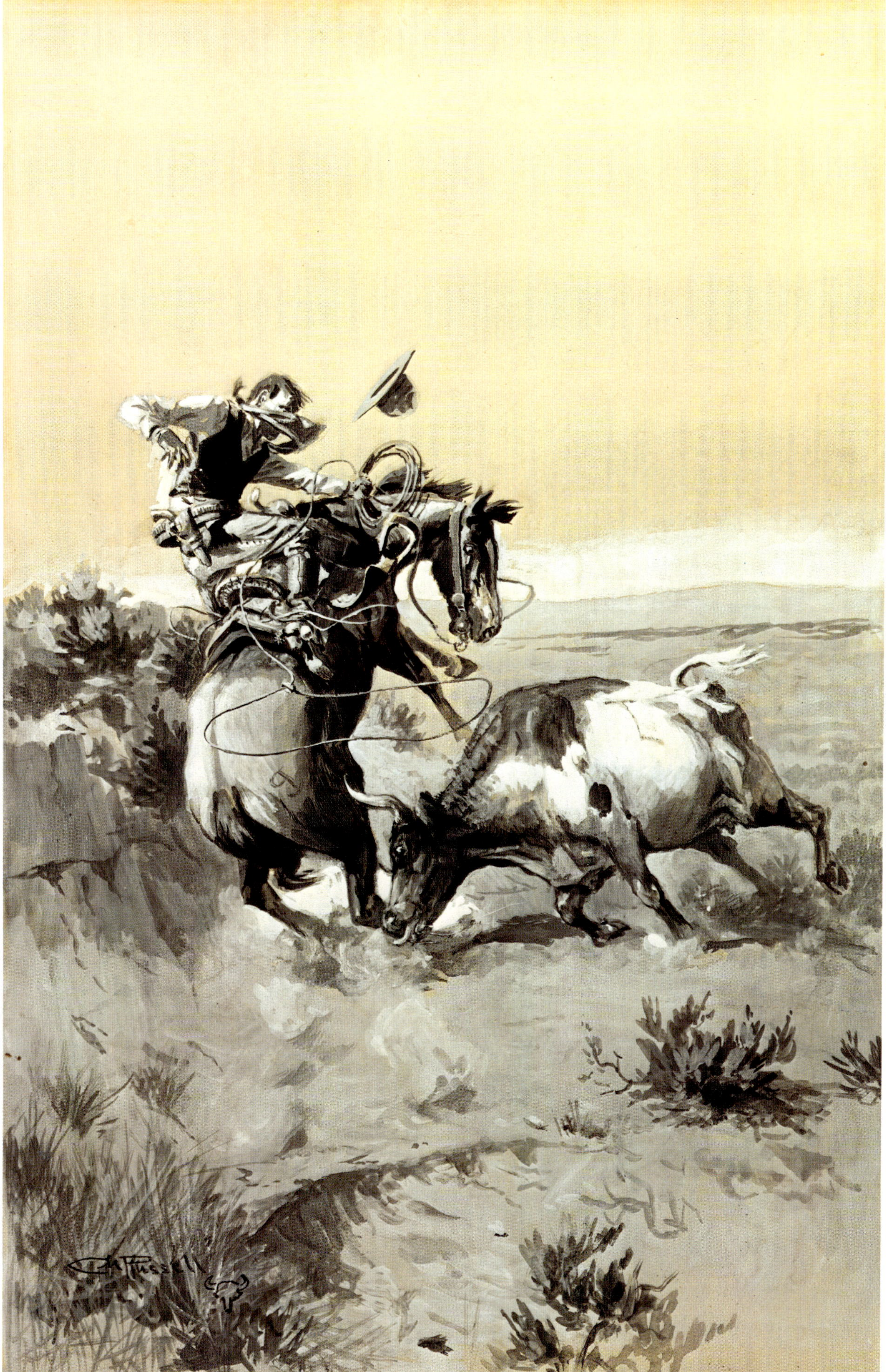

Tight Dally and Loose Latigo

1920 • 30¼ × 48¼ in. • Oil on canvas.

THIS RELATIVELY LATE roundup scene is another one that can be contrasted in its arrangement, coloring, and technique with those exuberant early efforts from thirty or more years past (such as *Cowboy Camp During the Roundup*, on page 43). The same energy is there, but tightened now into a taut interplay and connectedness of form that correlates with the literal connectedness of cowboy and cattle. In this instance of the author's mature style, the almost expressionist interplay of orange and blue coloring in the three horses also acquires energy; and so does the flickering texture of brush strokes.

The result is of course neither abstract nor expressionistic; but the surface narrative is now being underlined—consciously or not—by these aesthetic ingredients: which means that the narrative goes under the surface of forms and figures and finds roots in form itself. Notice the subdividing of landscape to help identify the areas of action and so to clarify the story.

As always with Russell, then, it is a story picture, showing the problems that a cowboy faces when his dally (the half-hitch of rope he takes around his saddle horn to secure a catch) is tight and his latigo (the strap connecting his cinch-belt to the base of his saddle) is loose. The horn is being pulled to the left, while the cowboy and his mount—like good sailors offsetting the windblown tilt of a sailboat—are throwing their weight to the right. He's in for clear trouble if the saddle keeps going where it's headed; and that upended calf may break away toward the loops of one or both circling cowboys.

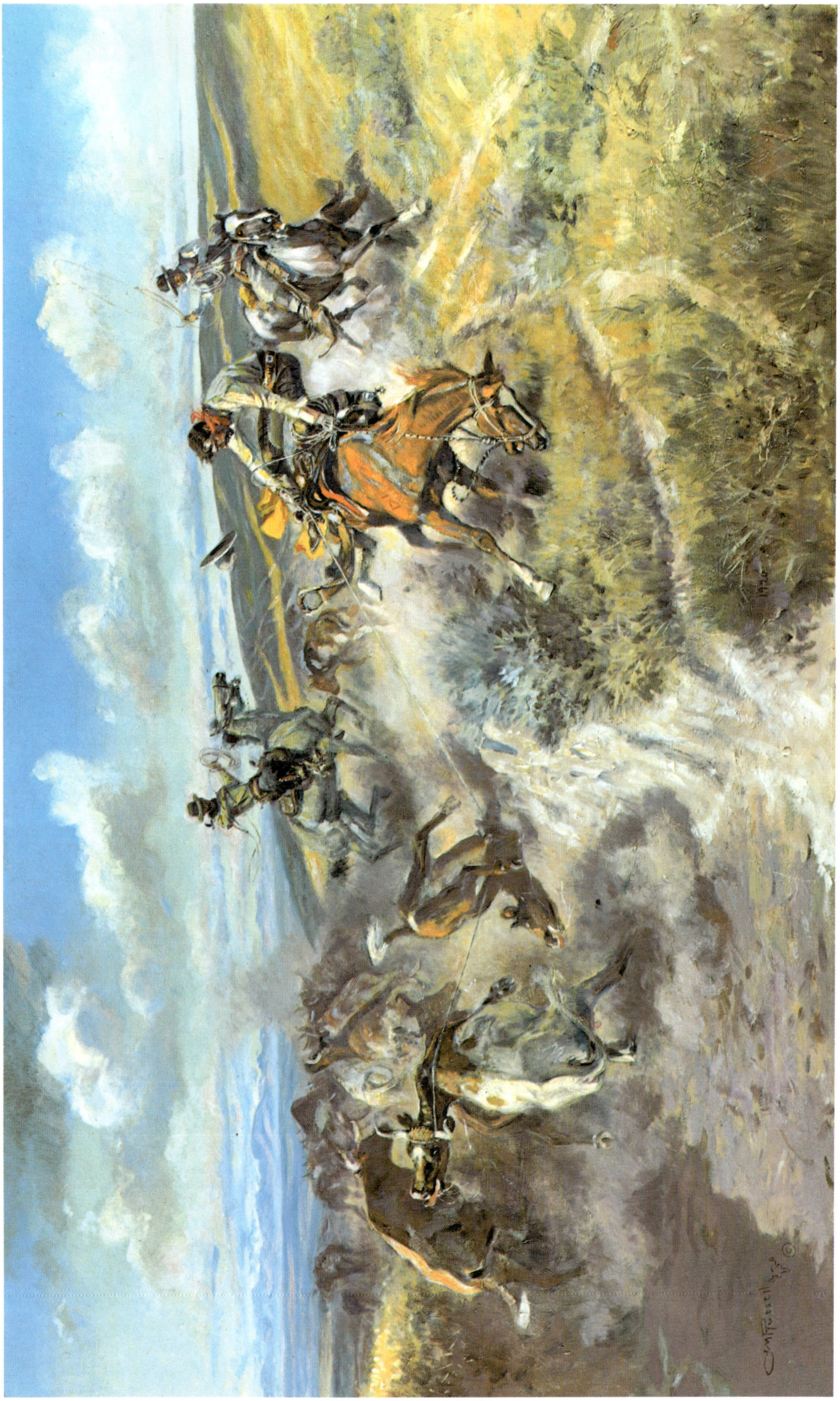

The Broken Rope

1904 • 24 × 36⅛ in. • Oil on canvas.

RUSSELL PUT SUCH A SWING into this oil—and not only into the figures themselves but into the scooped-out terrain precipitating the fall as well—that we really should have the swing of his words to accompany it. The painting brings together cowboys from Montana and Texas (to the right); and in "The Story of the Cowpuncher" from his book, *Trails Plowed Under,* Russell puts these words into the mouth of his protagonist, Rawhide Rawlins:

> "Texas an' California, bein' the startin' places, made two species of cowpunchers; those west of the Rockies rangin' north, usin' centerfire or single-cinch saddles, with high fork and cantle. . . . These fellows were sure fancy, an' called themselves buccaroos, coming from the Spanish word, *vaquero.*
>
> "The cowpuncher east of the Rockies originated in Texas and ranged north to the Big Bow. . . . He wasn't so much for pretty. . . .
>
> "I tell you right now, there ain't no prettier sight for my eyes than one of those goodlookin', long-backed cowpunchers, sittin' up on a high-forked, full-stamp California saddle with a live hoss between his legs."

That's the position the nearest, less-pretty cowboy here would like to get into instantly, if he could—and the lift of the painting seems capable of taking him up there. But meanwhile, he might prompt Rawhide's earlier reminiscence of "the eastern girl that asks her mother: 'Ma,' says she, 'do cowboys eat grass?' 'No, dear,' says the old lady, 'they're part human,' an' I don't know but the old gal had 'em sized up right."

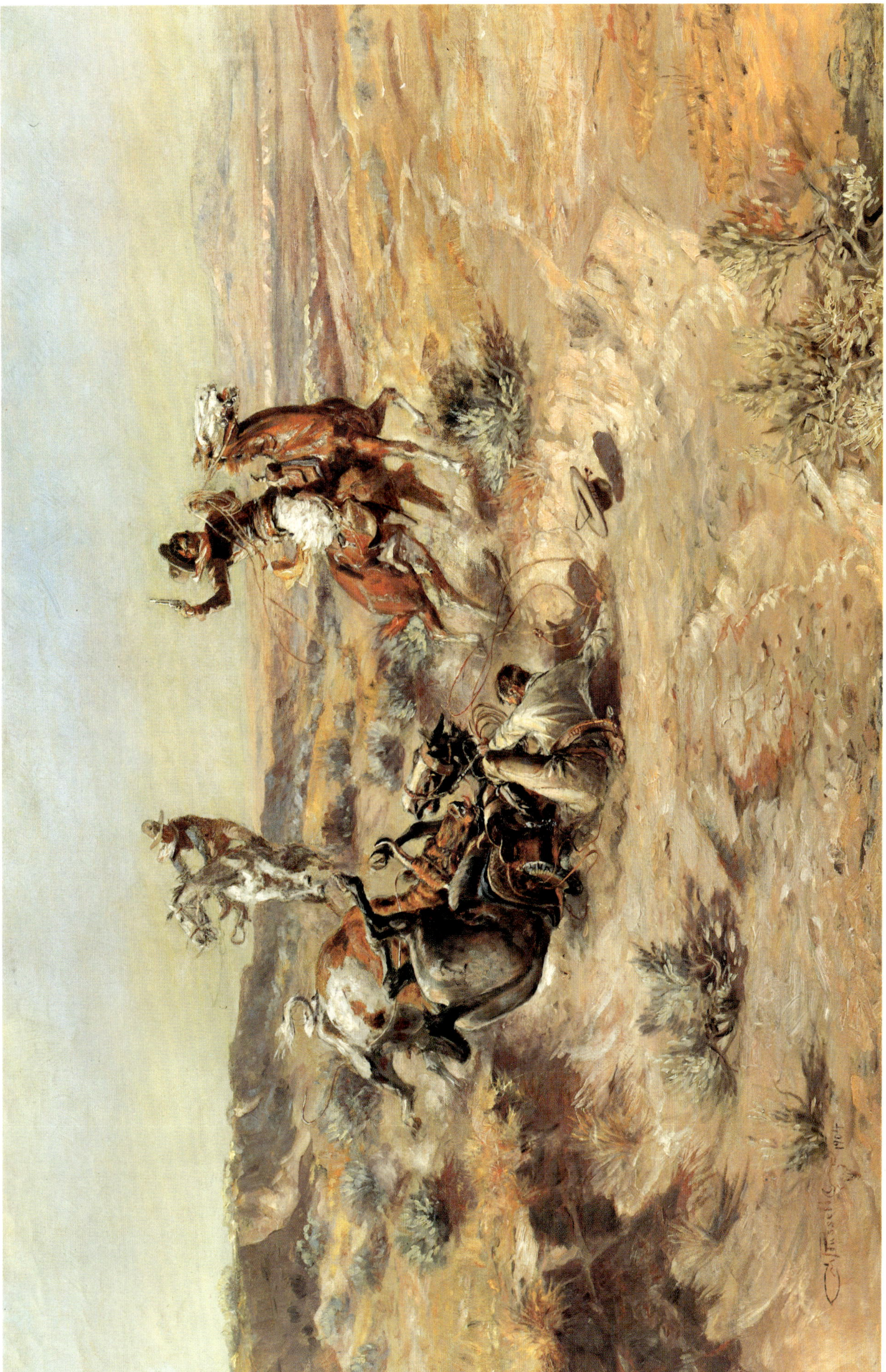

Smoke of a .45

1908 • 24⅜ × 36¼ in. • Oil on canvas.

THIS PAINTING AND THE NEXT ONE, *In Without Knocking*, have some scenery in common. They are set, for one thing, in different parts of the same early Montana cowtown of Stanford; they both show the off-duty cowboy's capability, as Duncan Emrich has put it, of "raising virtually every kind of hell imaginable"; and each scene is surrounded with a scattering of whiskey bottles, cards—and gunsmoke.

Yet the paintings are hard to identify in relation to each other, or even to a contemporary photo of Stanford's main street. All of which indicates that, like any good storyteller, Charlie Russell had a superb memory for the "right" details—verifiable or not. And since he was also an artist bent on the rightness of composition (his wife spoke of the hours of "big silence," when he'd spend long evenings with a pad on his knee, sketching and re-sketching the composition for a painting), those details were not allowed to detract from the way lines and forms hung and swung together—and almost blew apart.

For instance, the pivotal center of that careening tangle of horseflesh is the cowboy's head and shoulders, not to mention his .45-caliber pistol. To secure that center, and so give coherence to the surrounding action, Russell needed to frame the head and pistol in something as emphatic as the white hotel facade. The result of this kind of strategy is a picture of Stanford that might be less physically exact than a facsimile, but is distinctly more "lifelike."

Then no matter how you sort out the pieces of the story (who shot who, when, and why) you're dealing with people that breathe—or did, anyway. That may be why Will Rogers pursued this painting for 15 years or so, and finally (as Renner tells the story) had to settle for a duplicate.

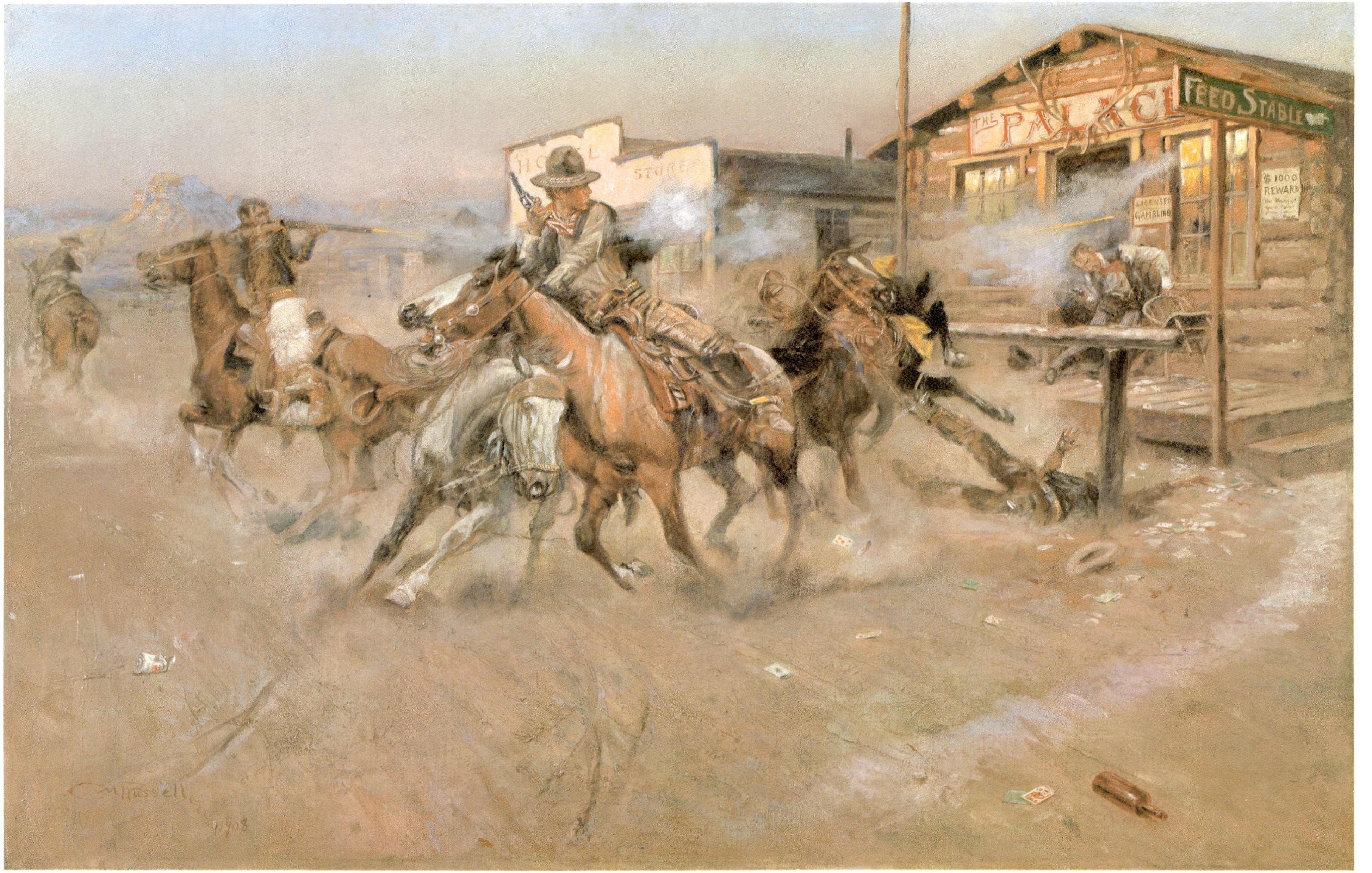

FEED STABLE
THE PALACE
HOTEL
STORE
$1000 REWARD
LICENSED GAMBLING
CMRussell
1908

In Without Knocking

1909 • 20⅛ × 29⅞ in. • Oil on canvas.

HERE'S ANOTHER OF THE GUSTY, noisy cowboy scenes that Russell enjoyed celebrating—at least in paint—and filling with people he knew, doing what he knew they'd done. These were colleagues of his on the 1881 cattle drive to the Northern Pacific railhead, so he might have joined them on this social round in Stanford, Montana. But he was working for them, "nighthawking" the horseherd, and had to get the details second hand the next morning.

He got them and kept them and, after more than a quarter century, painted them verbatim into his vivid picture—with its crackling forms and colors, its sprinkled cards and splintered porch—vivid enough to encourage the idea that cowboys carried on like this *all* the time. On the contrary, of course, it was those long, more or less solitary, most-of-the-time demanding days or nights on the open range that built up the steam for an occasional rampage on a nearby cowtown—when there *was* a nearby cowtown. However, one continually typical cowboy habit it does show results from what Harold McCracken in *The American Cowboy* calls "a haughty disdain for using his legs in the normal fashion of a biped, except when he stood with one foot on the foot-rail of a cowtown saloon, or made an awkward attempt at participating at a very infrequent dance."

Dance? In Russell's hands, it could be argued, that's the most continual cowboy habit of all.

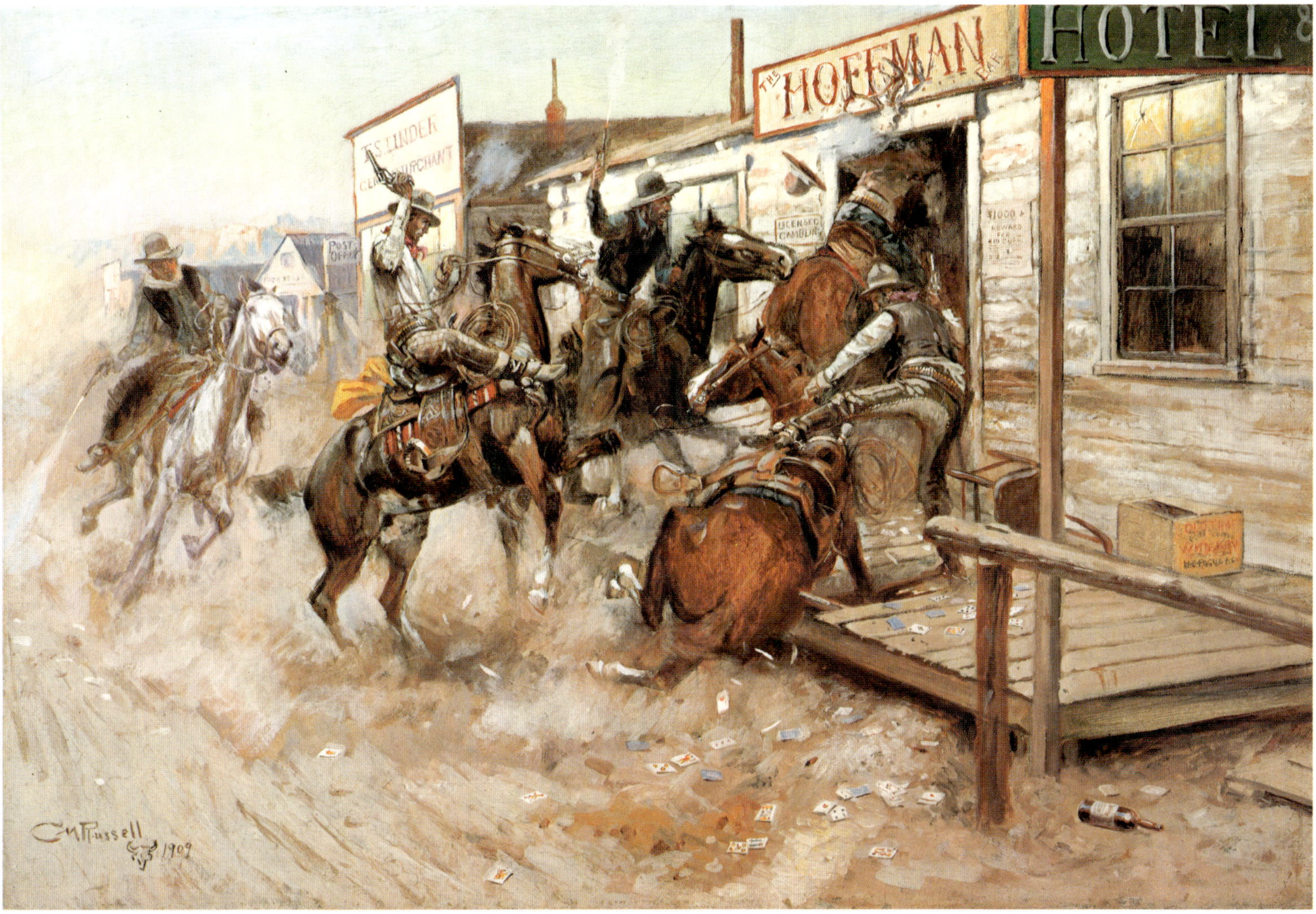
HOTEL
THE HOFFMAN
CMRussell 1909

Just a Little Sunshine

c. 1898 • 13⅛ × 9⅞ in. • Watercolor on paper.

THE CONTRASTS OF LIFE, the dualities, and especially the ironies that play back and forth between them, were latent to the drama that infused most of Russell's paintings. Occasionally he balanced them off in pairs; and when William H. Rance, proprietor of the Silver Dollar saloon in Great Falls, asked for a series of four paintings about cowboy life, Russell was ready to oblige.

If the titles he chose weren't lines from a song, some lyricist has missed an easy bet:

Just a little sunshine,
Just a little rain;
Just a little pleasure,
Just a little pain.

The first pair, included here, are visual weather reports almost as graphic as that *Waiting for a Chinook* that started Russell on his amble toward fame in 1886.

The cowboy in this one is using his horse as a slight shade from a whole lot of sunshine. It is one of the artist's stiller pictures: neither man nor beast seems inclined to move more than is absolutely necessary, so that at least the shade stays put. And the two of them, as an island of dark, sharply drawn color, seem all but baked by the heat-bleached sky and land around them.

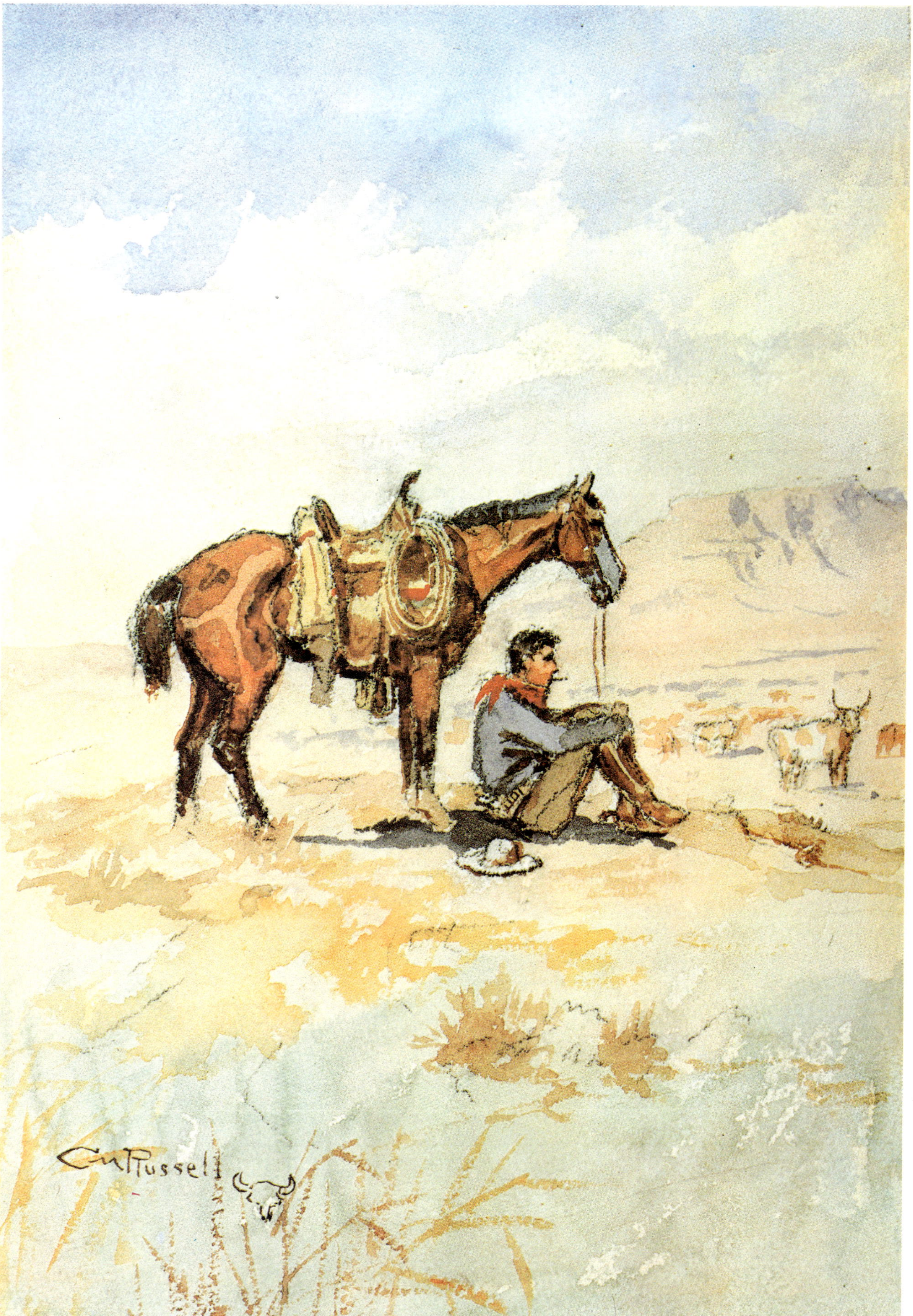
CMRussell

Just a Little Rain

c. 1898 • 13⅛ × 10¾ in. • Watercolor on paper.

SUNSHINE IS AND WAS a familiar enough phenomenon to the Montanan. Sometimes a bit too familiar, when as one of thousands of homesteaders he watched his free farmland blow away in dust. How he might have thirsted for the inches of rain Russell is sloshing down—*wasting*—on this miserable-looking cowboy and his soggy herd.

Watercolor can lend itself admirably to communicating the spongy sky, the sudden puddles—the whole heavy wetness weighing on a scene like this. But of course it doesn't do so automatically. Though Russell could hardly have used actual "wet paper" technique (some artists let the rain itself soak their paper) he seems to have loaded the sky area with some quantity of water.

Yet he's kept it from running over into his mounted figure, and has even managed the trick of the dripping hat-brim. This almost has to be done by letting the white (and dry) paper show through, as it also does here and there on the horse and in the puddles. With true watercolor, you don't add white.

Completely wettened paper would have made those vital touches impossible. And even the wetness he did use had to be under expert control. This must be one of Russell's most idiomatic, even virtuosic, watercolors.

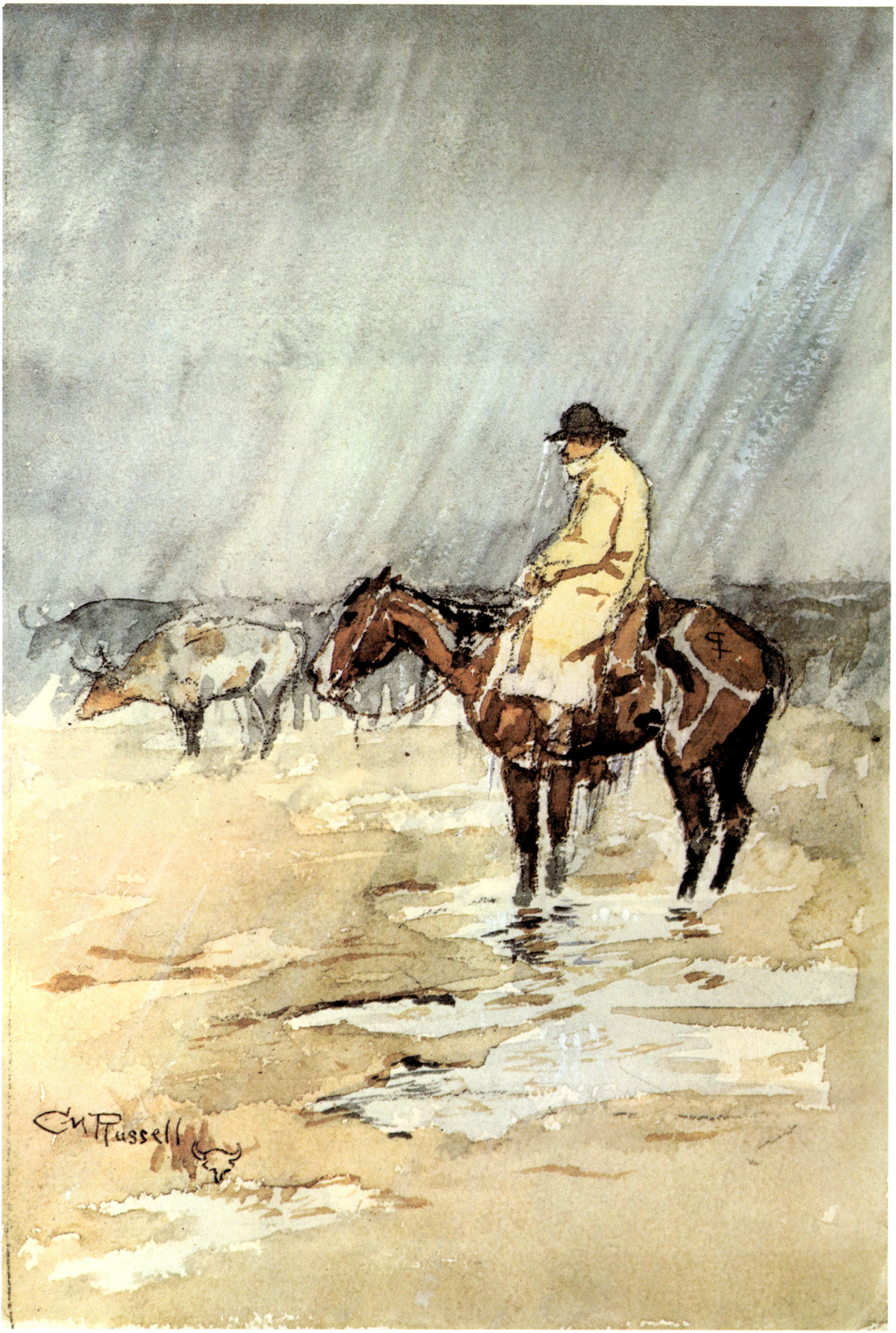
CM Russell

I Beat You To It

1908 • 8 × 19⅝ in. • Pen, ink, and watercolor on paper.

One of Charles Russell's closest long-time friends was Sid Willis, erstwhile sheriff of Valley County, Montana, and proprietor of The Mint saloon in Great Falls. Beginning with *The Hold Up* in 1899 (see page 91), Willis became a steady and enthusiastic collector of Russell paintings and modellings. Since almost every piece he bought or was given found a place somewhere in his roomy establishment, The Mint became widely known as an art gallery.

It was Willis's unfulfilled hope that the collection would always stay in Montana. But he was not in a position to make a gift of it, and soon after the saloon changed ownership the paintings and sculptures were purchased by M. Knoedler and Company in New York, which in 1952 sold all the Russell works to Mr. Amon G. Carter in Fort Worth. They then became the nucleus of the collection drawn on for this book, now installed at the Amon Carter Museum.

In 1908 Russell did this watercolor for use on The Mint stationery. It shows the big billboard that used to stand as a landmark on the outskirts of Great Falls. The cowboys who have raced each other that far are obviously going on to the place itself.

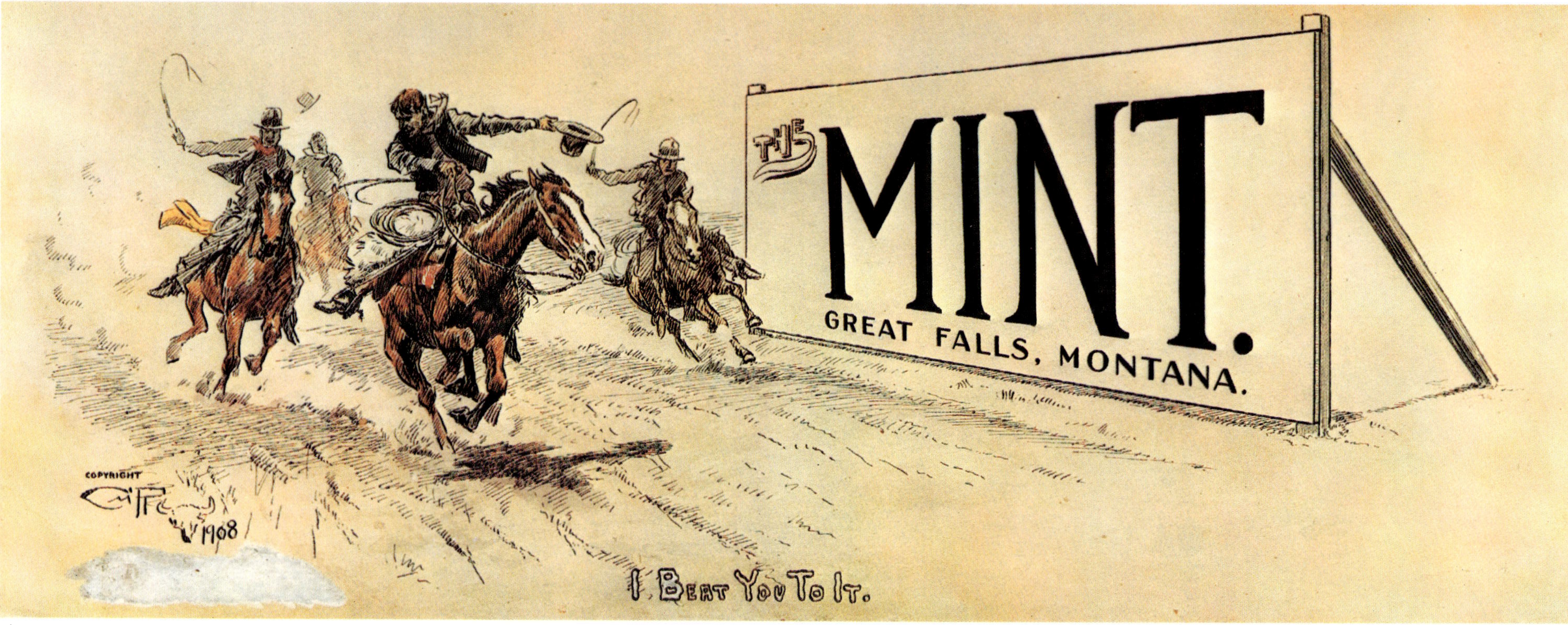
THE MINT.
GREAT FALLS, MONTANA.
COPYRIGHT
1908
I BEAT YOU TO IT.

Christmas at the Line Camp

1904 • 14¼ × 20⅝ in. • Watercolor on paper.

CHRISTMAS WAS A TIME and place of warmth in Charlie Russell's sentimental heart, and he shows it here as a warm haven for cowboys "riding line" after the fall roundup through Montana's white vastness. They've brought fresh venison with them and so will be extra-welcome around the fire inside.

With a characteristic Christmas poem to his Great Falls friend and neighbor A. J. Trigg, Russell included a small watercolor showing something like this same cabin, but more fancifully: the moon is rising, and Santa Claus has just pulled up with his full team of reindeer and a heap of presents in the sleigh behind him.

In the poem, under this same title, Charlie is dreaming of his own childhood Christmas: "I've said my prayers, blessed all my kin/I'm good as good kin be."

Then he hears the jingle outside, stumbles through the door, ("I ain't no kid no more"), and finds Santa ("the same old cuss / Maw tells me about, . . . aholding his ribbons like an old timer would"). But he's "way off the trail"—of the stork ("there's no sign of youngsters, I see"). He reminds these bachelors that however well they may do on the Fourth of July, "or Paddy's Day, / A-passing the drinks around,"

> . . . to get the joy that Christmas brings,
> You must be acquainted with three,
> A home's but a camp without these things:
> A wife, the stork, and me.

Then Charlie's bunk-pal wakes him, cold and cranky, pulling the bedclothes back over himself:

"I wonder what day is today."

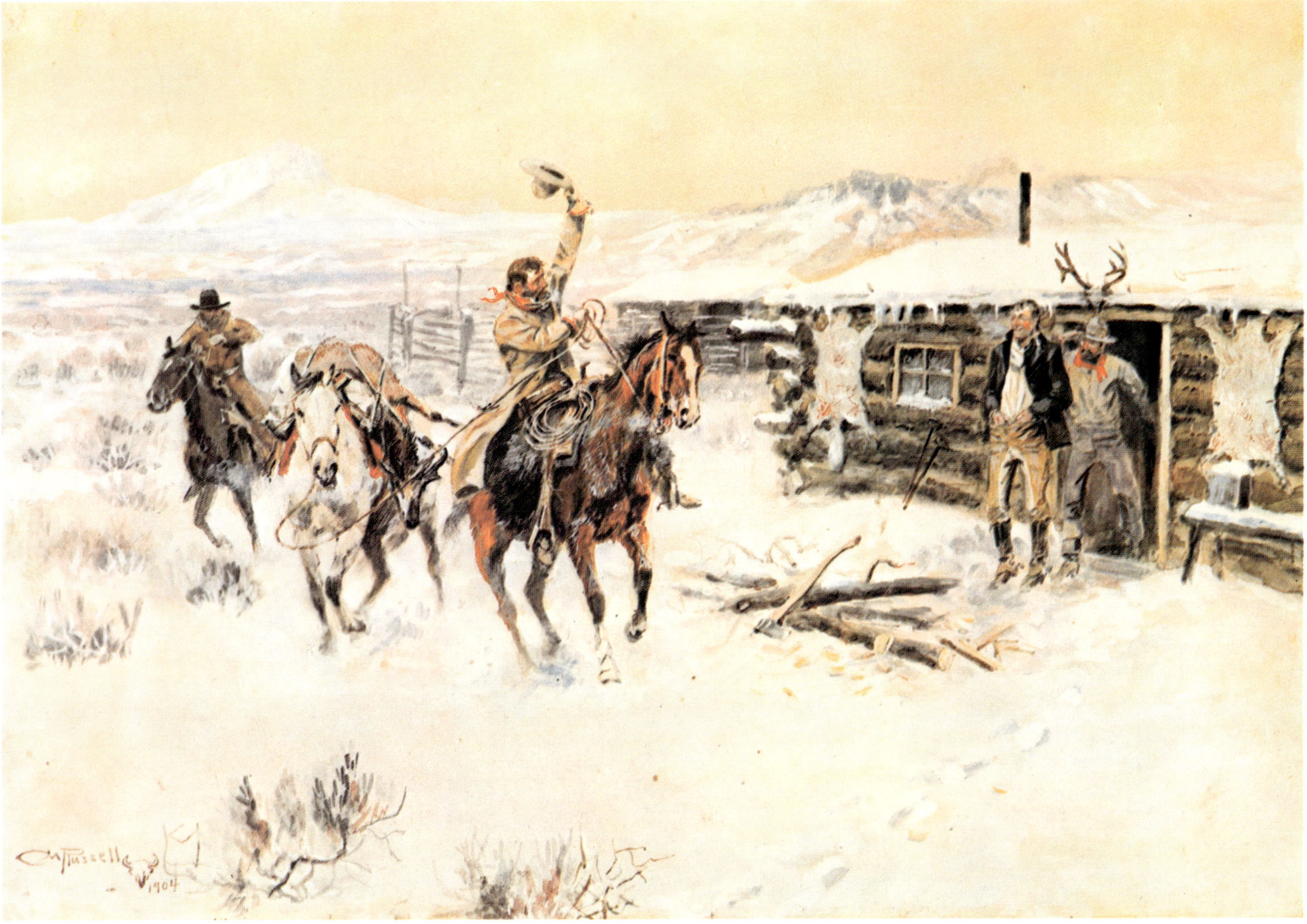

CM Russell
1904

Stagecoach

1920 • 3¼ × 5⅛ in. • Pen, ink, and watercolor on paper.

THIS COLORED PEN and ink drawing, crackling with economy and pungent with nostalgia for its subject, was made in 1920 and sent from Pasadena to the artist's old friend Sid Willis in Great Falls, as a small visual assurance that the old days were not forgotten—including the sharp Montana winter against which the drivers are bundled.

The stagecoach reached its peak as a means of transcontinental travel during the 1850s, just before the gradual encroachment of the railroads. The two systems, however different their motive power, had in common a dependence on freight and mail subsidies for their uncertain livelihood. Passengers were hardly more profitable for the stages than they were later to be for the railroads.

Yet it was the passengers who could talk. Waterman L. Ormsby, a *New York Herald* correspondent who covered the 24-day, 2,866-mile maiden trip from St. Louis to San Francisco of the South-circling Butterfield Overland Mail stage in 1858, could somehow report feeling "almost fresh enough to undertake it again." (I would surmise that "almost" was the operative word.)

Not so Frances M. A. Roe, an army officer's wife, after traveling a mere 140 miles up North, 20 years later. "I was glad enough to get away from that old stage," she wrote. "It was one of the jerky, bob-back-and-forth kind that pitches you off the seat every five minutes. The first two or three times you bump heads with the person sitting opposite, you can smile and apologize with some grace, but after a while your hat will not stay in place and your head becomes sensitive, and finally you discover that the passenger is the most disagreeable person you ever saw. . . ."

Big Nose George (next page) could be a blessing in disguise.

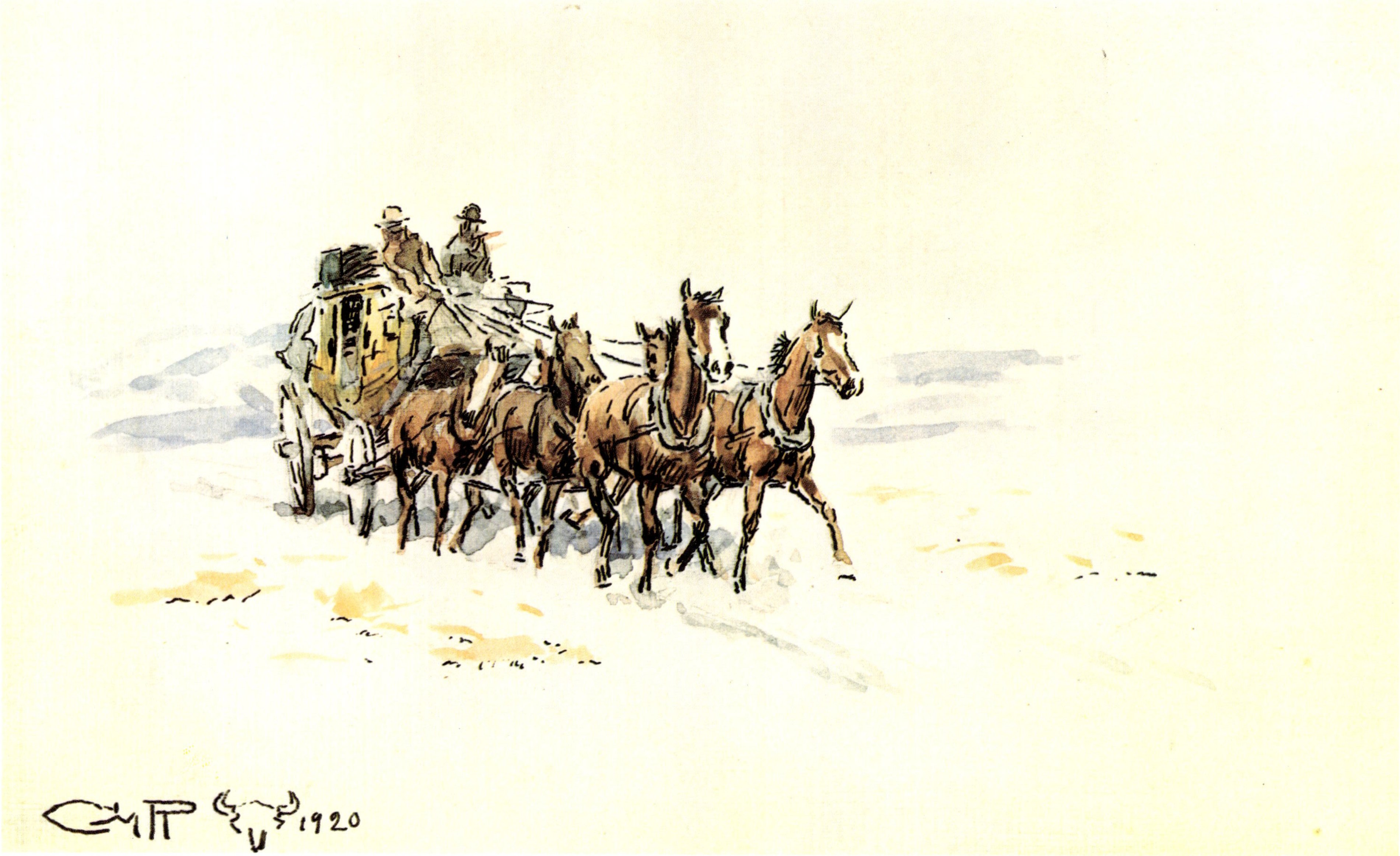
1920

The Hold Up

1899 • 30⅜ × 48¼ in. • Oil on canvas.

Charlie Russell was famous for his stories, whether in words, in pictures, or both. But here's a painting whose main story—with a little help from the imagination—seems to give birth to a dozen more, needing perhaps a Chaucer or Boccaccio to develop the possibilities of its assorted characters.

What we know of the actual incident here centers on the career of an early 1880s outlaw called Big Nose George, whose distinguishing feature Russell has carefully silhouetted against the glow of autumn foliage at stage center. This holdup of the stage between Miles City and Bismarck, North Dakota, is the scene of his last crime: he was arrested in Miles City, and taken for trial to Rawlins, Wyoming, where he was ignominiously lynched by outraged citizens.

But this final time around he nabbed quite a cross section of the citizenry—some of them friends of Russell's. There's a minister, a prospector, a schoolteacher, a Chinese. And there's Isaac Katz, who had recently come from New York to open a men's clothing store and was on this occasion relieved of quite substantial winnings from playing faro. And next to the more professional gambler at the center is the Widow Flanagan, proprietor of the Miles City boardinghouse, whose distress could also be disillusionment at the quantity of cards extricated from her neighbor's tailcoat.

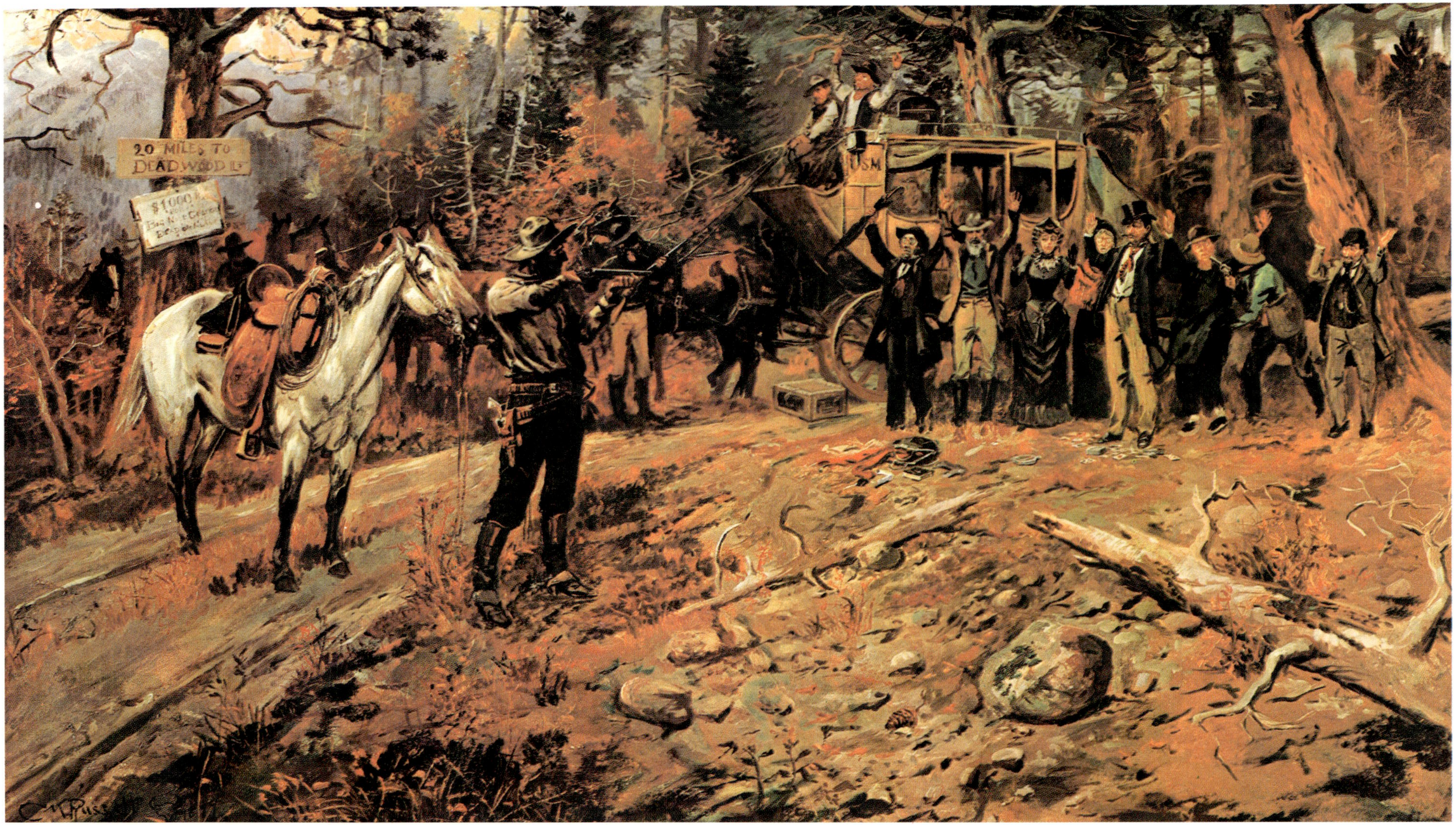
20 MILES TO
DEADWOOD

The Horse Thieves

1901 • 24⅛ × 30⅛ in. • Oil on canvas.

HORSE THIEVING WAS for the white settler a sometimes flourishing but always despised occupation. When a thief was caught in a community aroused to action he was likely to be tried and hung within hours.

For the Indians, however, horse raids were generally important tribal pursuits, and the brave's success in stealing the "god dog" would mean not only the acquisition of wealth, but a strong proof of manhood. Furthermore, immense skill might be involved.

The Piegan raider White Quiver, shown in this moonlit scene of Russell's, is a case in point. On one occasion he took fifty Crow ponies—including their chief's favorite buffalo horse—was apprehended and jailed by the authorities at Fort Benton, escaped and restole all the horses, and then repeated the performance when he was again captured by the Canadian Mounties. He finally found his way safely to the Blackfoot Reservation on the Montana side of the border.

One of the ponies taken in that raid ended up in Russell's hands as "Monte," to be ridden by the artist for twenty-five years.

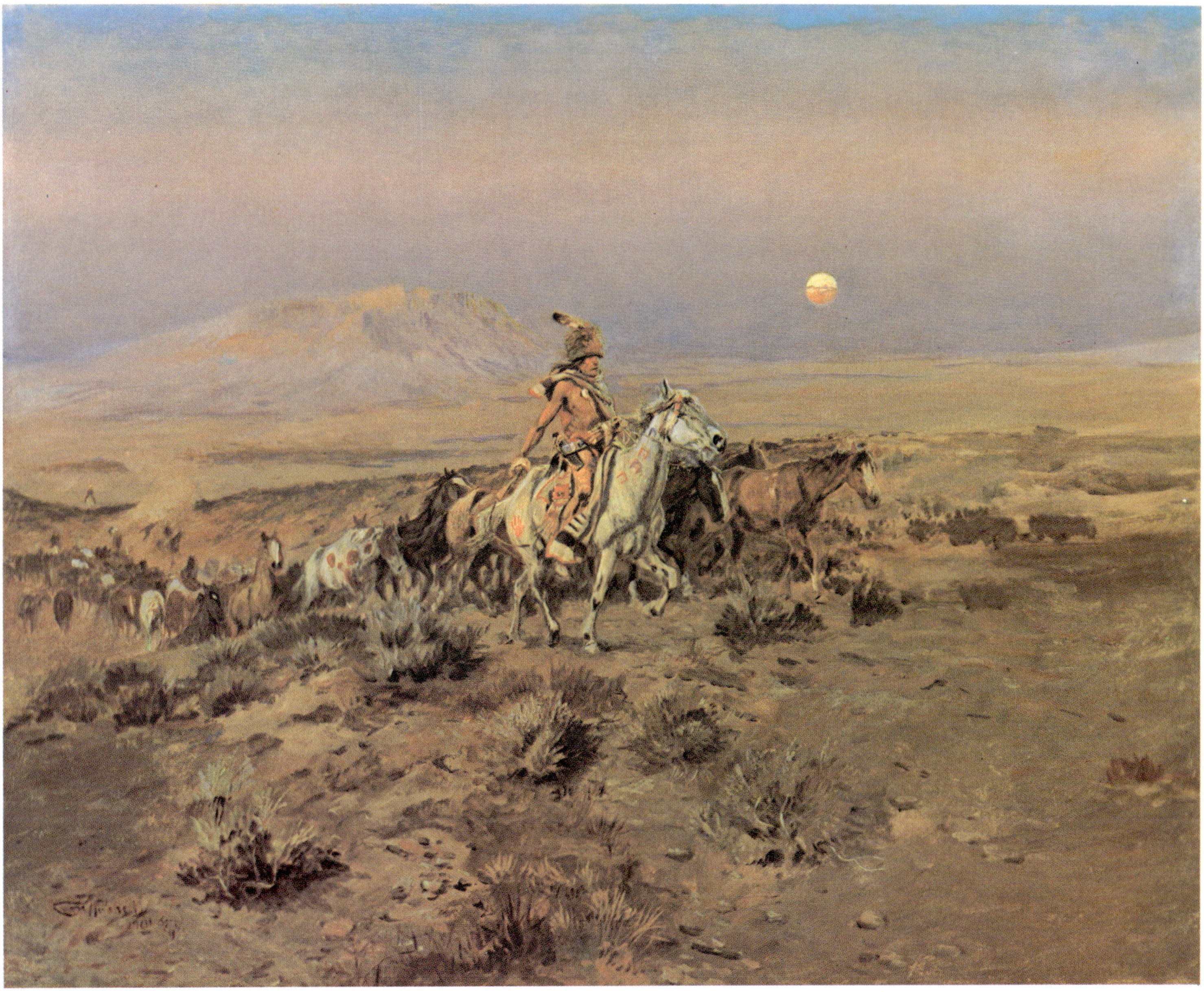

Navajo Indian Horse Thieves Hotly Pursued by Robbed Mexicans

1904 • 25¾ × 19⅛ in. • Gouache on paper.

THE NAVAJOS LIVED considerably south of Russell's usual territory as an artist, being centered well down towards the Mexican border—though at one time they had been in the habit of making long summer journeys as far north as Kansas. The Spanish *conquistadores* had brought horses into their lives, and guns—with some help from the French—and the Navajos learned to make expert use of both. Horses became for them, as for other "horse Indian" tribes, not only a crucial means of mobility but a unique measure of wealth and status. To acquire them and keep them, by whatever means possible, was a high purpose in their lives.

Russell found his way this far afield in 1904 while he and Nancy were all the way East in the "big camp," struggling to make some inroads in the New York art market. One of Nancy's few successes on that trip was with *Leslie's Weekly,* which ran a story about her husband—including reproductions of a few paintings—in its March 3 issue, and picked this lively scene for the April 21 cover.

A few months earlier, under the optimistic headline, "Smart Set Lionizing Cowboy Artist," a reporter for the *New York Press* had more soberly sized up Russell's yearning to be anywhere rather than where he was: "Taciturn as a Sioux chief, self-contained and impassive, he is hardly the man to care for pink teas. He will remain a Westerner of the old school to the end. . . ."

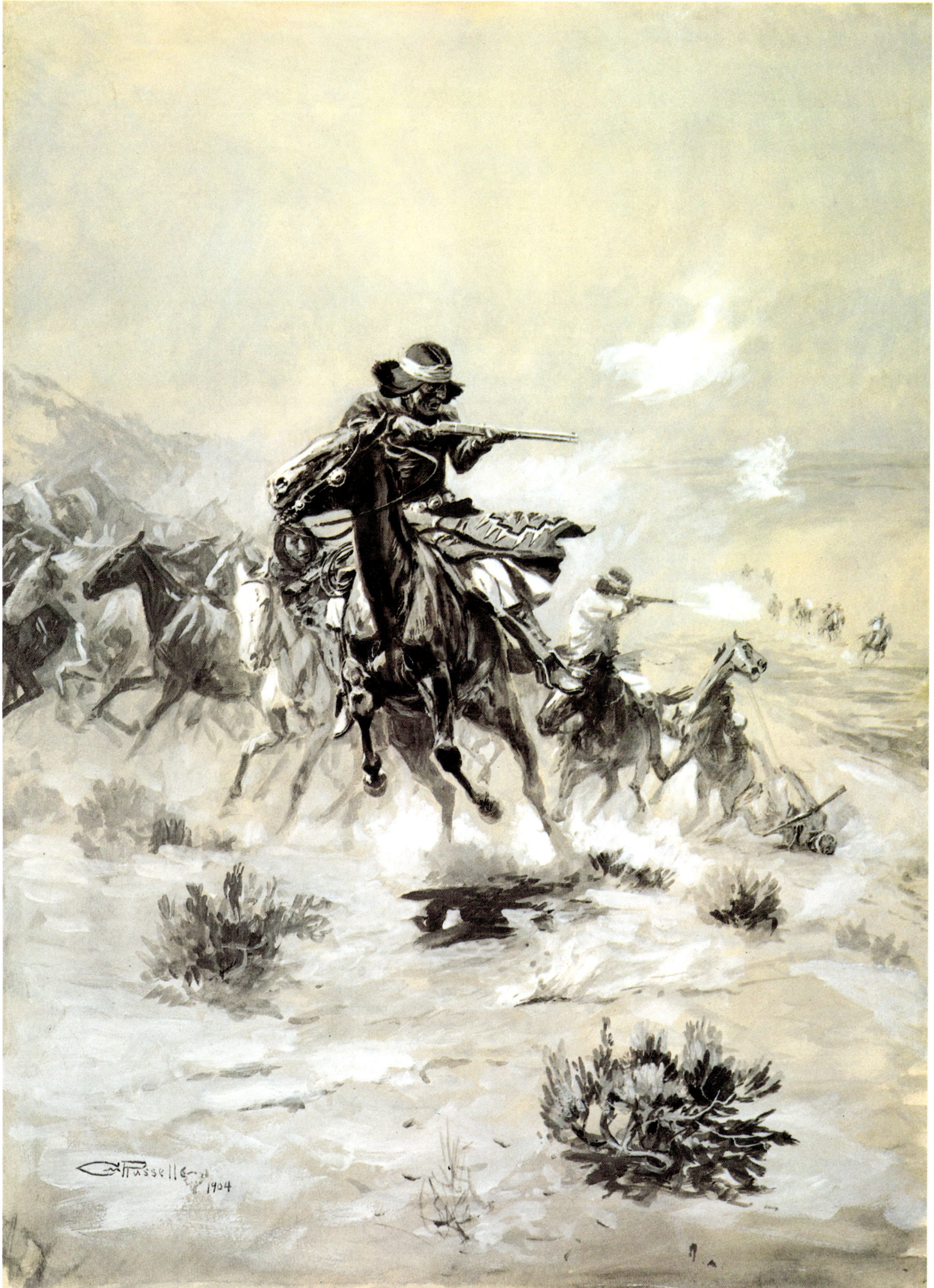
CM Russell
1904

The Posse

1895 • 14 × 20⅛ in. • Watercolor on paper.

DURING THE EARLY YEARS of cattle ranching in the Northwest, with the range open and the laws all but unenforceable, horse thieves and cattle rustlers had a relatively easy time of it—as did, for that matter, murderers and highwaymen. Montana's first "vigilance committee" was forced into existence in 1863 and established a quick reputation for justice, its rancher members pledging themselves to "violate no laws of right." It was some time after that before the regular process of law became effective.

In 1881, for instance, facing heavy cattle losses and with stolen horses being run north and sold to ranchers in North Dakota and Canada, cattlemen in the Judith Basin took matters into their own hands. They rounded up the culprits, tried them by jury, found them guilty, and allowed them twenty-four hours to leave the country (the alternative sentence was what one contemporary called "purification by hemp").

The work of these committees, with or without a sheriff in charge, clearly demanded courage, alertness, and tight discipline. Russell's posse of five, with a sixth as rear guard, seems eminently equal to the demand. His energetic bunching of them and their spirited horses is typical, against the distant buttes; through the sprung rhythm of line and the heightening of color, and through the bursting effect of the grass and scrub underfoot, he gives them a concerted impetus of explosive force. Yet they strike us as individuals, with sharpest focus on the leader—men who share a single urge for justice but who would speak to us, if they could, with a wide range of accent and attitude.

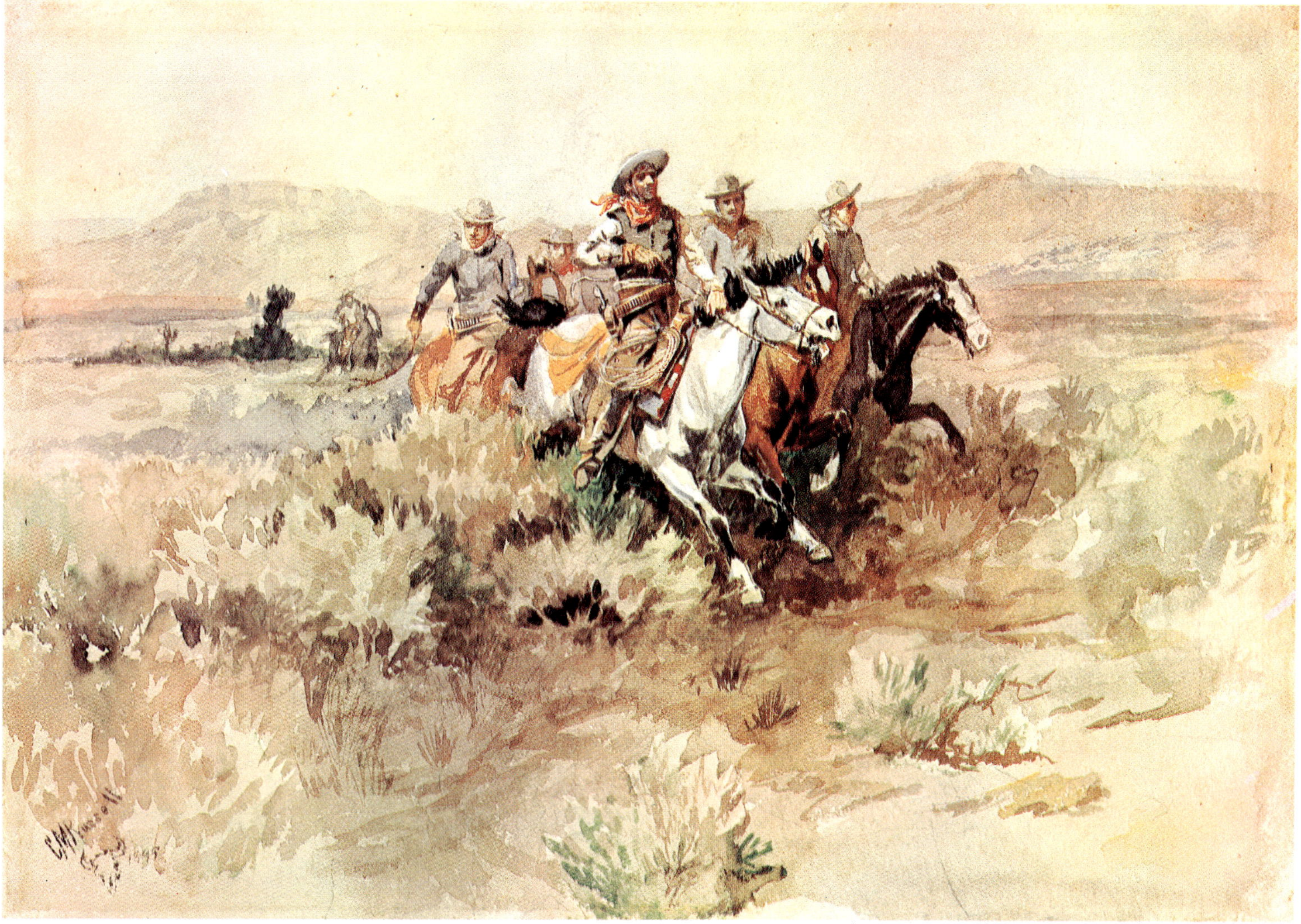

When Horseflesh Comes High

1909 • $24\frac{1}{4} \times 36\frac{1}{8}$ in. • Oil on canvas.

SOMETIMES CHARLIE RUSSELL'S URGE for excitement in a picture raises questions which the picture itself may not answer. Yet that may be part of the picture's life. Frederic G. Renner, in his monograph, reports a conversation with John R. Barrows of Ubet, Montana, concerning this particular oil. Barrows had known and admired Russell since their days together in the Judith Basin, and vouched for the authenticity of detail: "Look at the saddle, it was built in Cheyenne on the old half-breed tree and the strings look real enough you could tie your coat on with 'em."

But to have a posse riding directly into rifle fire from a couple of horse thieves was too much for Barrow's tolerance. The members of a posse, in his view, would have shown more consideration for their own lives.

With all respect to this experienced eye, there are other questions that come to mind. Was the posse actually chasing outlaws, for instance, or might it have come upon them unexpectedly?

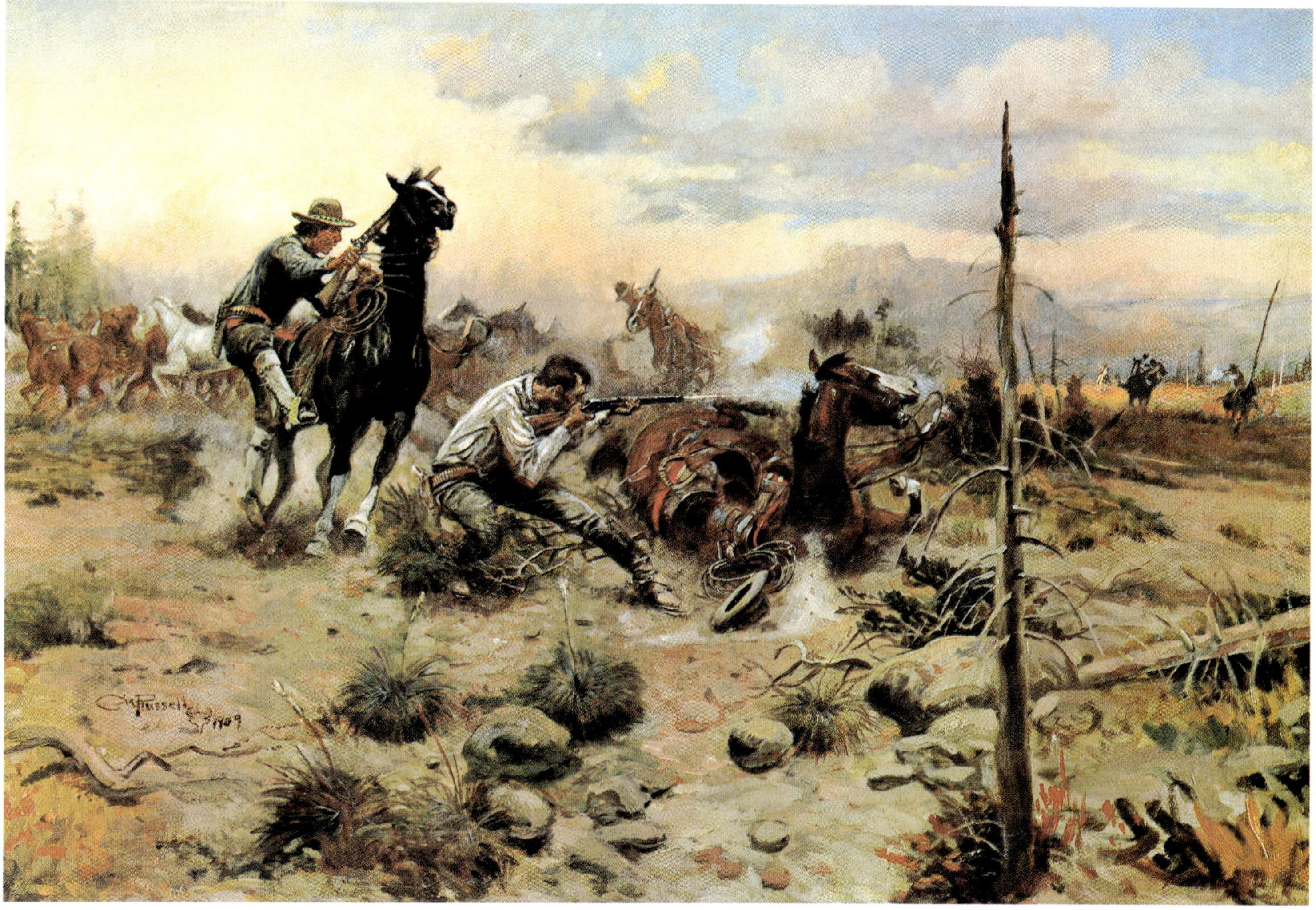

Bested

1895 • 23 × 35 in. • Oil on canvas.

THE HIGH DRAMA OF THIS SCENE, though inspired by the wiping out of a number of horse thieves under "Stringer Jack" by cattleman Stuart Granville and his Vigilance Committee in July 1884, is in certain respects a creation of Russell's own imagination. He shows the wounded remnants of the outlaw band signaling surrender to the oncoming vigilantes—an unusual act, which was unreported in Granville's account and attributable not so much to lost men as to spent ammunition. (A thief sure to be hung would never give up as long as he could shoot.)

Russell has chosen the scene itself as well. Actually, the decisive shootout had occurred in and around a cabin and corral of one of the accomplices, near the mouth of the Musselshell river—except for the later hanging of four fugitives at another settlement. But the artist prefers this rolling battleground and this vantage point, as the desperate survivors gaze mutely across bodies of men and horses toward their own steadily approaching fate. The intensity with which they do so is sharpened by the general counter-movement of those fallen bodies—and of the seated man apparently too exhausted to look.

The painting was titled and published as an illustration in the September 1897 issue of the magazine *Western Field and Stream.* During the same month, Russell signed an agreement with W. B. Cameron, the magazine's editor, providing for a series of twenty black-and-white oil paintings plus twenty pen sketches.

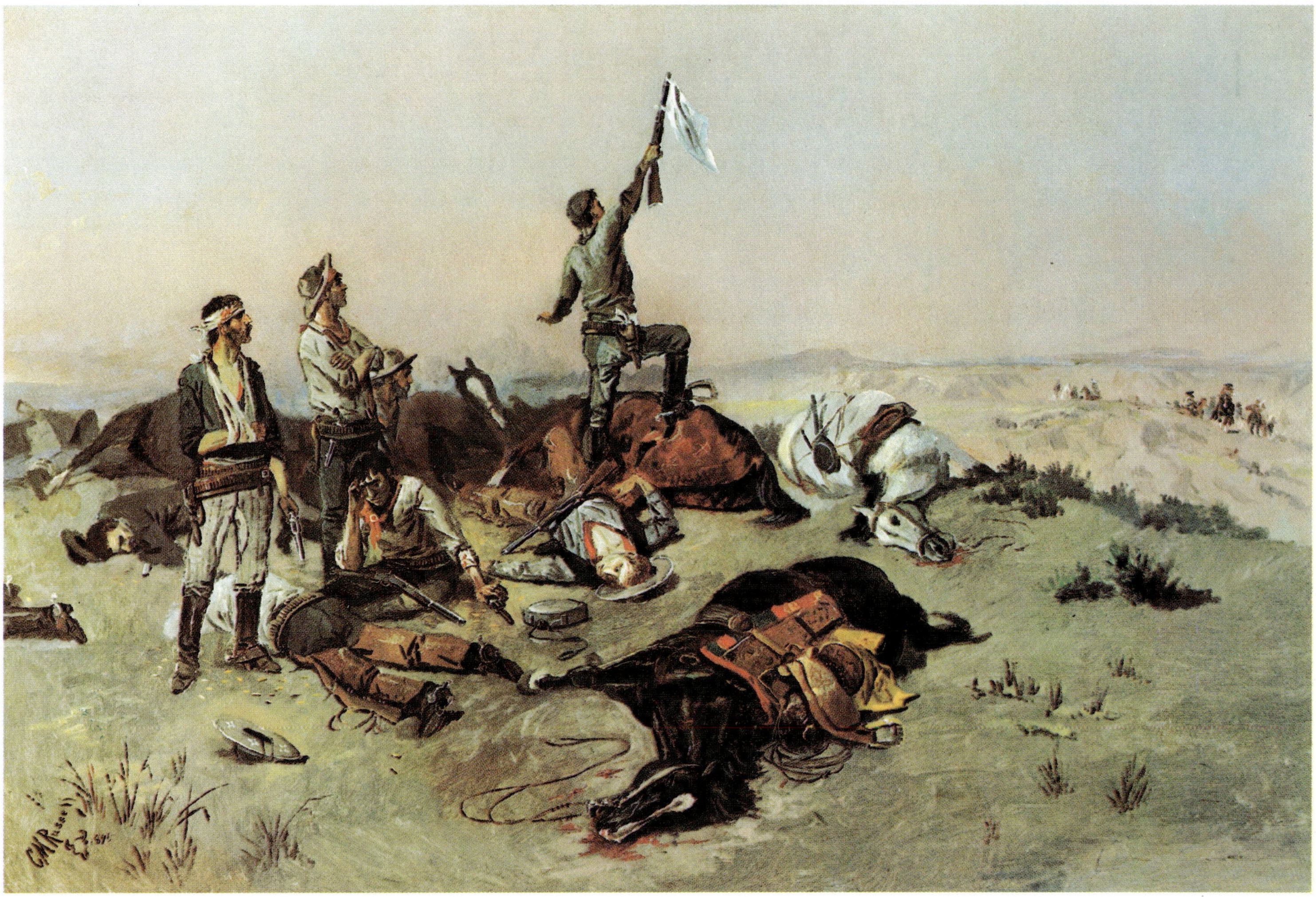

The Medicine Man

1908 • $30\frac{1}{8} \times 48\frac{1}{8}$ in. • Oil on canvas.

THE MONUMENTAL DIGNITY of this Blackfoot medicine man, leading his tribe to their fall hunting grounds, is backed by long tradition and supported by deep respect. He and his tribe have just taken part in their late summer Sun Dance, a ceremony of self-mortification and renewal designed to assure continuance of health and fertility. Since then they have been told by returning scouts of the first sighting of buffalo. Now, an hour or two after dawn, the entire camp has started moving. The men have prepared their weapons and their mounts; the women have struck the lodges and packed up their furnishings and small children; the scouts have gone ahead; and this medicine man—followed by the chiefs and their families—is leading the main body of the tribe.

Such leadership came naturally to a person (older women were occasionally qualified) who had special rapport with the supernatural and could be used not only during tribal ceremonies, but whenever there was call to foretell the future, cast love spells, find lost animals, or bring about good weather. He might also function as tribal physician.

His calling had at some time come to him through a dream or trance, including rather specific directions, and it was ordinarily confirmed by the success of his ministrations and by such an aura of authority as Russell has portrayed here.

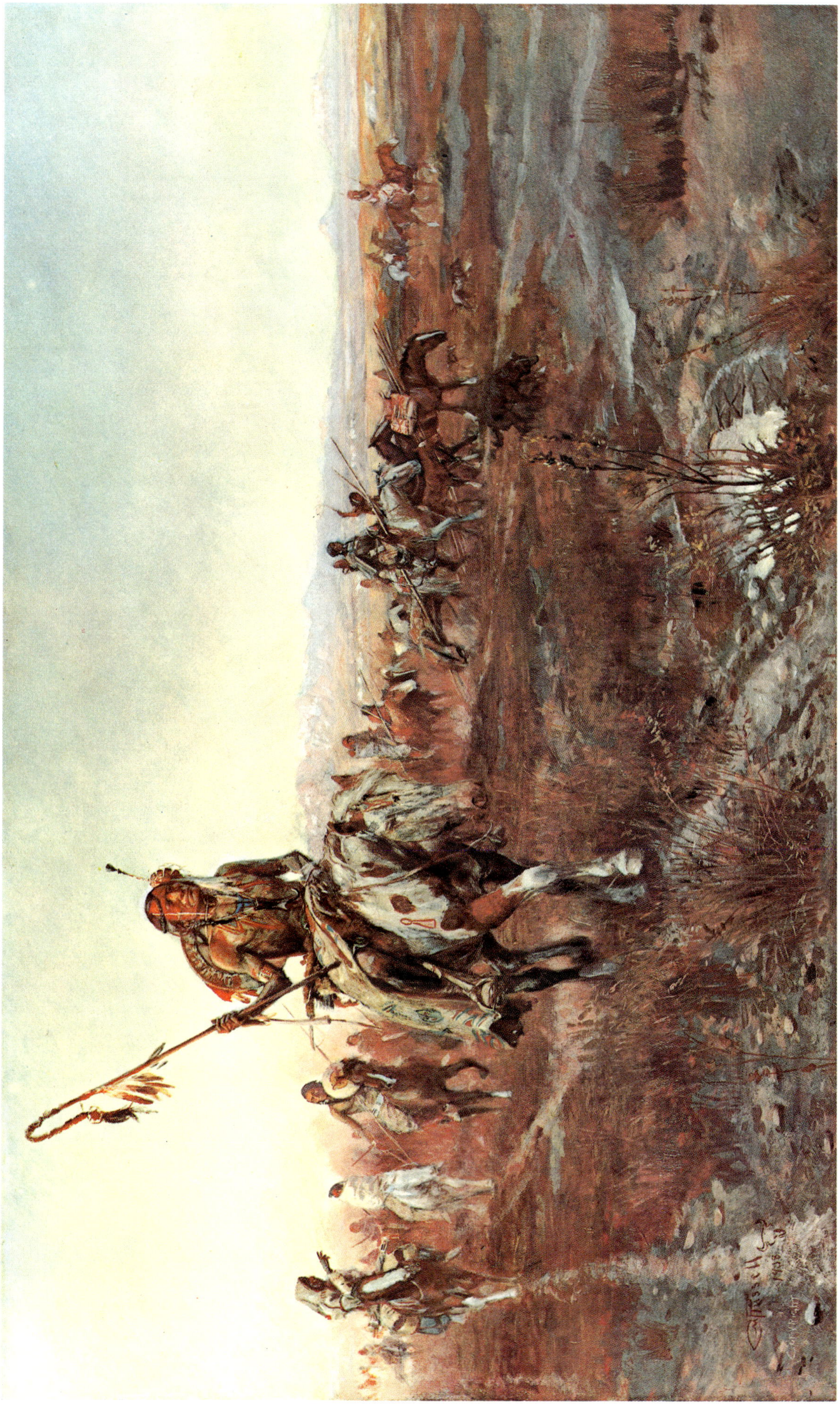

Indians Sighting Buffalo

c. 1896 • 13⅛ × 23¼ in. • Watercolor on paper.

THE MILLIONS OF BUFFALO that once roamed the plains—Ernest Thompson Seton estimated their peak number at sixty million—provided a resource of crucial importance to the Indians, who not only needed their flesh for food but had a use for virtually every other part as well. Many of the great buffalo herds migrated south into Wyoming during the winter (some Indians believed they hibernated in a huge cave), and it was a time of tense excitement in the spring when tribal scouts laid eyes on the first to return. Soon one of the year's major hunts would be underway—and for some tribes this could mean an expedition covering several hundred miles.

After each hunt came a feast at which as much of the fresh meat as possible was eaten, with dancing to celebrate and to stimulate the appetites. The rest of the meat was preserved through drying and taken home to be stored against the coming winter.

Given his continual interest in the subject, it was natural that in addition to his dozens of paintings of the hunt itself Russell would provide this scene as a kind of dramatic prologue. And what a stage is set: it reaches from the near rise of ground with its sharply drawn scouts, across the vast river valley to where the first of the herd are refreshing themselves—and of course includes the ever-present backdrop of buttes and mountains beyond.

And for all the distance that reduces these big animals to a cluster of specks, Russell has given them full reality against the light ground, to us and to the gazing Indians. What's more, the deftly painted cloud of dust lifts over the herd with faint but unmistakable thunder.

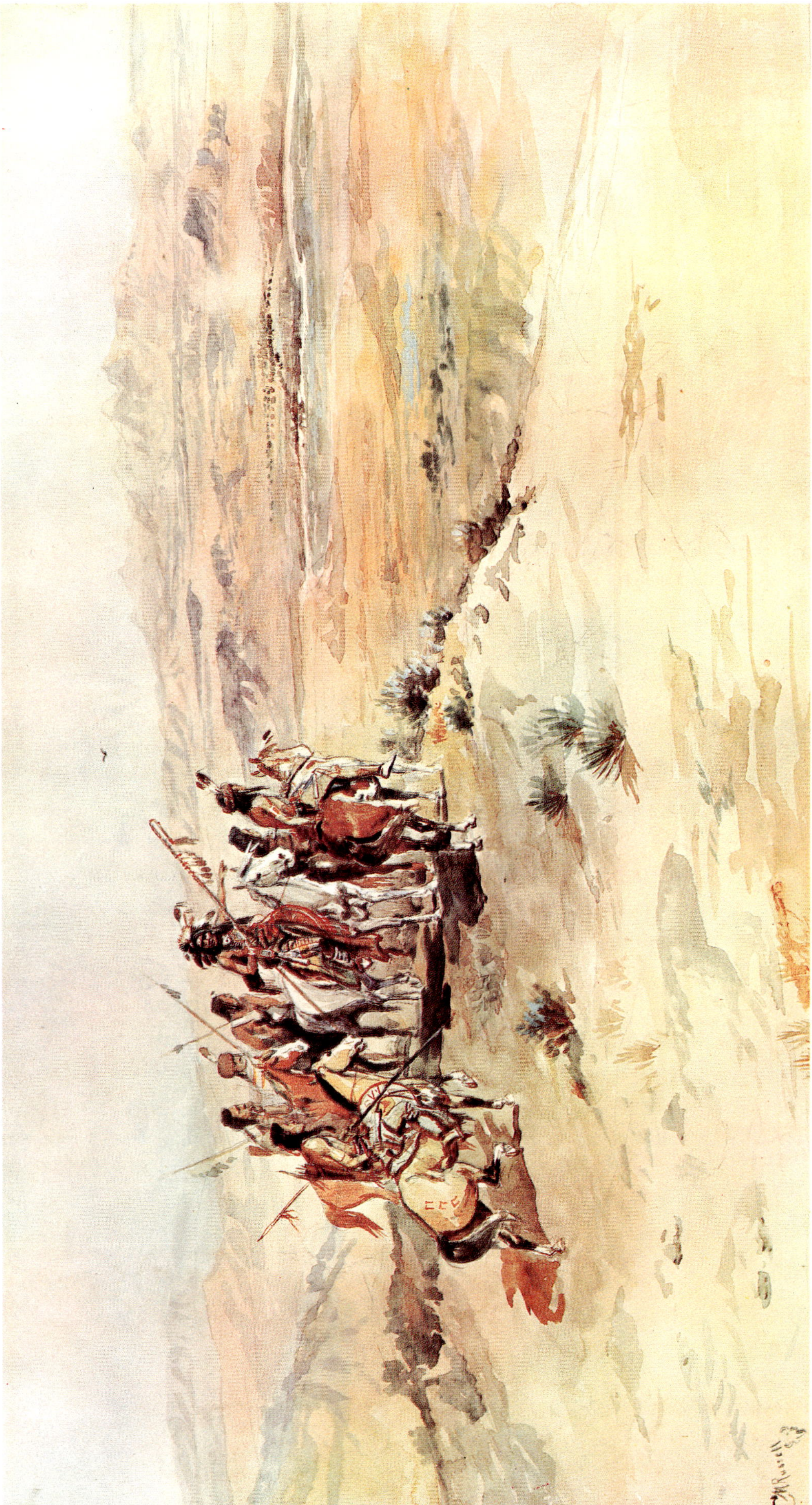

Wild Meat for Wild Men

1890 • 20¼ × 36⅛ in. • Oil on canvas.

THE INDIAN BUFFALO HUNT was a subject which fascinated Russell throughout his career. In this early effort the artist has not yet found the later balance between convincing detail and convincing movement. His studious care with the detail of his foreground hunter has lost him some momentum; while his more distant Indian seems to show difficulty on both counts.

Even so, Russell has realized a powerful spread of action, illustrating the Indians' practice of working around the fringes of a herd and picking off individual beasts before they swung off together in a stampede. One reason for many Indians' preference for bows and arrows over firearms was that their quietness might enable more beasts to be brought down before the whole herd was disturbed.

Although most of the animals here—and a third hunter—are blurred by the rush and the dust, Russell has given sharp reality to the clumps of grass that provided the buffalo's staple diet. It was a tough, nourishing part of the region's whole ecology, thriving not only on a minimum of moisture but even from the pounding buffalo hooves, which helped to scatter its seed.

The general location of this scene is clear as well: in the left background is Square Butte, mentioned by Captain Meriwether Lewis when his party was exploring near the Great Falls of the Missouri.

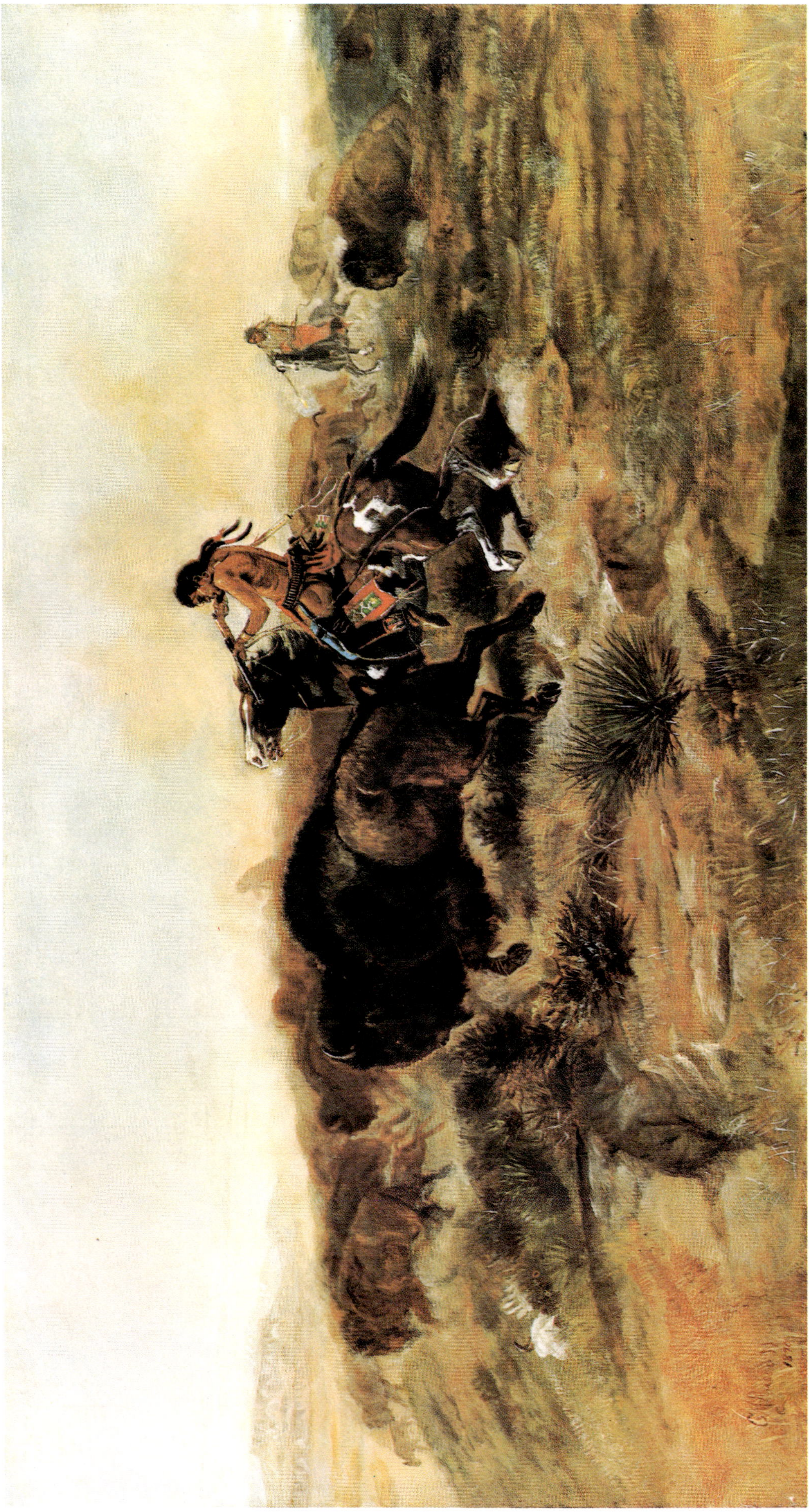

Buffalo Hunting

1894 • 20⅛ × 24⅛ in. • Oil on canvas.

DURING HIS MORE formative years as a self-trained artist, Russell generally preferred—as here—to show moving animals from the side, and so to minimize problems of foreshortening. Yet at times he was more adventurous; and he has given quite a swing even to this relatively "primitive" treatment by swerving his buffalo on a slightly diagonal course while the horse and rider seem about to veer the other way. The contrast of hulking darkness and swift lightness in the two animals quickens the drama.

What communicates above all, however, is the special skill and great courage required of both the Indian hunters and their mounts. Although dim-witted and weak-sighted, the buffalo was as fast as a horse and something like a ton in weight, with a hide that could be inches think—no easy prey for a man with a bow and arrow. And even if the first arrow found its way, as intended, through the skin just ahead of the hip bone, the buffalo might still run a mile before dropping. If it was less mortally wounded, this animal could become a four-footed cyclone with horns.

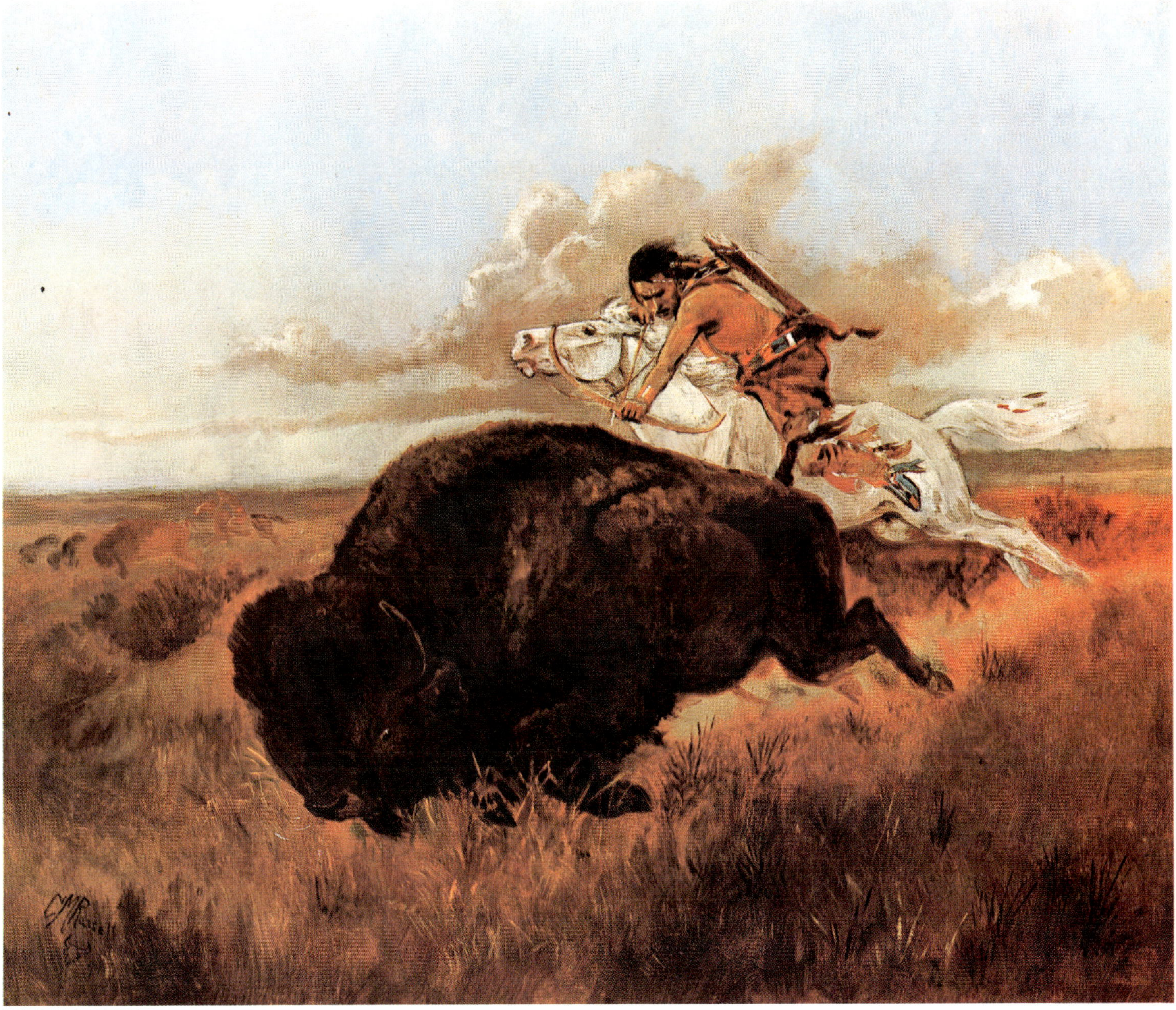

Buffalo Hunt No. 15

1896 • 14⅜ × 21 in. • Watercolor on paper.

By this time, Russell is equal to picturing almost any combination of brute power and human agility that a buffalo hunt might bring about: the excruciating moment here, in which one Indian doesn't seem to have been quite agile enough, has more twists and lurches than the famous statue of the Laocöon—and they all come off with ample reality.

The buffalo's unfortunate victim was apparently caught by some sudden burst of speed in the wounded animal—notice the dust still hanging behind—and the concerted efforts of the three others seem helpless to save him.

A far cry this, in its ever-present danger and its necessity, from the killing of buffalo "purely for sport" by the wealthy Irish hunter, Sir St. George Gore, in 1854. This gentleman of leisure brought along a few friends and Indian guides, about 40 servants, 112 horses, 24 yoke of oxen, 14 dogs, 21 carts, and 6 wagons. He momentarily mollified the Crow Indians with the guns and ammunition he provided them as he went about scattering and demolishing their game, and his two years' bag was estimated at 105 bears and some 2,000 buffalo, elk, and deer.

But he never got his picture painted by Charlie Russell.

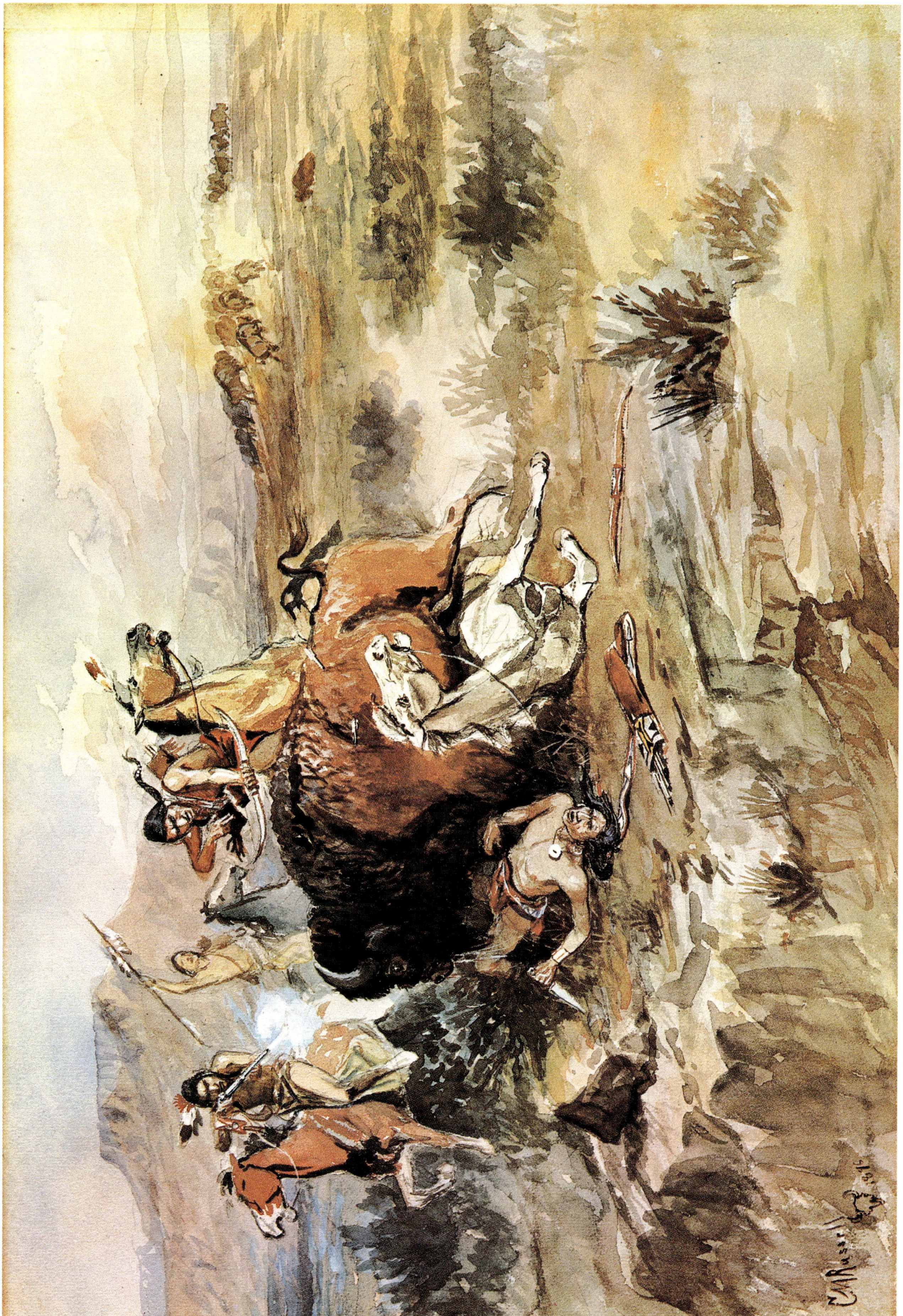

The Buffalo Hunt No. 26

1899 • 30⅛ × 48¼ in. • Oil on canvas.

RUSSELL GAVE FAR GREATER attention to the hunting of buffalo by the Indian than to the more massive assault on them by the white settler. His preference is hardly surprising. For the Indian, the taking of buffalo was a matter of his own survival, yet posed no threat to the animal's survival. For the white newcomer, on the other hand, wholesale slaughter seemed justified, even mandated, by the opening up of the Western "wilderness" for his safe settlement and development.

So the artist turned with a kind of vehemence to a phase of Indian life that by 1899 had passed into history—the buffalo, in a sense, having taken that full-dimensioned Indian life with them. But the Indians themselves were, and are, still with us, and Russell felt impelled to do honor to their cultural integrity. His attitude seems to correspond to that of Mari Sandoz in her *Love Song to the Plains:*

> "Given iron, powder, and the luxury of the horse, and saved the temptations and the pressures of the white man's whisky and ambition, the Plains Indian, north and south, could have lived an enviable life for a long, long time, husbanding his buffalo, developing his gentleman's life and his increasingly close relationship with the earth, the sky and everything between, a deep personal identification with all the universe around him, a oneness with the buffalo, the rock, the cloud, the tree."

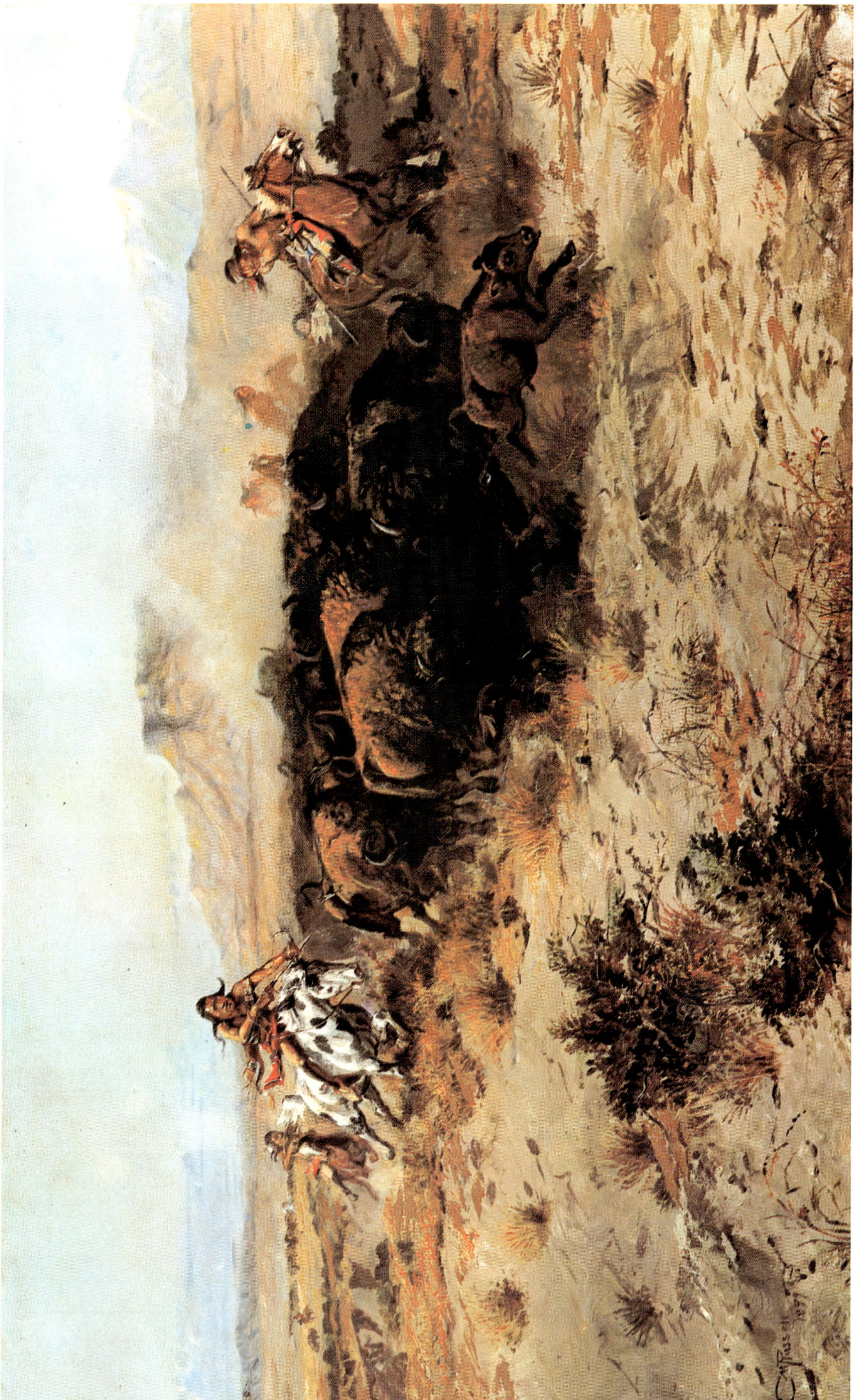

The Buffalo Hunt No. 40

c. 1919 • 30 × 48½ in. • Oil on canvas.

THERE ARE SO MANY paintings of this favorite Russell subject, each carrying the same title, that they've been given catalog numbers for sure identification, like Mozart symphonies or Bach cantatas.

This rather late one shows the same general scheme as No. 26 (previous page), with three hunters working to surround and confuse the herd.

But this painting—No. 40—is no mere replica of earlier paintings. It heightens the excitement by lowering the viewpoint and giving a livelier, more crackling color and texture to the grass and sagebrush of the foreground.

And it brings with it, as always, the skill and aptitude not only of the Indian himself but also of his extraordinarily qualified horse. In addition to possessing unusual speed and endurance, a good horse had to be able to hold steady while stalking a grazing herd, for all of the six-foot height of the mature bull buffalo; and then, when the buffalo crowded together for protection, the horse was expected to dart in among them, dodging horns and positioning the rider for his best aim.

When horse thieves were rumored to be around, everyone in a household understood that it was the buffalo horse that slept inside the tepee, and the women outside. The buffalo itself, however, was in its own way prized above all as the Indian's greatest resource, providing him not only with meat but with tools, housing, furnishings, clothing, fertilizer from the bones, and even fuel from the dung. It was, at the same time, the most hunted and venerated of creatures; its spirit was invoked in dance whenever a hunt was in prospect. And its formidable power is surpassingly conveyed in this symphonic movement of Russell's.

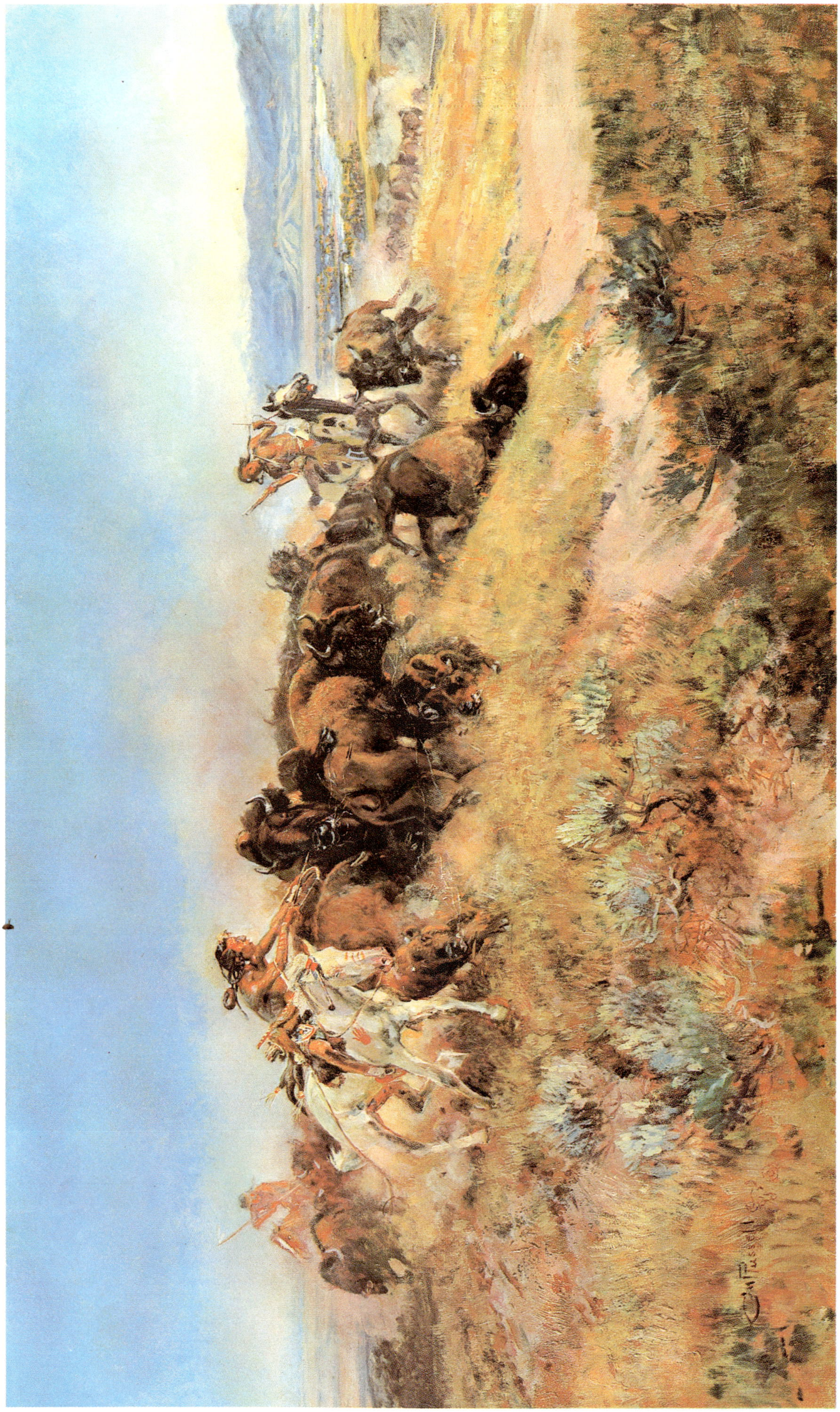

Flintlock Days—When Guns Were Slow

1925 • 20 × 29⅞ in. • Watercolor on paper.

THE FLINTLOCK GUN was one of those single shooters that came at a relatively early stage in the "arms race" of the Old West. It was startling, noisy, and effective if the first shot went home. But it was clumsy to load and fire from horseback; for one thing, the ball and powder had to be tamped down. An Indian, meanwhile, could return fire with about twenty arrows.

And a buffalo? He might have been mortally wounded by that first shot, but there was much too much time in which desperate anger could send him hurtling and tearing against horse and rider.

So there was special danger in those early days. But Russell is painting this watercolor during his later days, in 1925, and in his nostalgic way seems to prefer this mountain man's single possible calamity to the loss, over a half-century, of that whole region's natural and free character, including the balance of man and nature, cowboy and Indian.

His painting here has less organizational compactness and power than many earlier examples. Yet the "glaring defiance" of its buffalo, as Frederic Renner suggests in his monograph on the artist, "might well express Russell's own defiance at the thing he hated most—the advance of civilization."

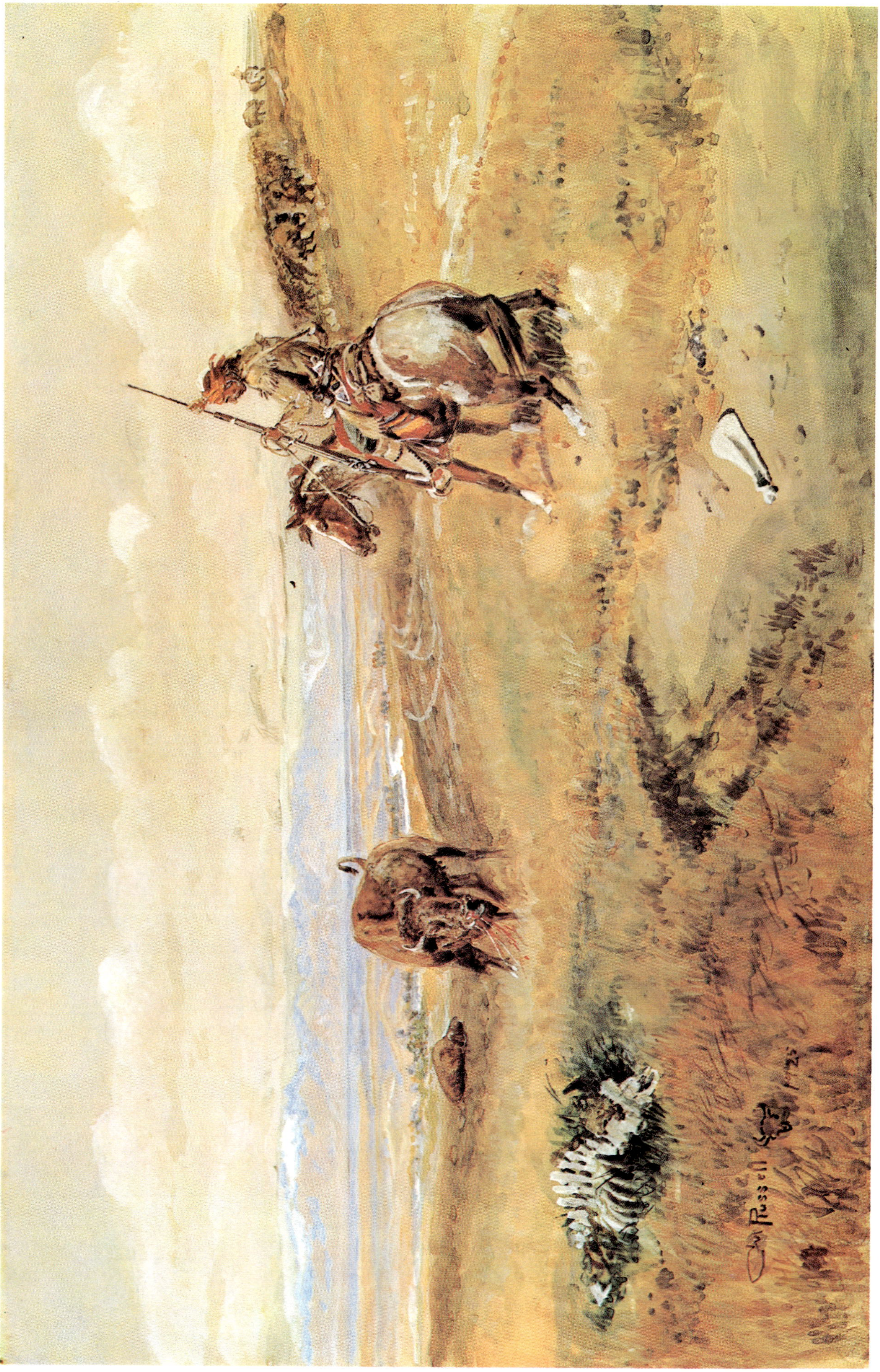

The Stand. Crossing the Missouri.

c. 1889 • 20⅛ × 30⅛ in. • Oil on canvas.

SOMETIMES, DURING those early years in Montana, there were just too many pictures for the canvas at hand. So the sky of one scene made room for the ground of another related one—and another sky. Both, in this case, treat of the buffalo, and complement each other most pointedly.

The large scene shows a herd on its way through the Badlands during the annual migration, silhouetted on this huge slope approaching to the distant Missouri and the hills beyond. It is a time, obviously, when the buffalo and the Indians still own the land. (And at this early stage, incidentally, Russell's buffalo-skull trademark is still realistic: by the next year it is reduced to a quick outline.)

The other scene depicts one of many changes that in the course of a few short years was to end all that—and had almost done so several years before Russell had painted this picture. It shows a "skin hunter," working very likely for the railroads' bounty money, firing from downwind into a herd with a long-range repeating rifle that could kill perhaps twenty animals before the rest realized the danger and moved away.

The change that this hunter represented was so massive in its effect on the tens of millions of buffalo that by 1900 only twenty animals were known to exist. In 1908 the American Bison Society was founded and a range of 18,540 acres established near the Mission Mountains in western Montana. Today a herd of three to five hundred or more is free to roam in the National Bison Range, environed by other congenial animals.

Pictures such as this no doubt contributed to that recovery.

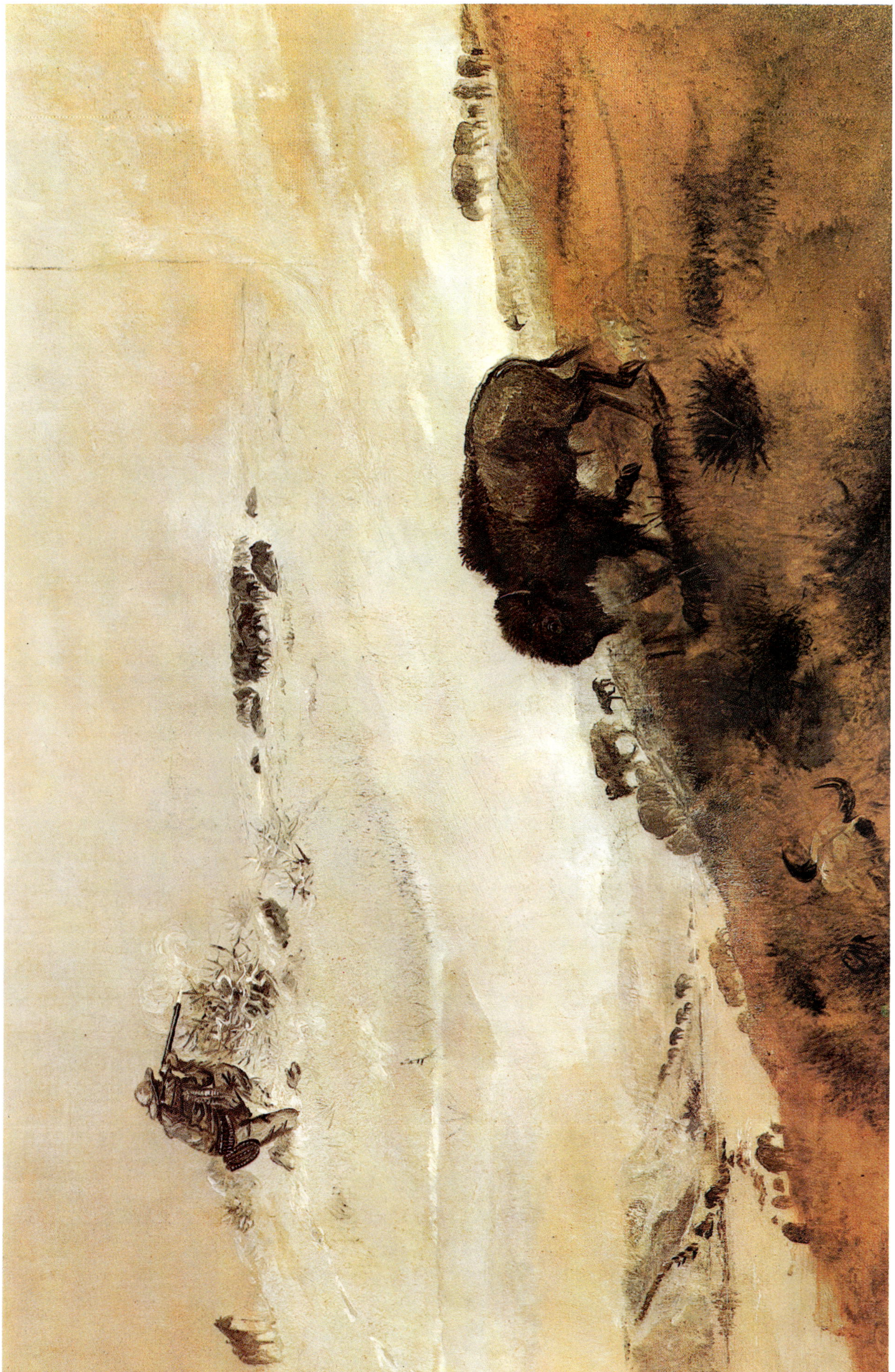

Bringing Home the Meat

c. 1891 • $36\frac{1}{8} \times 24$ in. • Oil on canvas.

INDIAN MEN, as everyone knows, did the tribe's fighting and hunting. Indian women did practically everything else. That meant, for example, not only the eventual cooking of the meat, but also bringing the carcasses home from the chase (four antelope in this case), skinning them, readying the meat for immediate or later use, and tanning the hides. Add this to the raising of their families, the erecting of tepees to house them, plus the gathering of wild plants to help feed them, and the Indian women might seem as burdened as the laden horses Russell has them riding here.

But by much of the evidence they took pride and even a degree of joy in their arduous, male-dominated round of work. Russell conveys this in the sturdy dignity with which these two negotiate the ups and downs of the rocky landscape. Putting space between them—which in its swinging curve enhances and balances the movement—he has also implied, out of his own observation, that they have managed to surround themselves with a certain independence.

The brilliant sunniness of atmosphere, and its effect on color, has been painted with a flair not entirely foreign to the impressionist techniques that Russell denounced roundly after sampling them in St. Louis ten years later: "Why, say, if I ever saw colors like that in a painting I would never take another drink" (from an interview in the Anaconda, Montana, *Standard* of December 15, 1901).

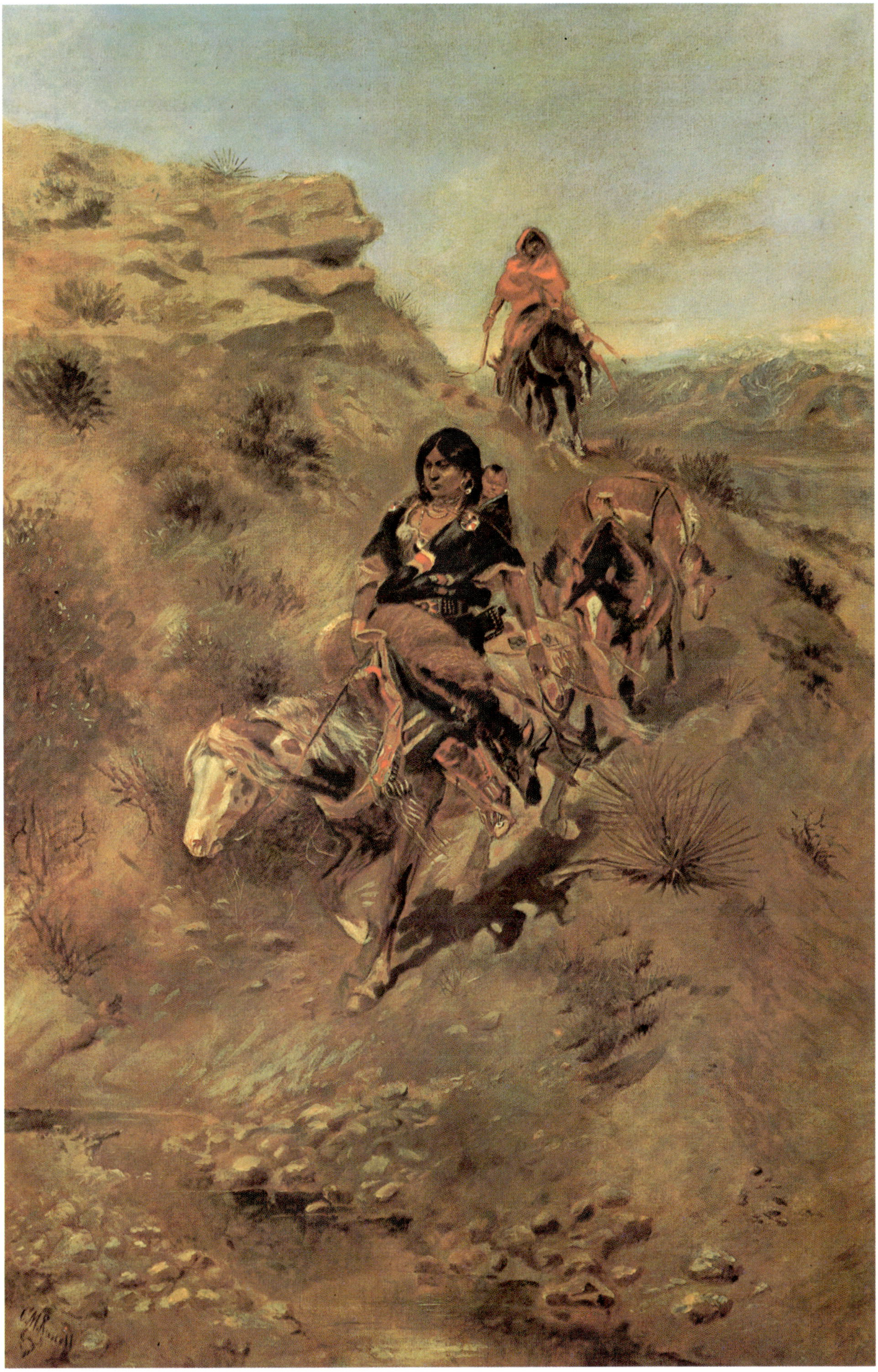

Following the Buffalo Run

1894 • $23\frac{1}{8} \times 35$ in. • Oil on canvas.

THE ROLE OF WOMEN in the Plains Indians' general system of hunting was especially important, of course, during and after the buffalo hunts. These were the hunts that involved not only the greatest quantity of animals, but the most complete use of them. In addition to food and clothing, then, the people here are helping to supply their families and their villages with tools and utensils, tepees, fuel and fertilizer, and much more.

The "shopping cart" they had used since long before seeing their first horses or wheels was called a "travois." By this time, it was an A-shaped arrangement of two light poles, crossed and bound together over the horse's head and spread out behind toward the poles' dragged ends to provide a sloping platform. The women not only loaded and drove these travois during any moving operation (see page 127), they also took great pride in making them. And for that matter the buffalo themselves contributed, since their hide was used both for the platform and for the binding together of all elements.

Though such scenes as this one are obviously less dramatic than those of the hunt, Russell seems to have taken special pleasure in painting their patient, processional solemnity—the women, children, and animals looking far before them, holding their heads as high as any Indian brave. Renner mentions having counted at least twenty treatments of the subject in oil or watercolor.

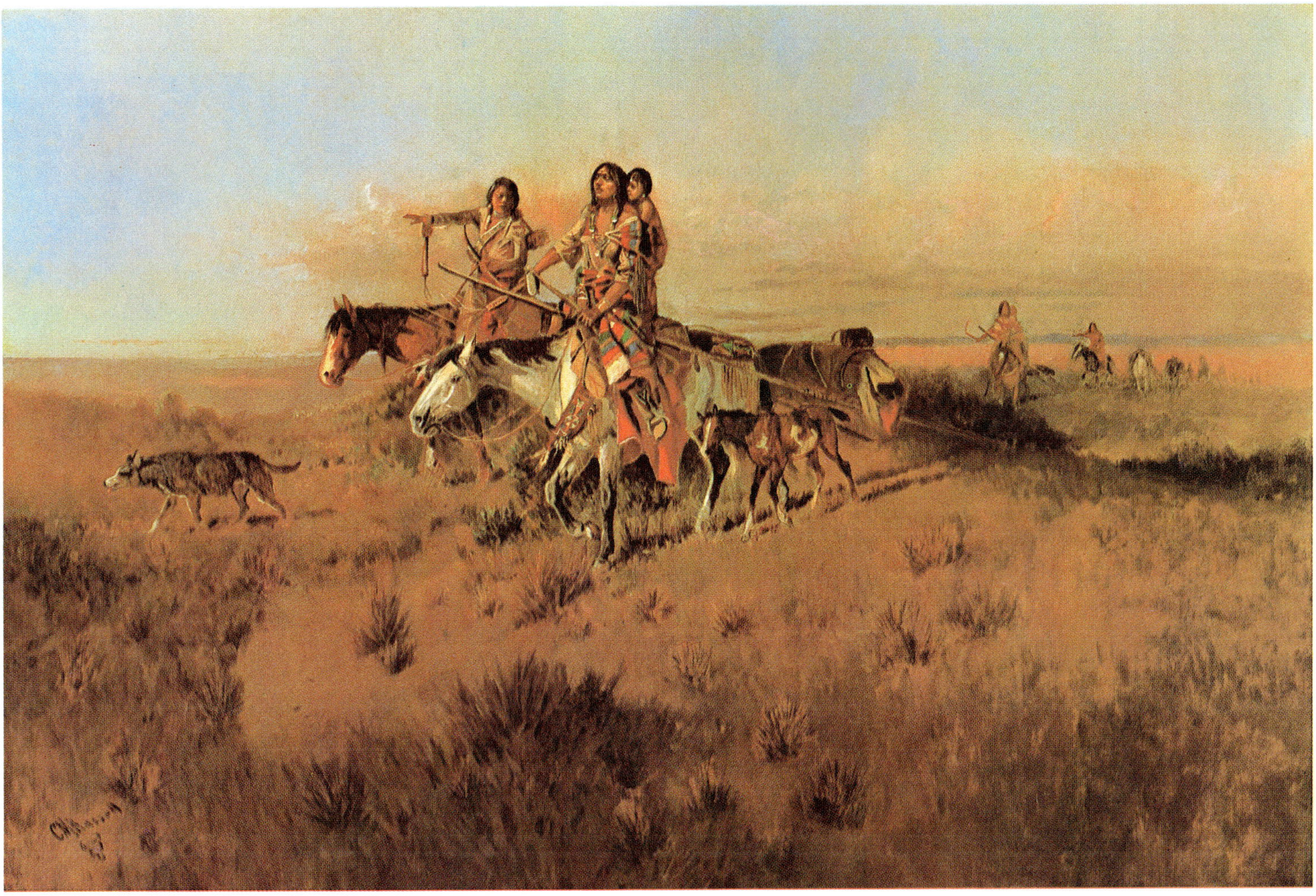

Squaws with Travois

1897 • $13\frac{3}{4} \times 21\frac{1}{4}$ in. • Watercolor on paper.

WHATEVER THE REASON for moving camp, the occasion itself was one of some moment, beginning when the chief sent his "cryer" around with the news, and continuing all through the packing and striking of tepees and the preparation of animals and children, until the exodus was actually under way. Central to it all, of course, was the conveyance known as a travois, built, loaded, and drawn by the women—if possible on horseback (see pages 122-123).

Once the tribe was moving, the bustle of preparation naturally gave way to steady progress along the trail, interspersed with moments that could be as idyllic as this one (in a watercolor once owned by Will Rogers). Having arrived at a tranquil stream, the squaws seem to be settling some matter of direction, perhaps where best to cross.

But meanwhile comes an instant of refreshment, at least for the animals and the viewer. A horse and a dog are drinking, a foal is nursing, and Russell has kept their disturbance of the water down to a slight, shadowed calligraphy of ripples.

Other horses and travois are following, however, and in the next instant these squaws and their weightless-seeming loads will be moving on, taking something of this peace with them.

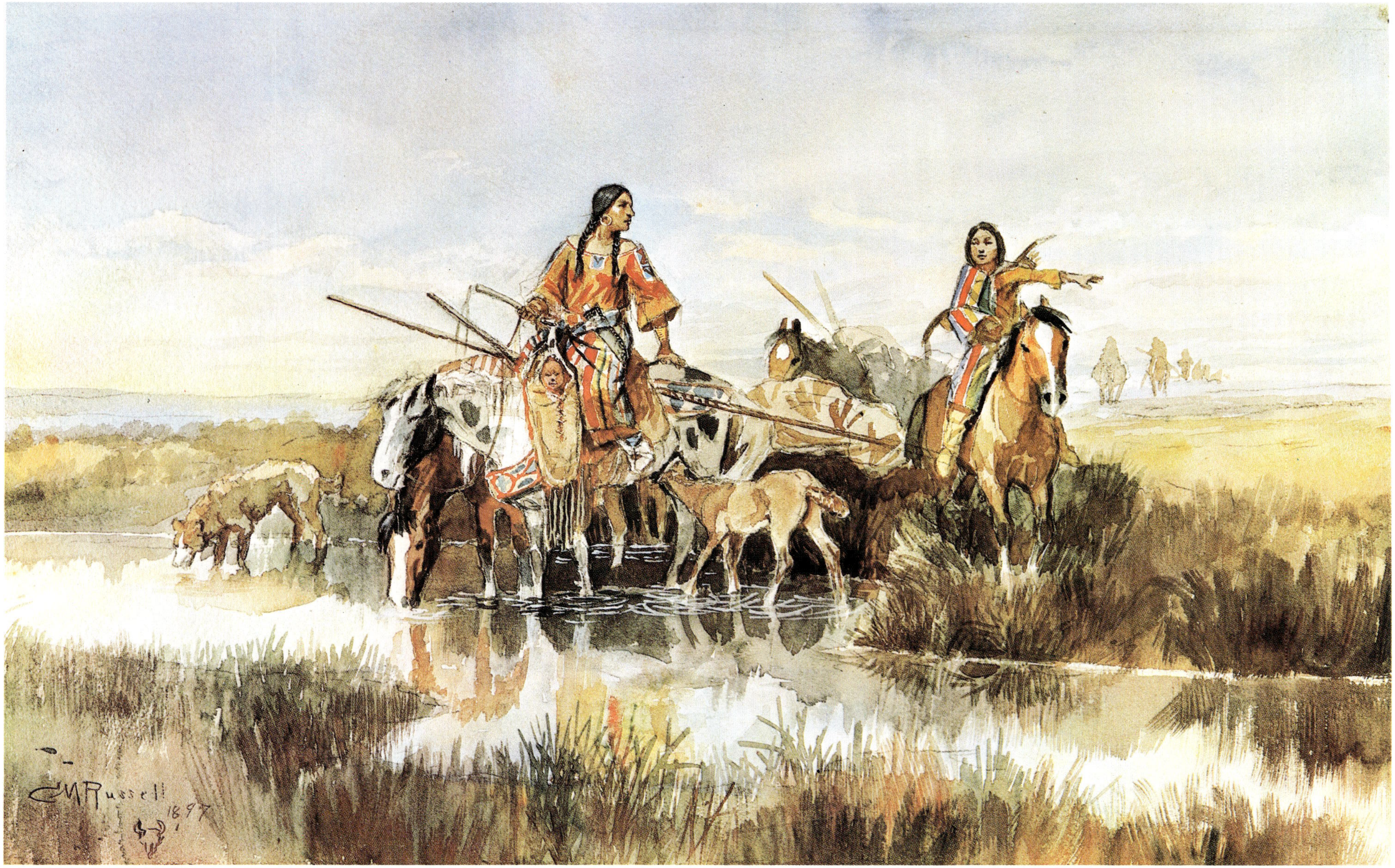
CMRussell
1897

Indian Women Moving

1898 • 24¼ × 36 in. • Oil on canvas.

To be successful as a nomad is to keep the dignity and integrity of your life intact as you move from camp to camp—even to confirm and nourish these essentials. Indian women, through the broad range of their responsibilities, were vital to this success, and gifted at it: when the menial task was part of a movement somewhere, it was no longer menial.

Russell shows perhaps three generations in this oil, each given the durability of a Mother Courage and something more than her grace. The women on their horses, with their parfleche bags and their travois, are loaded with the needed equipage of living. Yet they are lifted by obvious pride—theirs is no doubt a wealthy tribe, a successful tribe, and they move well.

It is a fact which appears not only in their faces and their bearing, but in the steady forwardness of so many rising diagonals—the travois poles in particular, that serve the eye's movement as they do the Indian's. The dog to the right is alone in turning slightly away from the forward course. But he too knows very well which way they are all going, and that they will quite surely get there.

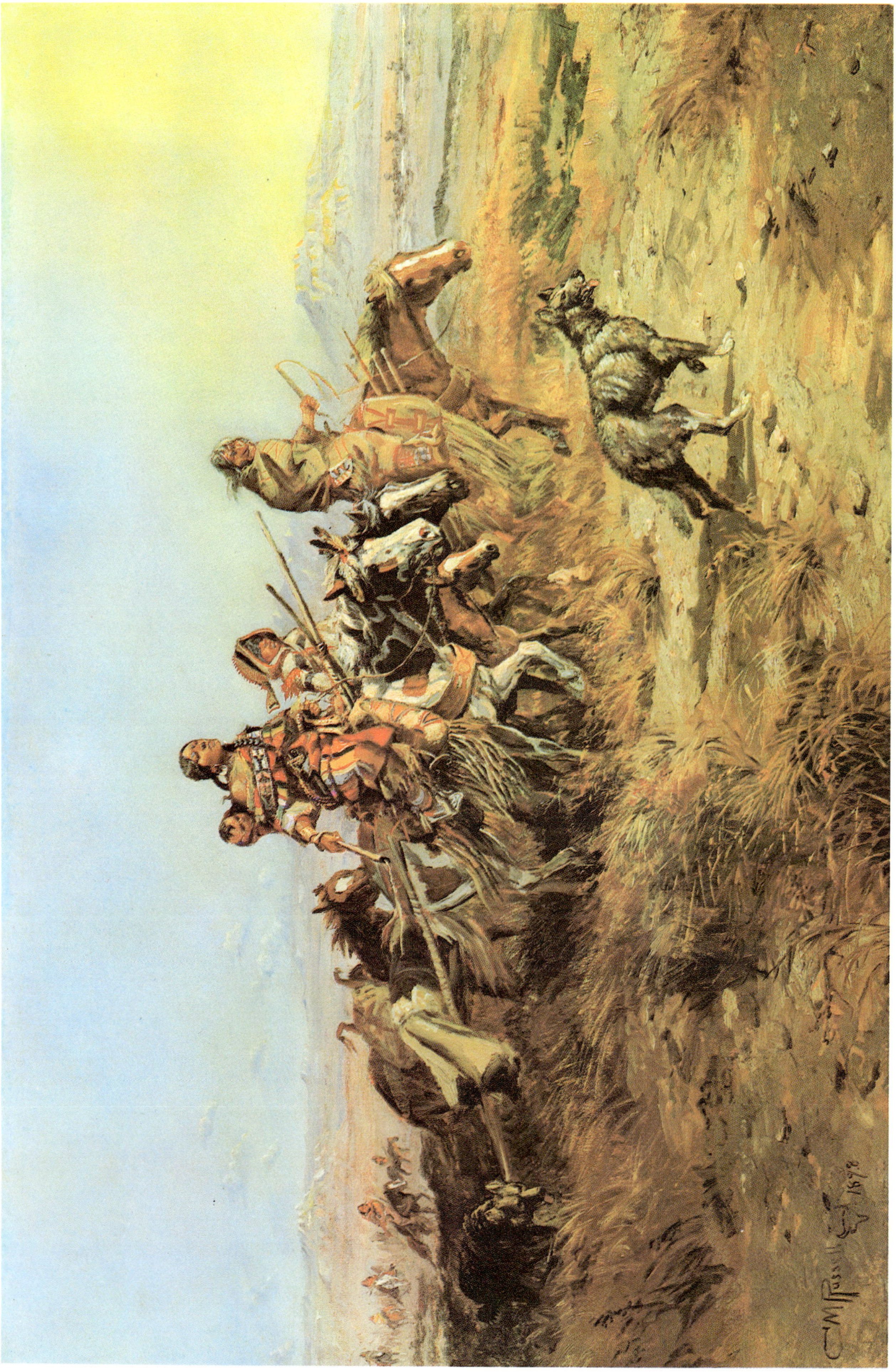

Indian Scouting Party

1900 • 30 × 13½ in. • Watercolor on paper.

Scouts were as much a part of Indian life as war itself. They provided an intelligence system as well as a kind of signal corps, and they needed to be even more mobile than the others in a nomadic Plains tribe. The Indian expert John C. Ewers once compared the Blackfoot war parties (often organized to steal the enemy's horses) to the operations of World War II commandos. Their theater of war was immense; and their scouts' objectives were to look cautiously and silently for horse tracks, footprints, decaying animal carcasses, fire hearths or any other evidence of the nearness of human beings. Once finding the enemy camp they would observe all they could of its size, its horse herd, and its surroundings, before reporting back to the main body and planning the stealthy "commando" raid itself.

Occasionally Russell ordered his own strategy according to a vertical scheme instead of the usual horizontal, and it seems to work well in this spirally composed painting. The wall of rock at the top begins the movement, which helps to propel the curved column of scouts and then curves back again through the foreground area.

A viewer who wonders why the artist left so much "empty space" at the top and bottom might try covering those areas with his hands. The figures of scouts and horses will not have changed; but without the slight propulsion above and below, they could seem suddenly not to be going anywhere.

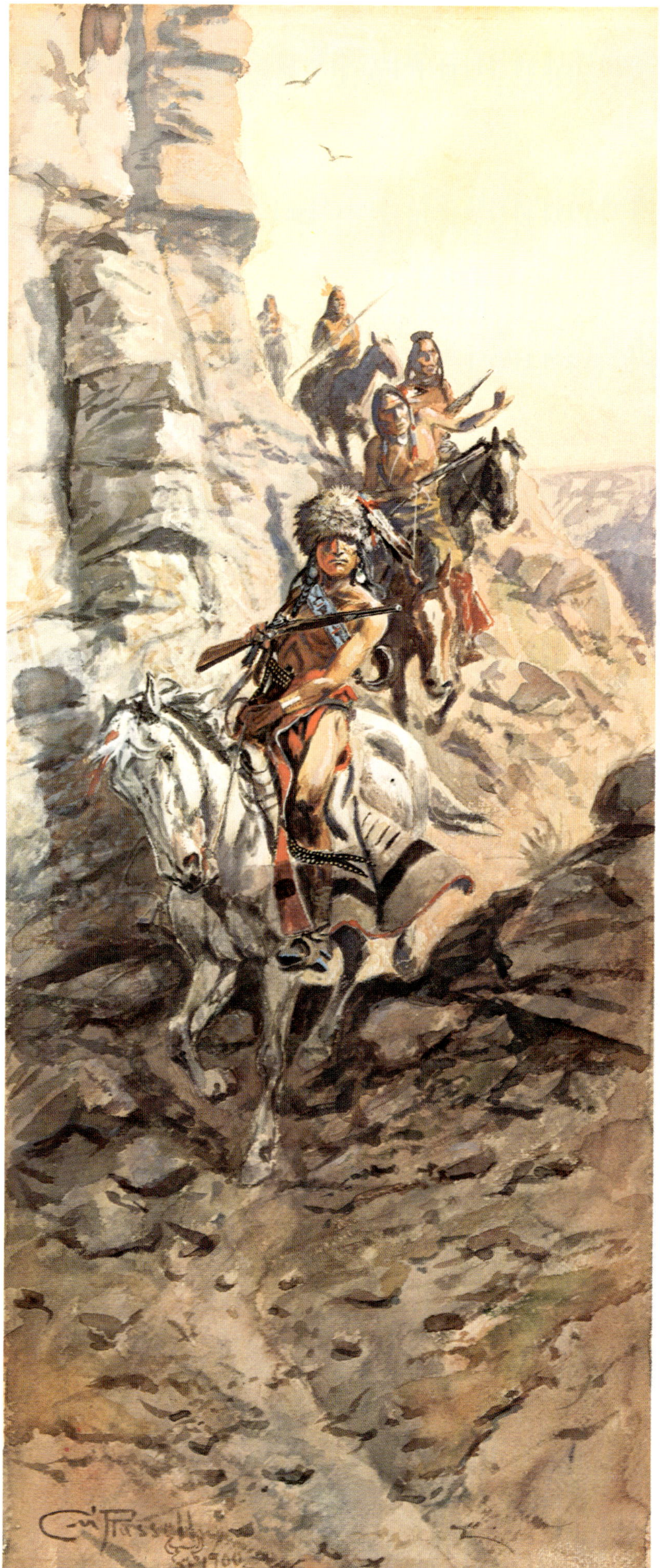

Indians On Horseback

1898 • 13¾ × 10½ in. • Oil on canvas.

NO MATTER HOW TENTATIVELY we may come to a Russell painting, we are seldom left in any doubt as to where to move into it or what to do. The artist almost literally seizes our attention here by the gesture of the nearest of these three Cree scouts on the trail. It's not that the gesture itself is exceptionally strong; but it is the focus for his bodily attitude of total attention, and so it does take the viewer's, and then direct its—as surely as if on the street one were to pass a fellow-pedestrian gazing fixedly at the top of a tall building. In that case we would look up, just as we look down towards the ground here.

The leader has evidently seen some suspicious-appearing tracks, has stopped his horse abruptly, and in the same movement is signalling the others to be cautious as well. We may not see what he sees, and it may be better that way: it puts us more nearly in the position of the other two Indians. Besides, we wouldn't be sure how to read the information anyway.

So our eye goes back to them, finds little to dwell on in their somewhat "out-of-focus" figures, and is carried up and held momentarily, at least, by the architectural majesty of that great Montanan butte.

Our curiosity about the footprints may not be satisfied, but we've found the subject behind the subject—so often part of the staying power of a Russell painting: the coexistential give-and-take between one human being and his immense environment.

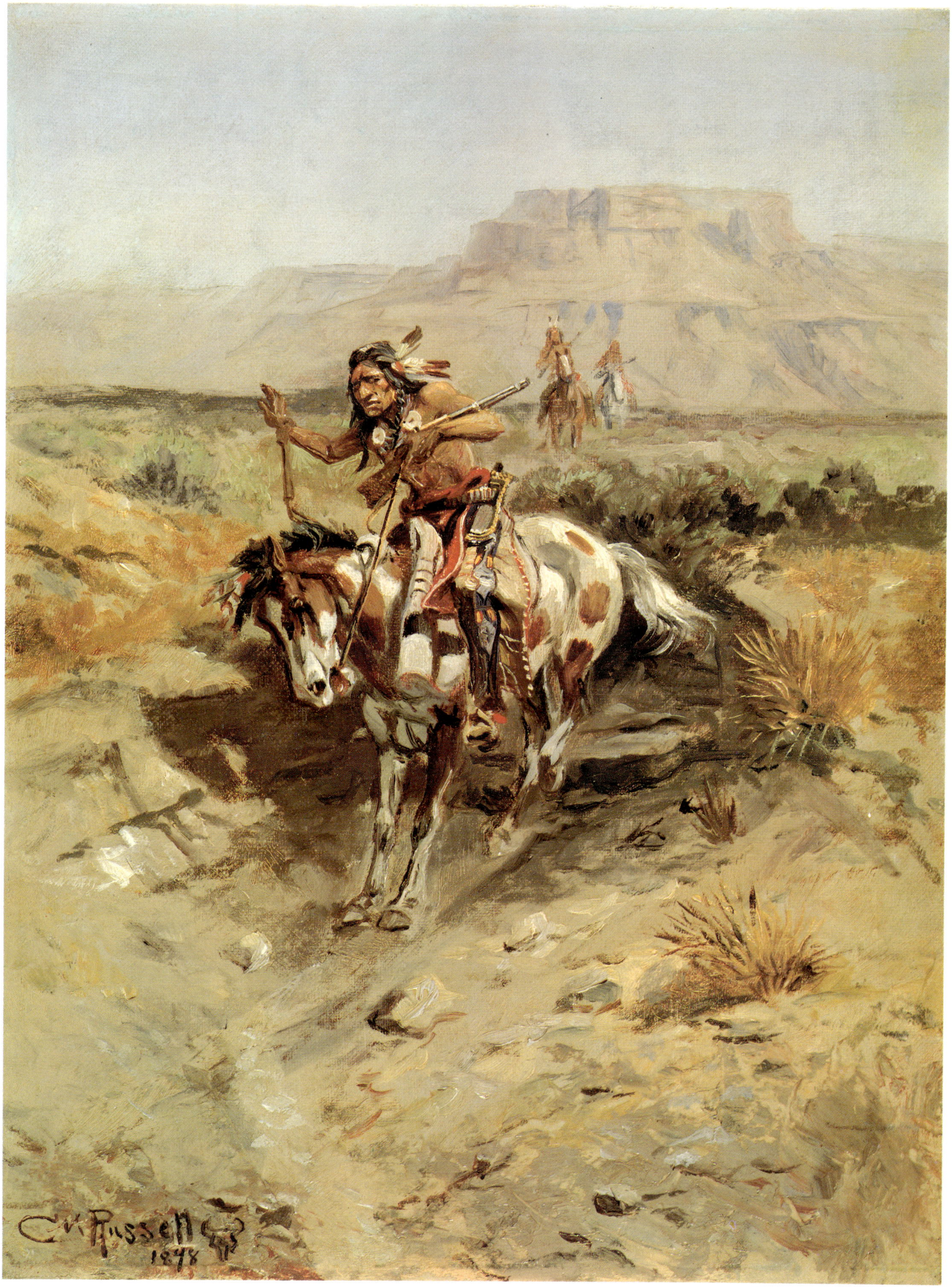
CM Russell
1898

Council of War

c. 1892 • $22\frac{5}{8} \times 34\frac{7}{8}$ in. • Watercolor on paper.

Between some Indian tribes and nations, peace was a continually precarious matter. Russell is here picturing the moment in which a peace council between the Piegans and the Crows reportedly became a council of war. Chiefs and subchiefs of the two tribes had been negotiating successfully toward a treaty when a Piegan medicine man's scalp was found in a bundle of moccasins, where Crows had hidden it.

At this moment a Piegan chief is confronting the assembled Crows with the evidence, leaving open no alternative to war. Russell has chosen to concentrate the drama in the sturdy figure at the center, holding out the scalp in one hand and grasping his coupstick—with its tally of battle-blows—in the other. At a later stage in his career Russell might have somehow taken this story outside to where he could see and feel the sky and mountains all around and find a reflection in them of the tense action that is present and the lively action to come.

That horizon of faces, however, with its slight variations of impassivity and concealment, does hold interest for the eye. And the coupstick, because it records the touching of enemy braves in battle whether or not they are brought down, is a reminder that, while the Indian's peace was precarious, his war represented something more than a desire to kill.

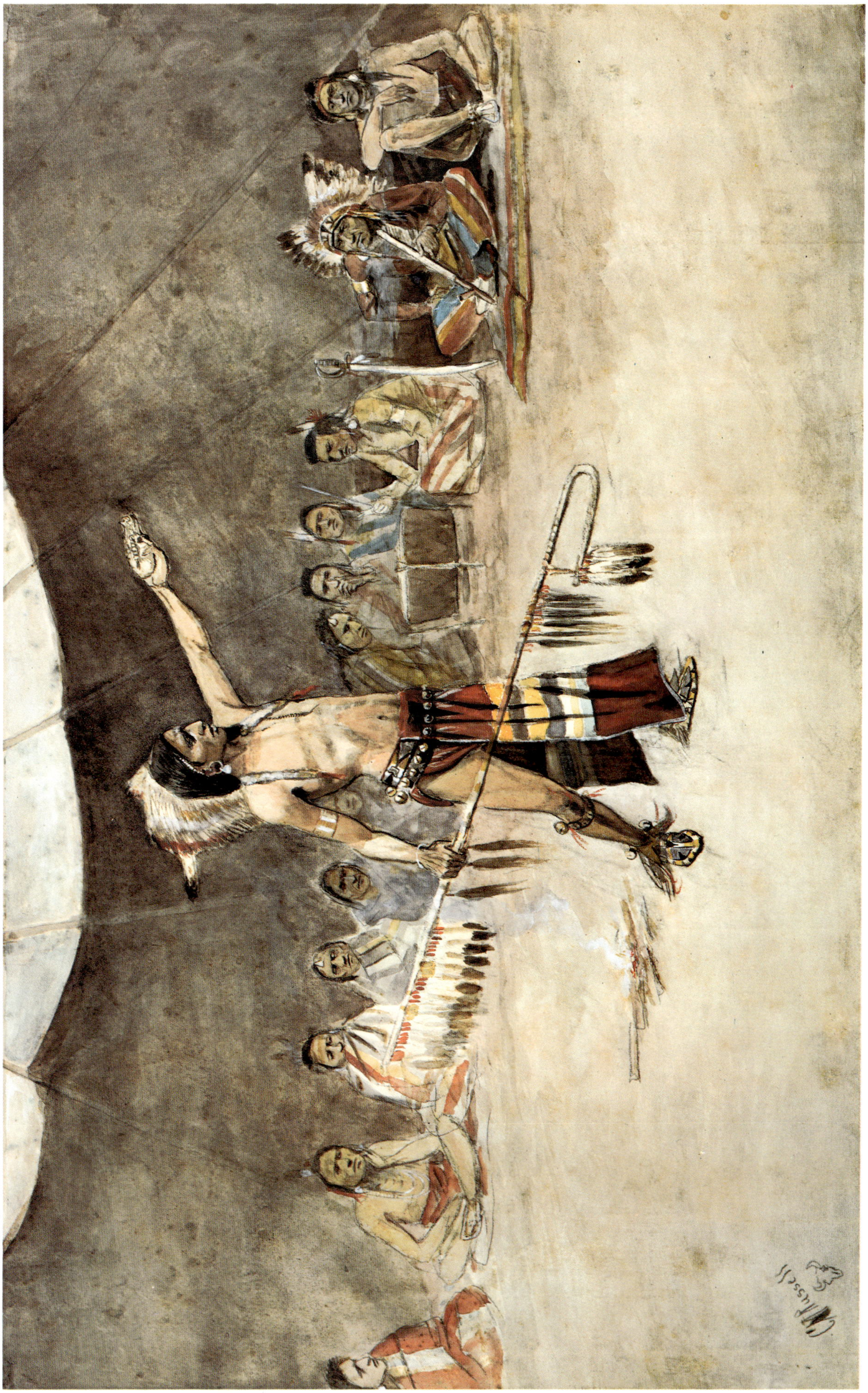
CM Russell

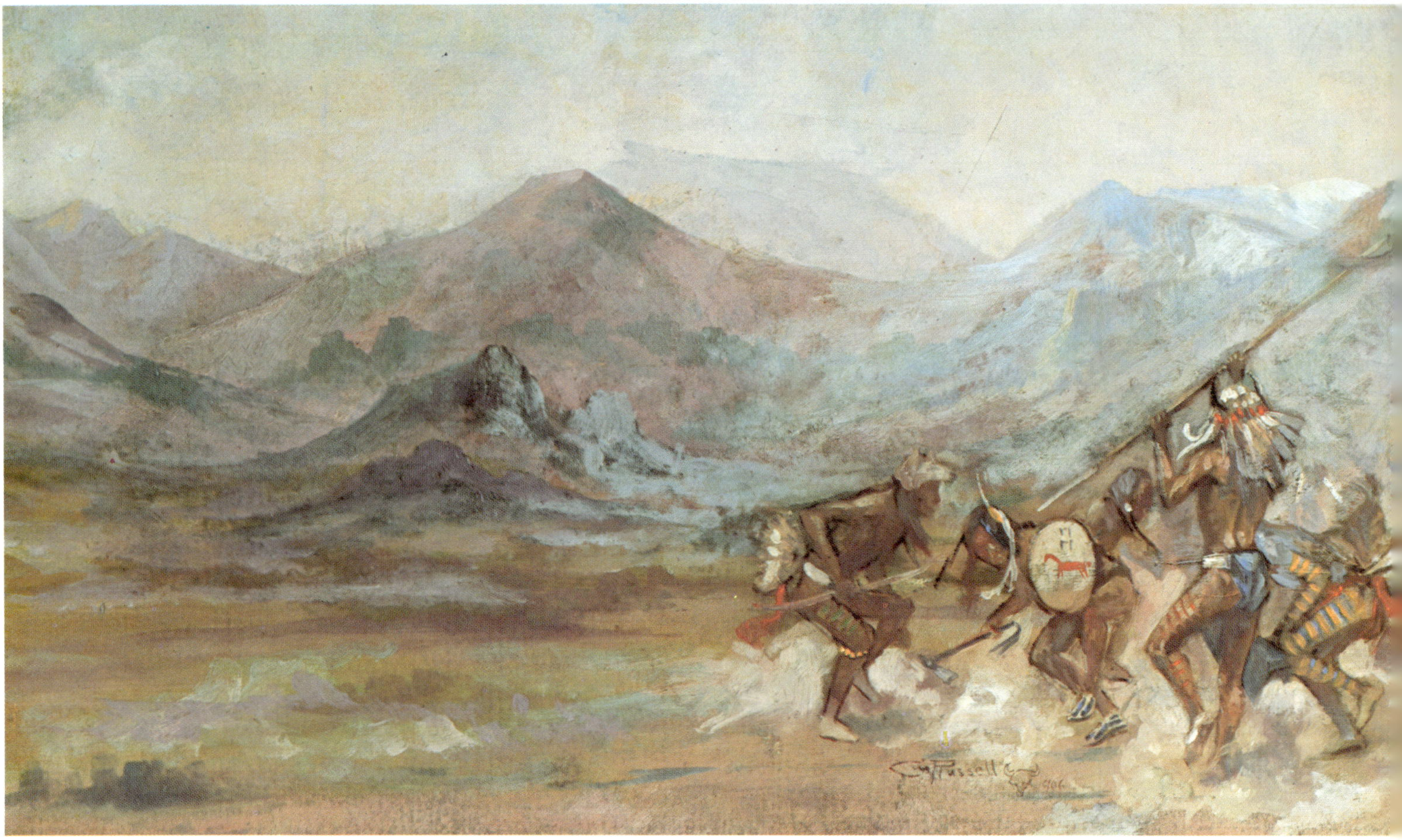

The Indian War Dance

1906 • 14¾ × 50⅛ in. • Oil on canvas.

THE ART CAREER of Charlie Russell had a distinctly sociable side to it. His spontaneous modelings in wax, for instance, or more careful watercolors at the heads of letters, all were intuitive, skilled elements in the way he talked and worked with others. The present painting is a special case in point.

Charles Schatzlein was a close friend, himself an artist and a dealer, who soon after Russell's marriage did his best to help by selling what paintings he could—even at the going price of twenty-

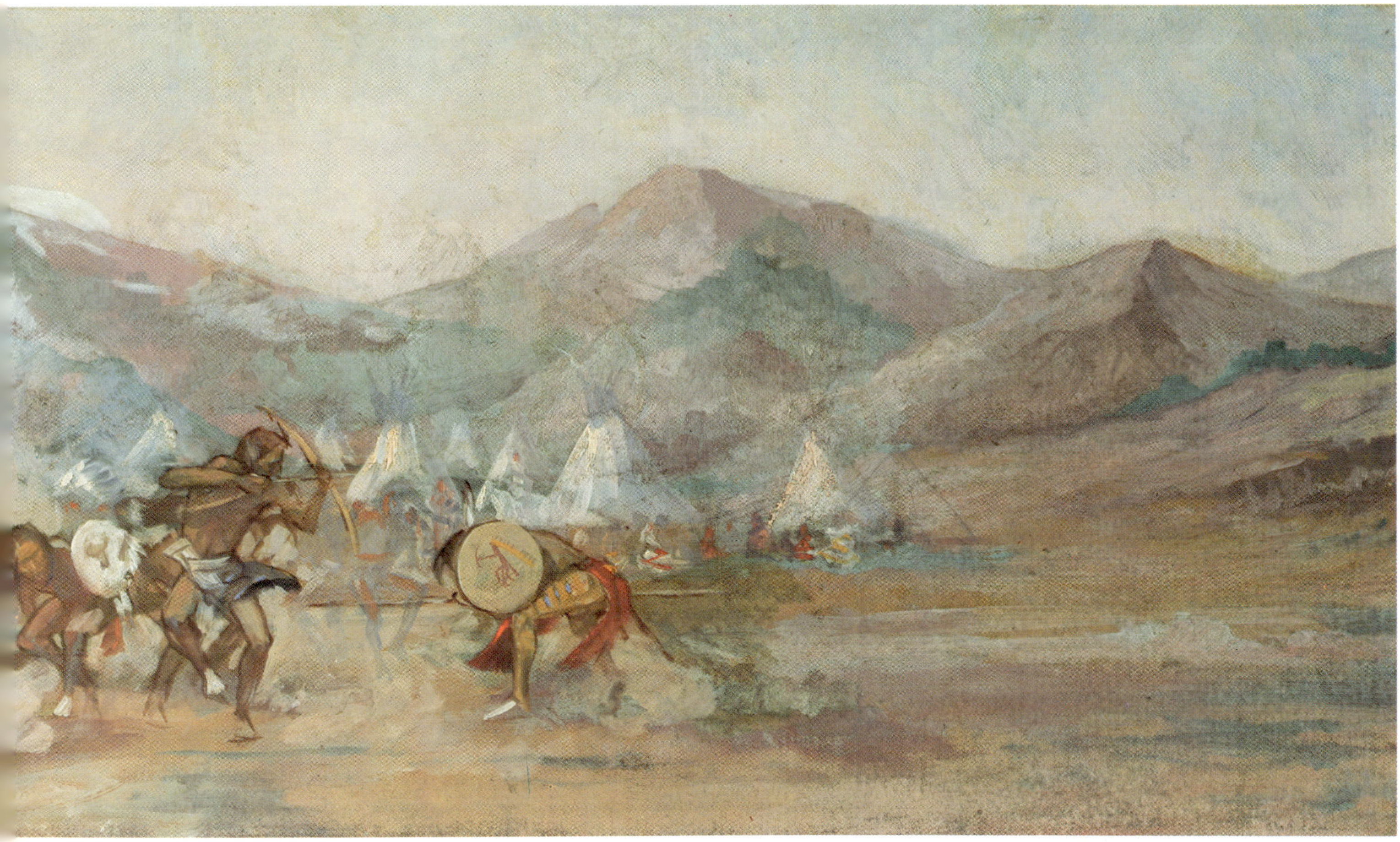

five dollars or so. Schatzlein, inspired by the mountains and canyons around his hometown of Butte, Montana, covered two walls of his living room with a forty-foot frieze of this landscape. When his artist friends came to visit he invited them to add scenes of their own against his background. The idea evidently appealed to Russell, and he brought on this handful of his Indians, and their tepees, giving immediacy to the distant dance of mountains. (After all, it was one of the ways he liked to work on his own: setting a scene first, and then populating it.) His section was later removed to become this separate painting.

Dance was an important embodiment of prayer for the Indian—in this case, of course, for victory over an enemy.

War Council

c. 1896 • 13⅞ x 21 in. • Watercolor on paper.

SOME COUNCILS—like the one on page 133—are held indoors in the tribal lodge, and are preliminary to a whole exploit of war. Others come together after the war has been undertaken and warriors are on the move, when interim decisions must be made as to the good or bad "medicine" of one strategy or another. The need may simply be for a sort of "vote of confidence" from the Great Spirit (coming by some inner or outer sign), lacking which the entire project might be given up. This particular venture seems to have reached a critical point; and the lookout in the background indicates that it may already have reached well into hostile country.

So the drama of the moment may involve more tension than communicates emphatically from this huddle of squatting figures, each somewhat self-contained, insulated against the flow of feeling and concern that must have existed. By this time in his career, Russell was manifestly expert at connecting and directing his drama when the action of its cast was mainly overt and perhaps quite strenuous. But the latent drama of people considering rather than primarily experiencing a crisis he sometimes found elusive—except as he could show it through facial expressions. The problem in a way is that of the medieval artist—who is not yet Giotto, and certainly not Leonardo da Vinci—tackling the Last Supper.

Yet with Russell the action is never far away, and we'll be snatched up into it the minute any battle is joined.

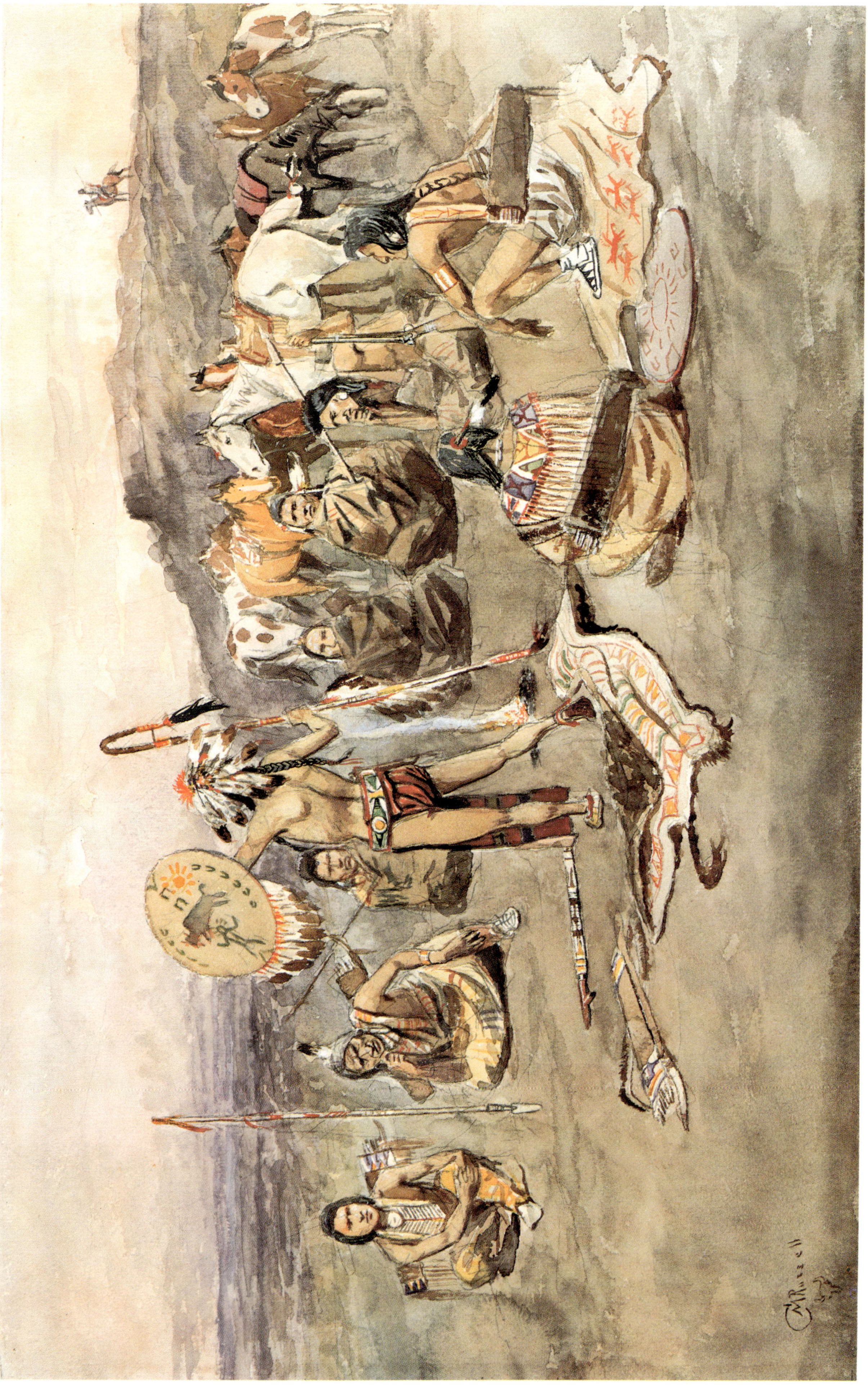

Indians Attacking

1895 • 13⅞ × 19¾ in. • Watercolor on paper.

At first glance this tightly composed watercolor can give the impression of a single body of fighters rushing toward some battle just off to the left. Then we notice the Sioux warrior in the left foreground shooting back while still riding ahead. His arrow is flying toward the Blood Indian who is coming furiously at him with his raised lance.

In his book *Trails Plowed Under,* Russell describes a battle that might have suggested his painting. After the Sioux burned the northern buffalo range, the angry and hungry Bloods had come after them; but their first encounter had been indecisive. Then there were taunts from the Sioux, saying (in Russell's words) "it ain't no credit to the Sioux to take the hair of a Blood, these trophies are only good to trim squaw's leggin's with."

This so riles one of the Bloods that he plunges into the attack with the vehemence we see here; his charge "rallies and nerves up his own men so they're right on his ponies tail when he hits the Sioux bunch, who are so busy dodgin' . . . they're all killed before they come to."

To help keep his picture from flying off the page, Russell reinforces the turning back of the three forward Sioux by the progressive downward movement of the lances arching overhead—which also, incidentally, give a kind of stopped-motion continuity to the thrust of the principal lance. Again, he has brought a degree of control to a scene of explosive energy.

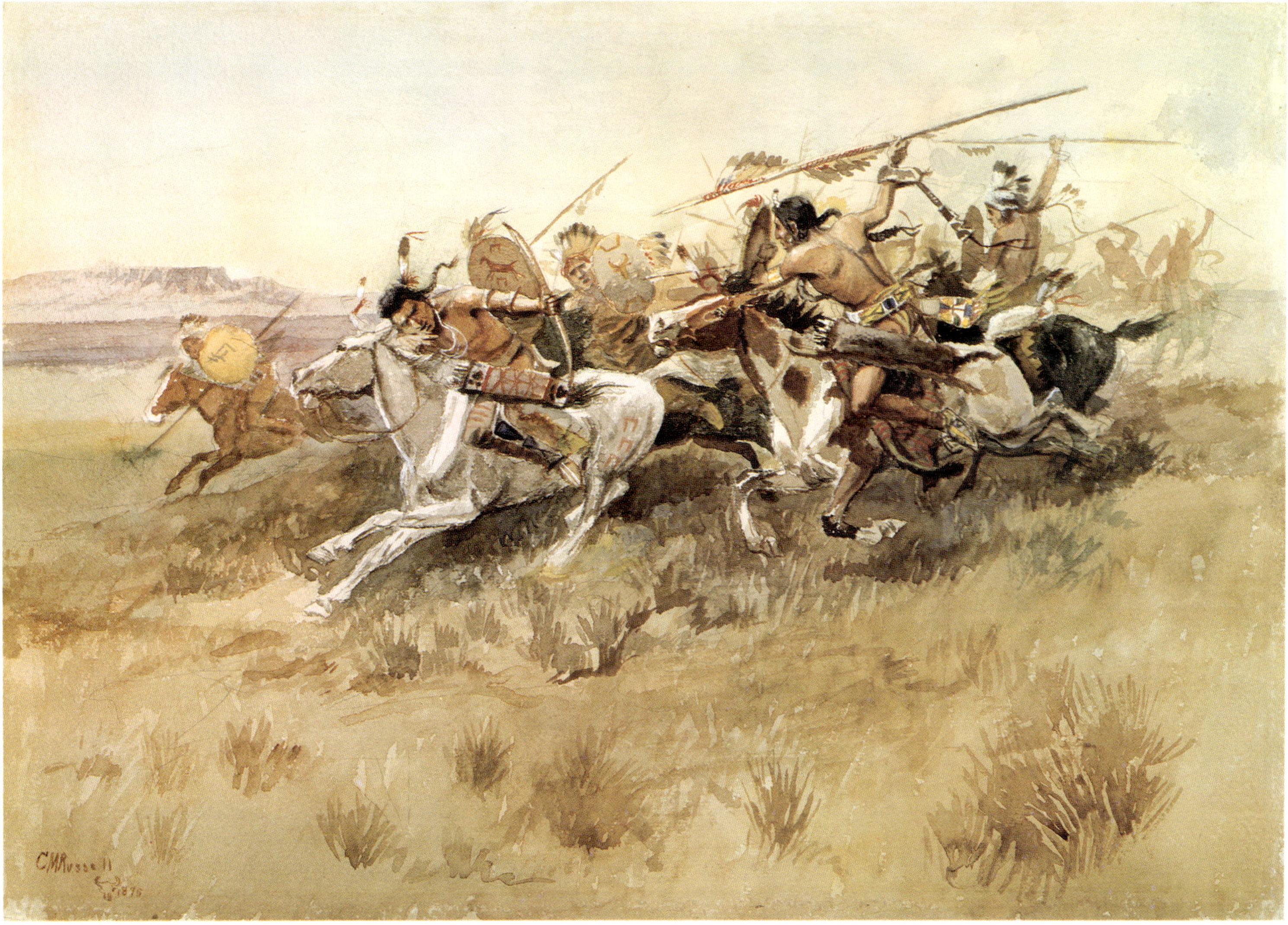
CMRussell

For Supremacy

1895 • 23⅛ × 35 in. • Oil on canvas.

HERE IS A CRITICAL MOMENT in the big battle between Piegans and Crows precipitated by the war council of page 133. The forces were large, and the losses reportedly heavy on both sides before the Crows—who had made the mistake of killing a Piegan medicine man on the way to the "peace" conference—were forced back across the Missouri. Russell has come in close enough to show individual encounters, while suggesting through the haze of dust and smoke the size of the whole battlefield.

The artist drew for vividness on his own experience whenever and however possible—a fact that is easier to demonstrate in regard to the cowboys than the Indians in his pictures. Yet not only were there his months with the Blackfeet in 1888, but before that his encounters with Indians during his first year as a cowboy in the Judith Basin. And the overland cattle drive down to the Northern Pacific Railroad later that year took him past the scene of a very recent Piegan-Crow battle. Then, as their drive passed through the Crow reservation, they were stopped by Indians demanding toll for the cattle, and came close to battle themselves.

These lusty tribal encounters therefore were far from being legendary concoctions for this artist. The men in them were from tribes he knew at first hand, and the country was his own country: he was equipped not only to portray but to stand up uniquely for them both.

This oil, by the way, is another of the few that he chose to sign with his name and customary buffalo skull in the bottom right-hand instead of left-hand corner—where it would be least likely to interfere with or be trodden on by the action.

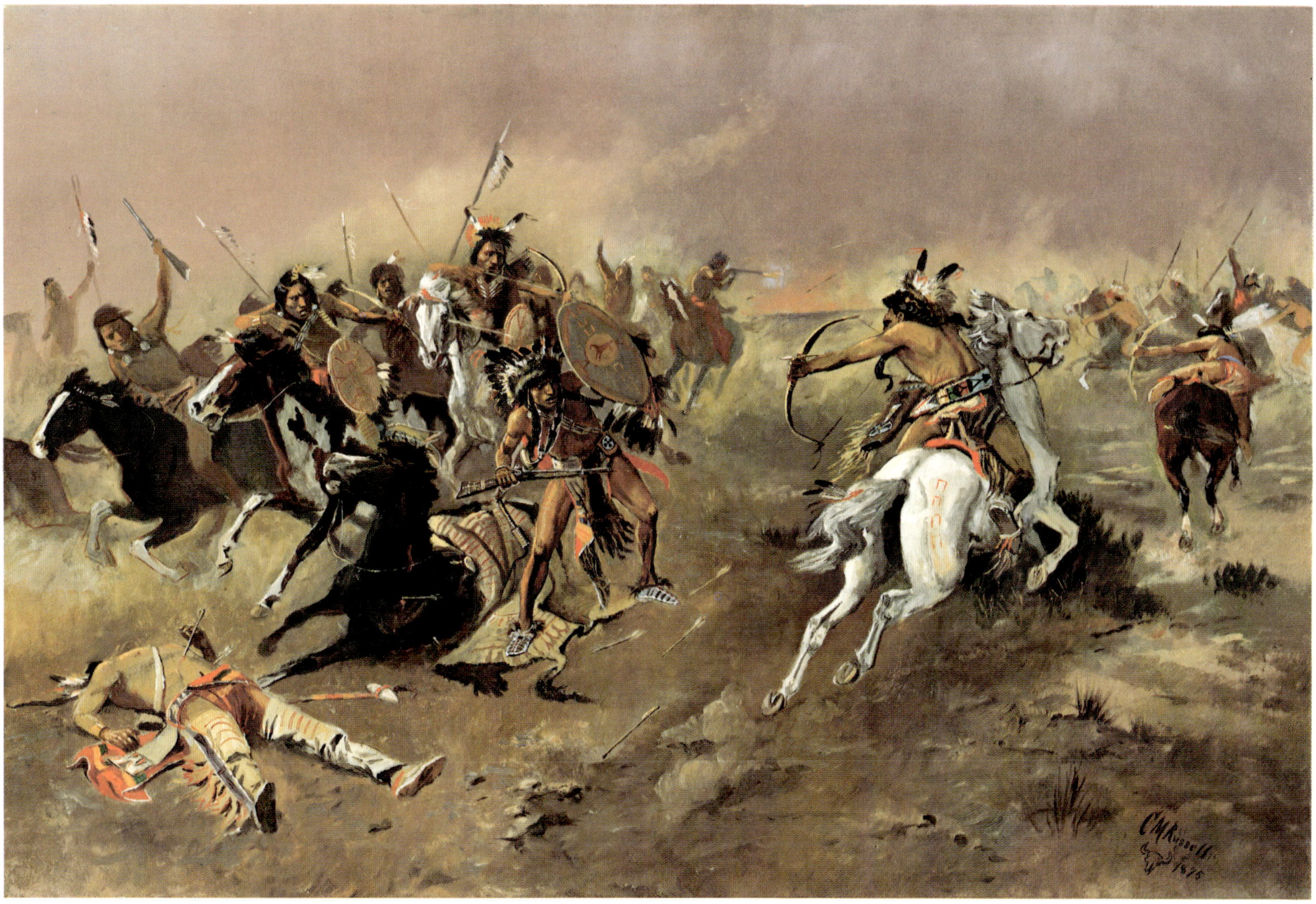
CMRussell

Wild Horse Hunters

1913 • 30 × 47 in. • Oil on canvas.

THE HORSE, in whatever situation, was almost as congenial a subject for Charles Russell as the cowboy or Indian on its back. And always as convincing. In most cases, however, the horse's action is altogether in the service of the rider's action.

But that's true on only one side of this superbly composed confrontation. And for all the skill required of the cowboy, the confrontation—as Russell has deployed it—is most centrally one of horse against horse.

The strategy really goes past deployment to something like choreography: those horses, the cowboy's red and the wilderness's black (.arched over by red), pull against each other with enough tension to snap any mere rope. The one Russell has painted is practically invisible anyway; but the whole space around it which is scooped out of the ground is taut with amazing tensile strength, and our eyes trust it to conclude successfully this contest between high-powered skill and instinctive power itself. It is a contest being fought in many Russell paintings, but nowhere more intensely than here.

There's special subjest-interest as well in the cowboy's technique, identifying him as a "dally-man." He has taken a dally, or half-hitch, around the knob called a saddlehorn, enabling him either to tighten up or slacken off on his rope, as the need may arise, like a sailor handling his main sheet in a stiff breeze. The alternative, as Renner points out, is to be a tie-hard-man, securing the end of your rope with a knot and so forfeiting all that give and take in the contest. As a cowboy, Russell came out at least once in favor of the tie-hard-man. But as the artist of these careening horses, he has made a lively case for the give-and-take.

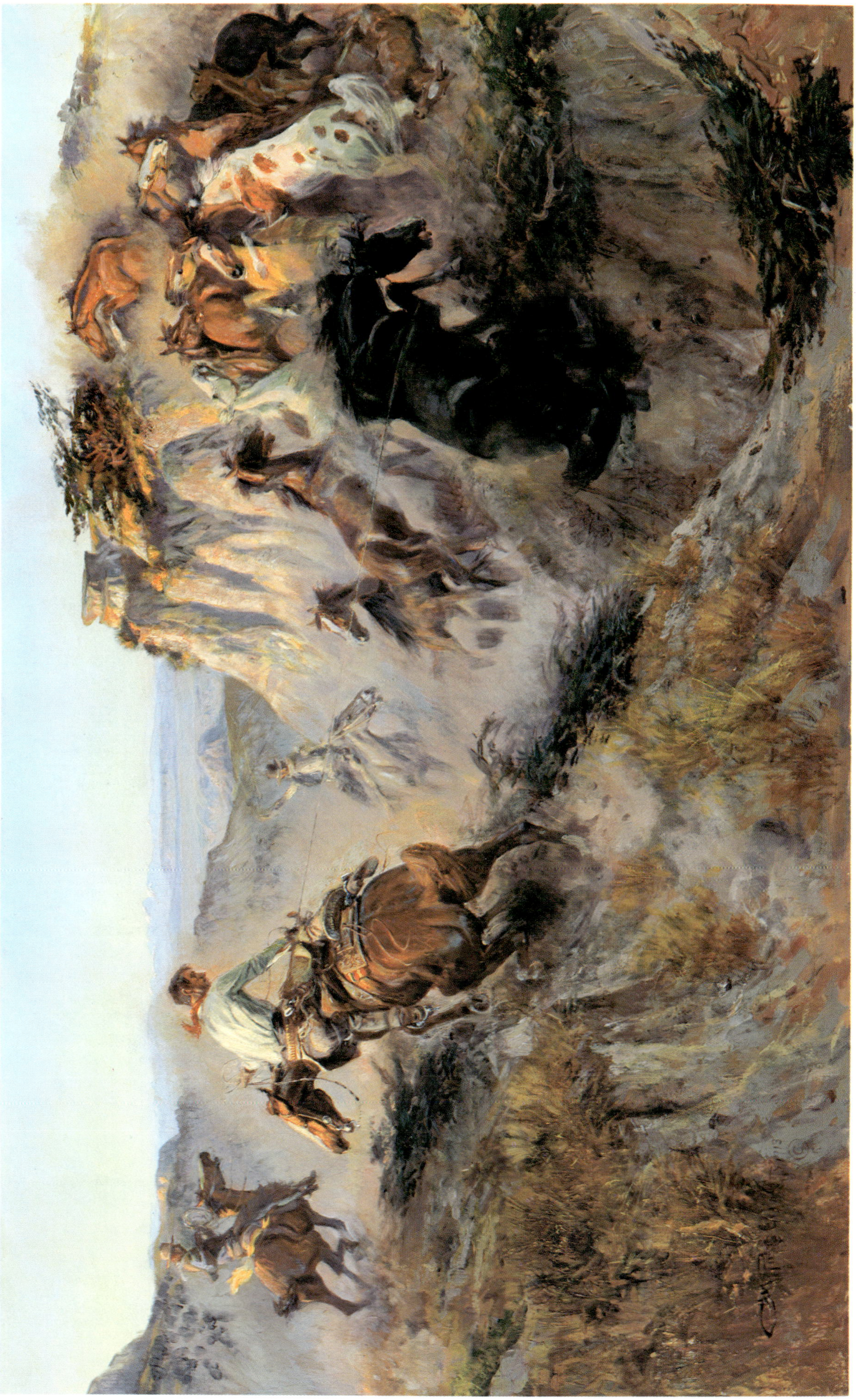

Sun Worship in Montana

1907 • 22⅜ × 17½ in. • Gouache on paper.

THE SUBJECT HERE is another one for which Russell could call directly on memories of his few months with the Blackfeet in 1888. Painting it almost twenty years later, he gives us the benefit of a color range that can intensify its sunlight with special warmth in the red surrounding this young mother and the infant she holds high. It intensifies her prayer as well, no doubt asking for him long life, vigorous health, and great success in war and in the hunt.

Russell's feeling about sun worship shows also in his story, "How Lindsay Turned Indian," originally written in this same year of 1907:

> "I remember one day we're sittin' outside the shack, clear of the eaves. There's a chinook blowin' 'n' the roof's drippin' like it's rainin'. It's mighty pleasant in the sun out of the wind. . . . [The] white Injun's smokin' his mixture of willer bark 'n' tobacco, while I' msizin' him up. . . . He says he's talkin' to the sun; he's thankin' him for the warm wind that melts the snow.
>
> " 'Don't you belive in God?' says I. 'Yes,' says he. 'What kind of one?' I asks.
>
> " 'That one,' says he, pointin' to the Sun. 'The one I can see 'n' have watched work for many years. He gathers the clouds 'n' makes it rain; then warms the ground 'n' the grass turns green. When it's time, he dries it yellow, makin' it good winter feed for the grass-eaters. Again when he's mad, my people says, he drives the rain away, dryin' up the streams 'n' water holes. If it wasn't for him, there couldn't nothin or nobody live. Do you wonder that we ask him to be good, 'n' thank him when he is? I'm all Injun but my hide; their God's my God, 'n' I don't ask for no better.' "

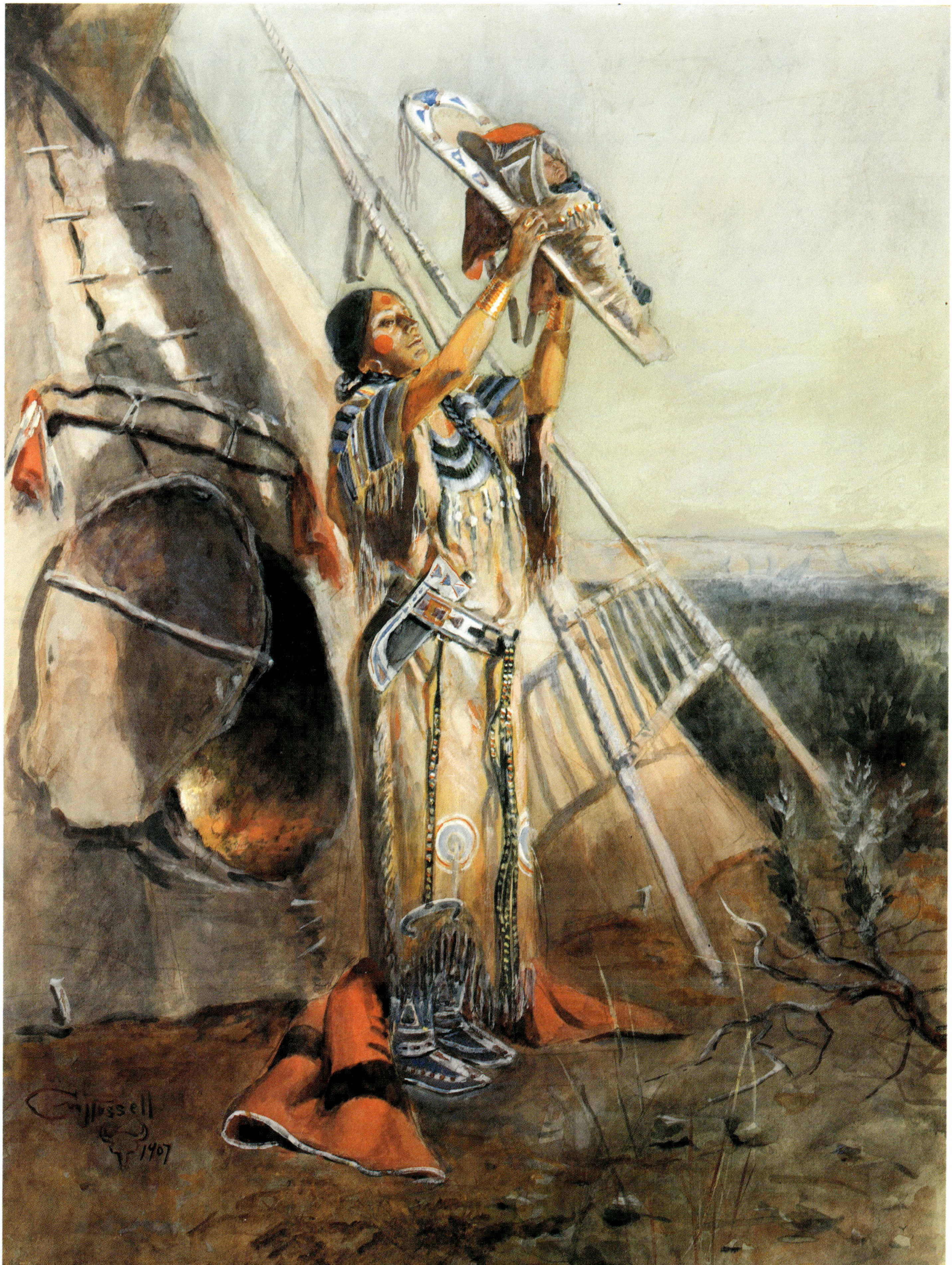
CMRussell
1907

Caught Napping

1898 • 11 × 15 in. • Watercolor on paper.

CERTAIN PAINTINGS suggest major options that Russell might have taken if he hadn't been rather well occupied with his first choices. His subject-matter departures from cowboy and Indian life resulted generally from assignments to illustrate magazines and books—of which this is one of the earliest. It was published in *Field and Stream* for January 1901, following an agreement with William Cameron, the editor, made in 1897. The initial batch of 20 black-and-white oils was to be paid for at fifteen dollars each, while each of twenty pen sketches was to bring only two dollars and fifty cents. Since this one is in color it may have done a little better for him. But it's hardly surprising that his young bride Nancy soon undertook to push the prices for his work up into a whole new range.

With its Indian guide this is of course still in familiar Russell territory; but the white hunter shooting moose, the birchbark canoe, and even the water are less typical subjects.

Noticing his sure, almost virtuoso, handling of shadows and reflections, we have to remind ourselves that Russell was entirely self-taught. Could he have held his own in a wider range of subject with a Homer or a Sargent? Perhaps so, perhaps not. But the fact that he didn't let even the transcendent popularity of a Remington bother him is part of what made him every inch a Russell.

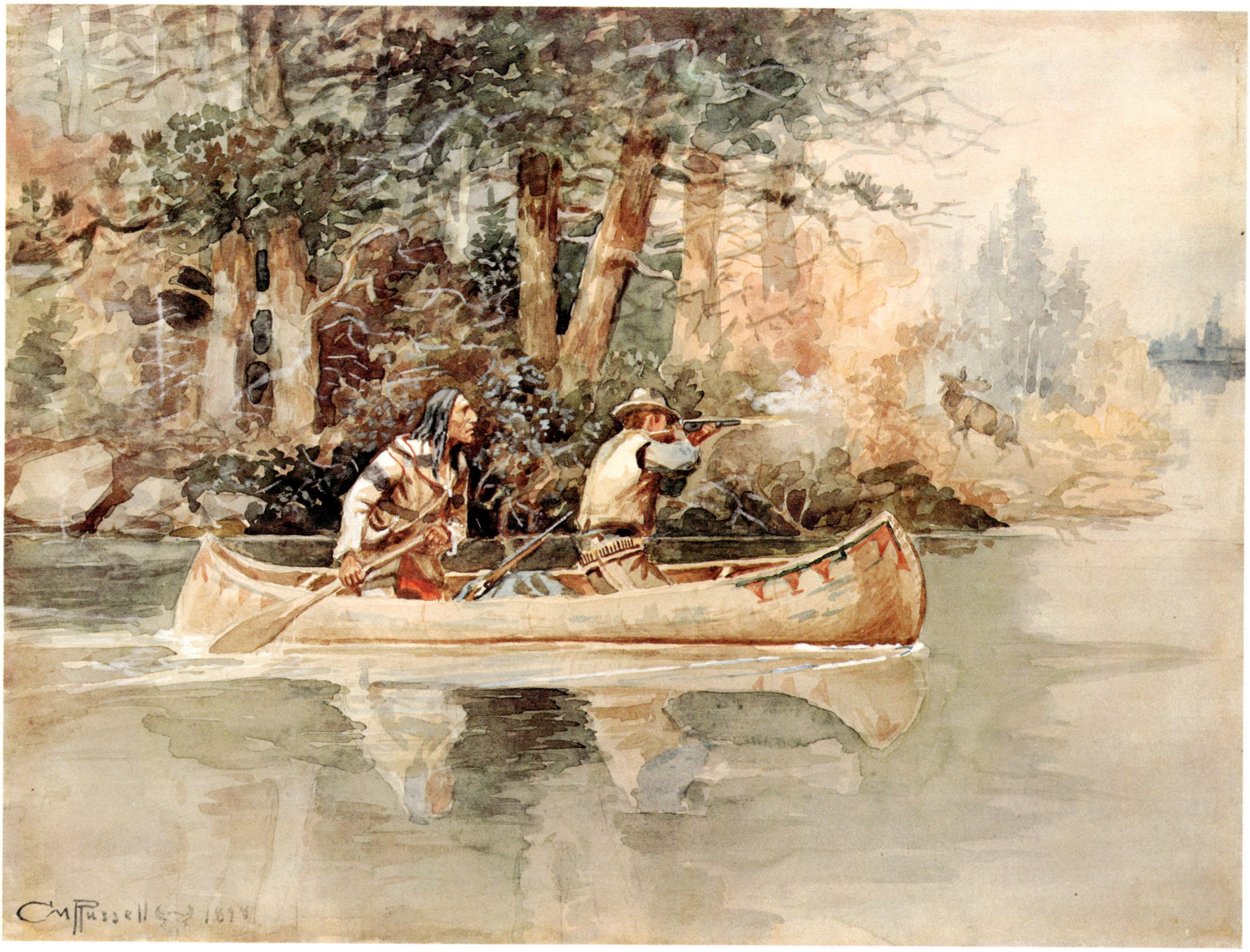
CMRussell 1898

Roping a Wolf

1901 • 10⅛ × 14⅛ in • Watercolor on paper.

THE DOMESTICATION of the Montana plains country along the Missouri River, carrying it from its old status of free, unfenced grassland to the inviting but sometimes calamitous status of farmland, was played out by successive casts of settlers. There were first the half-breed trappers; there were wood-choppers, needed to fuel the steamboats on which the trappers' furs began to be shipped; and then, when the railroads put the boats out of business and settlement began by the trainload, there were the wolfers, badly needed to secure the land against these peculiarly unpopular predators. Deprived of their natural prey—the buffalo—wolves were turning to cattle instead, and they had to go.

Wolfers generally used traps or poison—both of which incurred for them the arch-enmity of Indians. But cowboys, lured by generous government bounties, made this hunting into more of a sport during their off-hours, by going after the animals with ropes. The wolf was fierce and fast, outdodging if not outdistancing a horse. It was a rare trick to drop the rope as neatly as it's being dropped here—and this wolf isn't caught yet.

Montana's first bounty, in the early '80s, was a hundred dollars a head. Five thousand were soon turned in by one kind of hunter or another, and to avoid fiscal disaster the law had to be repealed. Later, the bounty grew more judiciously from three dollars to a 1911 high of fifteen—and even then the wolf was still going strong.

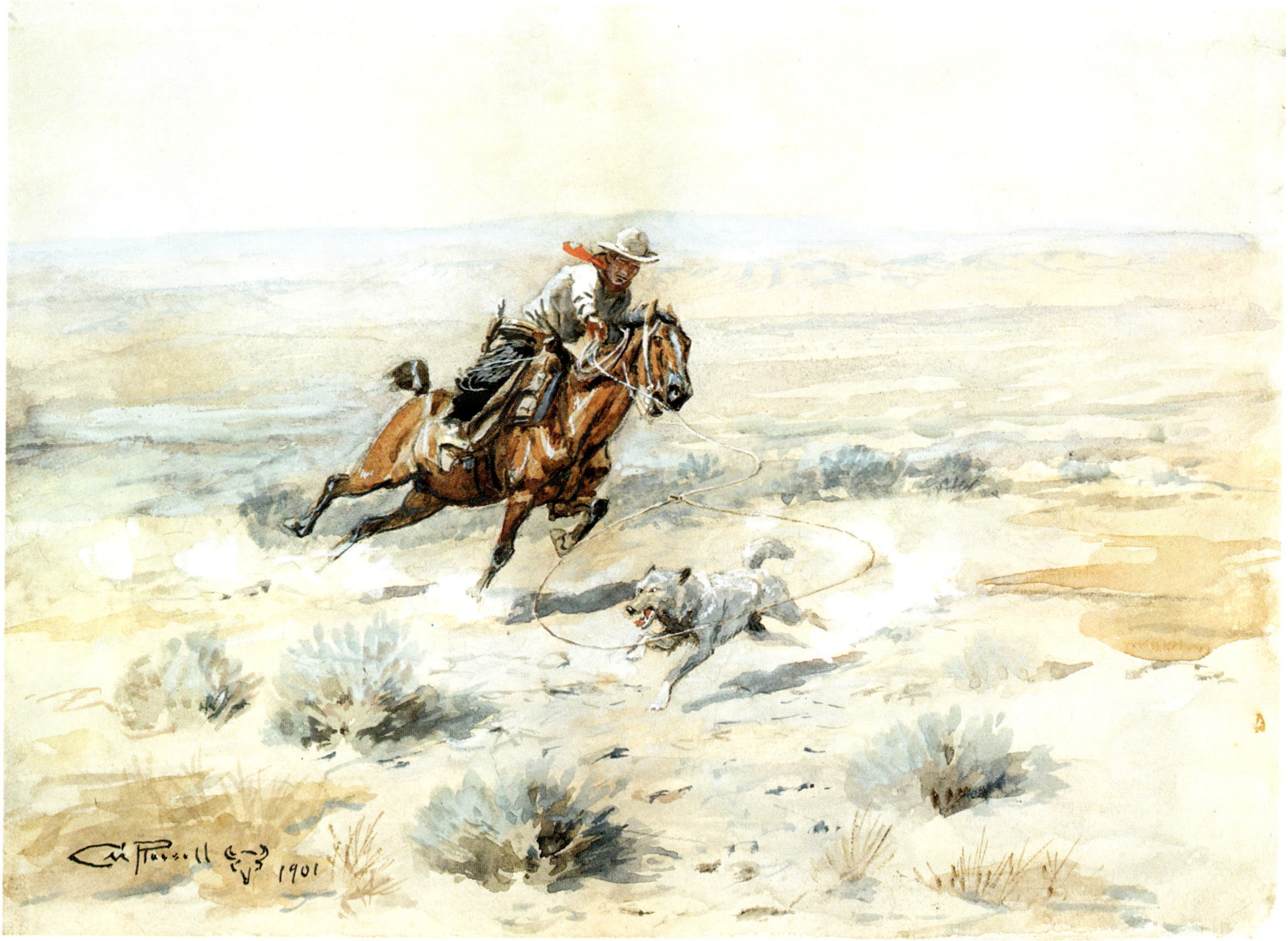

Roping a Wolf

1904 • 15⅛ × 20 in. • Oil on canvas.

RUSSELL SEEMS TO HAVE ENJOYED painting in oil and watercolor more or less equally. While it couldn't be said that he exploited the technical range of either medium to the full, he certainly knew the uses and special possibilities of each. This is one of several cases in which he treated the same basic subject in both media, perhaps at different times and almost always with different compositional results.

The earlier version of *Roping a Wolf* had been a watercolor in 1901, confining itself to a single mounted cowboy whose loop is just circling the fierce-looking "white wolf" (actually a silvery grey) hurtling across his path.

This oil, in 1904, might almost be an immediate sequel—except that two other cowboys have appeared to the right and left of the first, who is now wearing angora chaps on his legs against the presumably colder weather. Now the rope has tightened around the wolf's body and caught one of its legs, and the cowboy's horse is cooperating perfectly by pulling back on its own haunches. It looks as though one less wolf will be going after the range cattle, and one more five-dollar bill in bounty money will be paid this cowboy when he turns in the wolf's scalp.

Another difference between the two paintings is in the details of their broad landscapes. Yet each, in one way or another, uses successive clumps of sagebrush that seem to reinforce the rhythm of galloping horses and of the dust-puffs kicked up by their hooves.

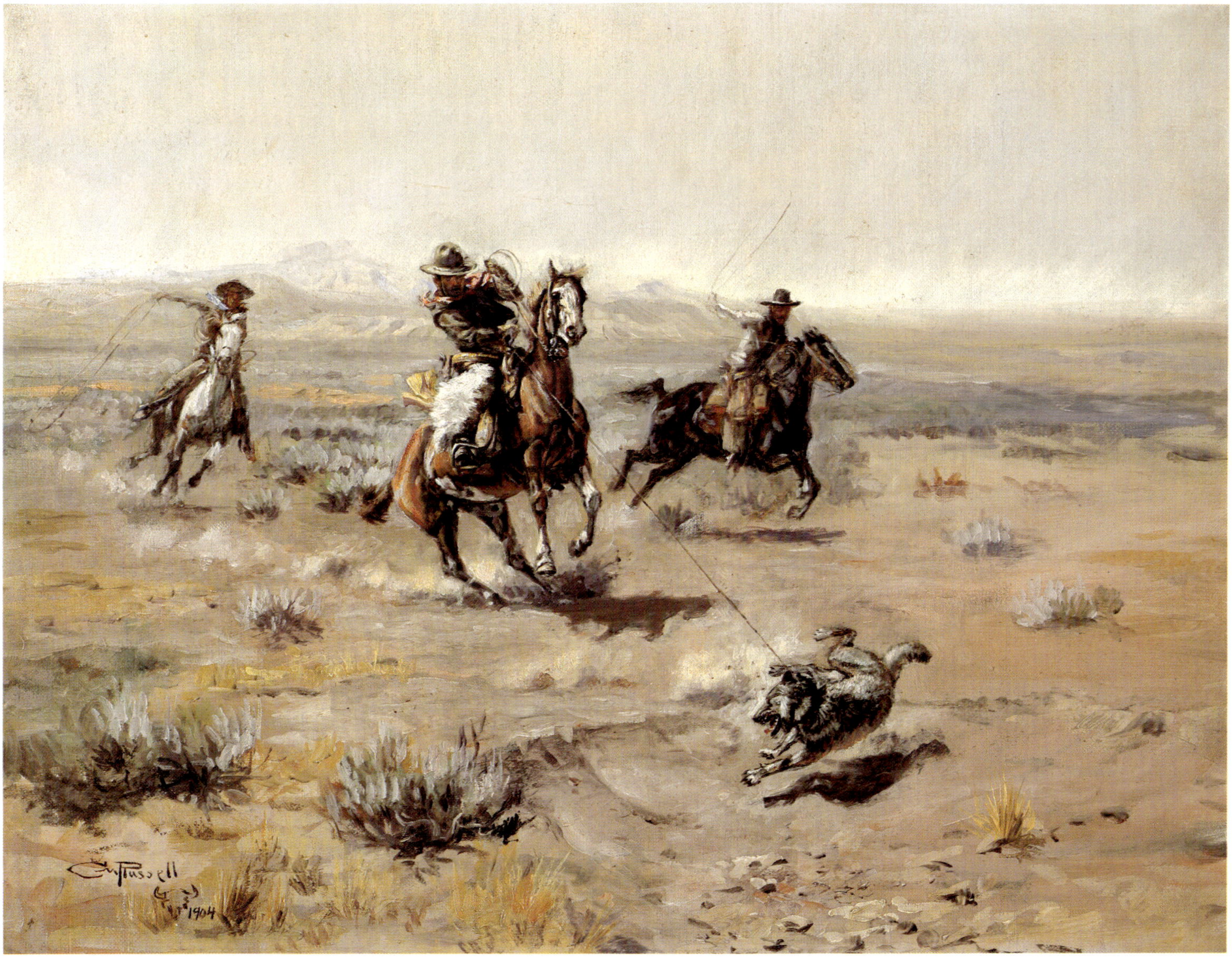

The Price of His Hide

1915 • $24\frac{1}{8} \times 36\frac{1}{8}$ in. • Oil on canvas.

When it came to stories of the Old West Charlie Russell had a double-giftedness—triple, perhaps, if you separate his way of telling them in conversation from his way of writing them down. More different from either, of course, was his way of painting them. But in any case it was a matter of touching those details which would pin down the unfolding reality of events, whether through a succession of words or an arrangement of images.

This one has to do with actual prospectors, Hank Winters and Bed-Rock Jim, and a bear that raided their camp one night in the Big Snowy Mountains. Early the next morning Winters decided, a bit recklessly, to go after the bear's hide. Frederic Renner found Winters's account of what happened in the *Plevna Herald* of June 5, 1920:

> "I plunge into the brush through the timber lookin' for trouble, and it ain't long till I find it. I hear a roar like all hell's turned loose, an' that bear's on me before I can bat an eye. I fire one shot but I'm so rattled that she goes wild. Before I can throw in another ca'tridge he knocks the gun loose from my hand, his claws tear my right sleeve from the shoulder down, cuttin' my arm plumb to the bone. Just as everythings turnin' black, I hear Bed-Rock's Winchester an' the way he throws lead shows he ain't no stranger to a gun.

Russell has picked the details needed to tell the story's essen-

> When I come to I ain't got rags enough on to pad a crutch."

tials against this chilly mountain sunrise. And the wondering horse acts as a kind of pivot between Bed-Rock's exhilaration and Winters's limp exhaustion.

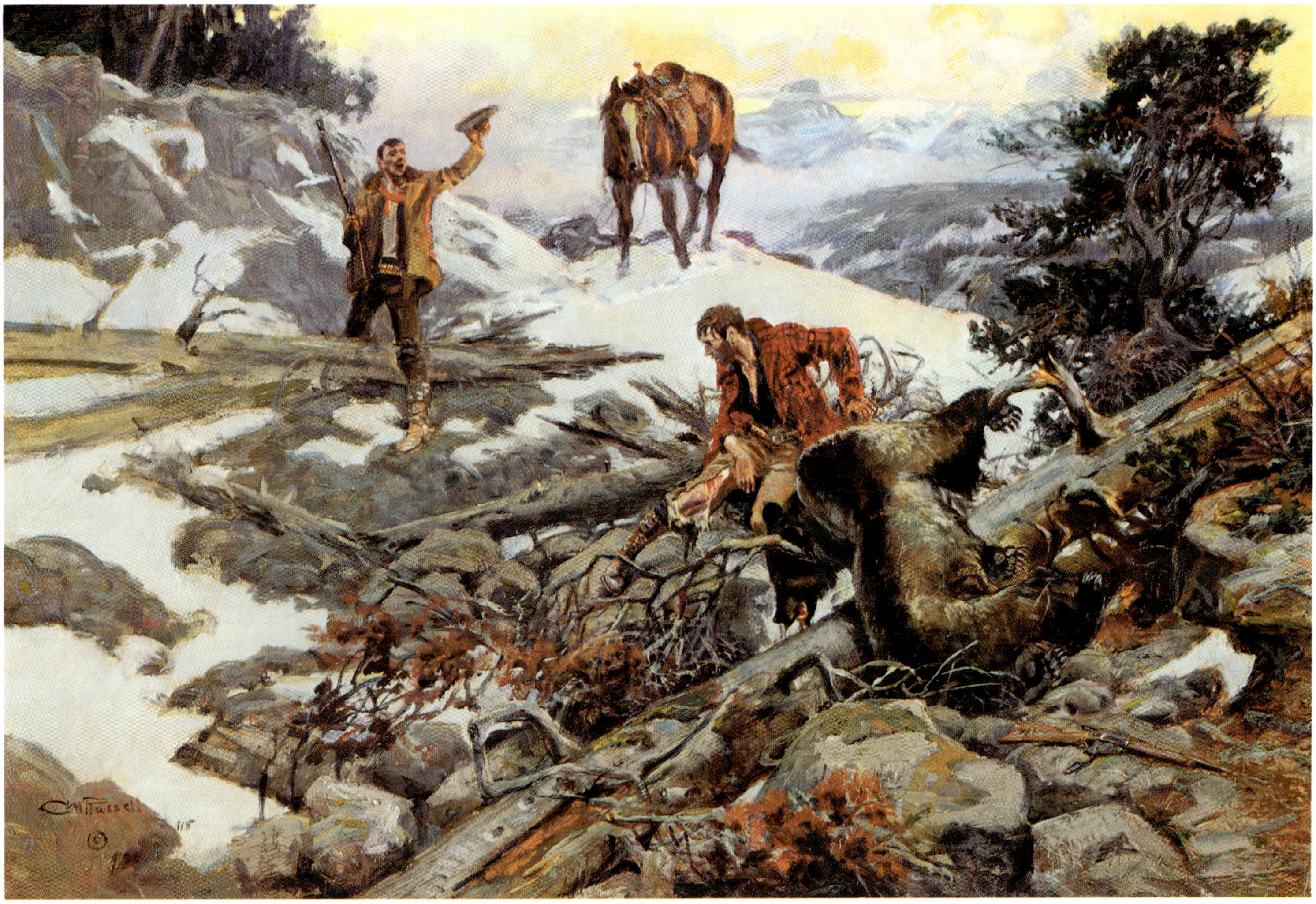

The Wolfer's Camp

1906 • 14⅞ × 21 in. • Watercolor on paper.

THE DISAPPEARANCE OF THE BUFFALO from the Northwest plains deprived the wolf of its natural prey; as a result, Montana cowmen began to experience serious losses among their herds. The bounty they offered induced cowboys, who in many cases were laid off for the winter, to get hold of a few traps and set up camp as "wolfers."

In this scene an Indian and his family have seen the campfire and have brought the carcass of an antelope; through sign language he and the wolfer are negotiating some kind of trade—maybe for tobacco or ammunition.

This watercolor is another in which Russell brings together warm, close details against a cold and vast expanse of landscape, with just enough color over the majestic mountains to echo the life nearby. The chosen details are of course pertinent and informative, such as the traps and the saddles (notice the simplicity, by contrast, of the Indian's saddle), the wolfskins hung up to dry, and the roaring fire that is warming as well as cooking.

He tells a story, as so often, which goes beyond such simple particulars to the essentials of an encounter: in this case the effort to communicate an arrangement which will meet human needs on both sides of a racial wall, with mutual respect and the sense of belonging to the same country.

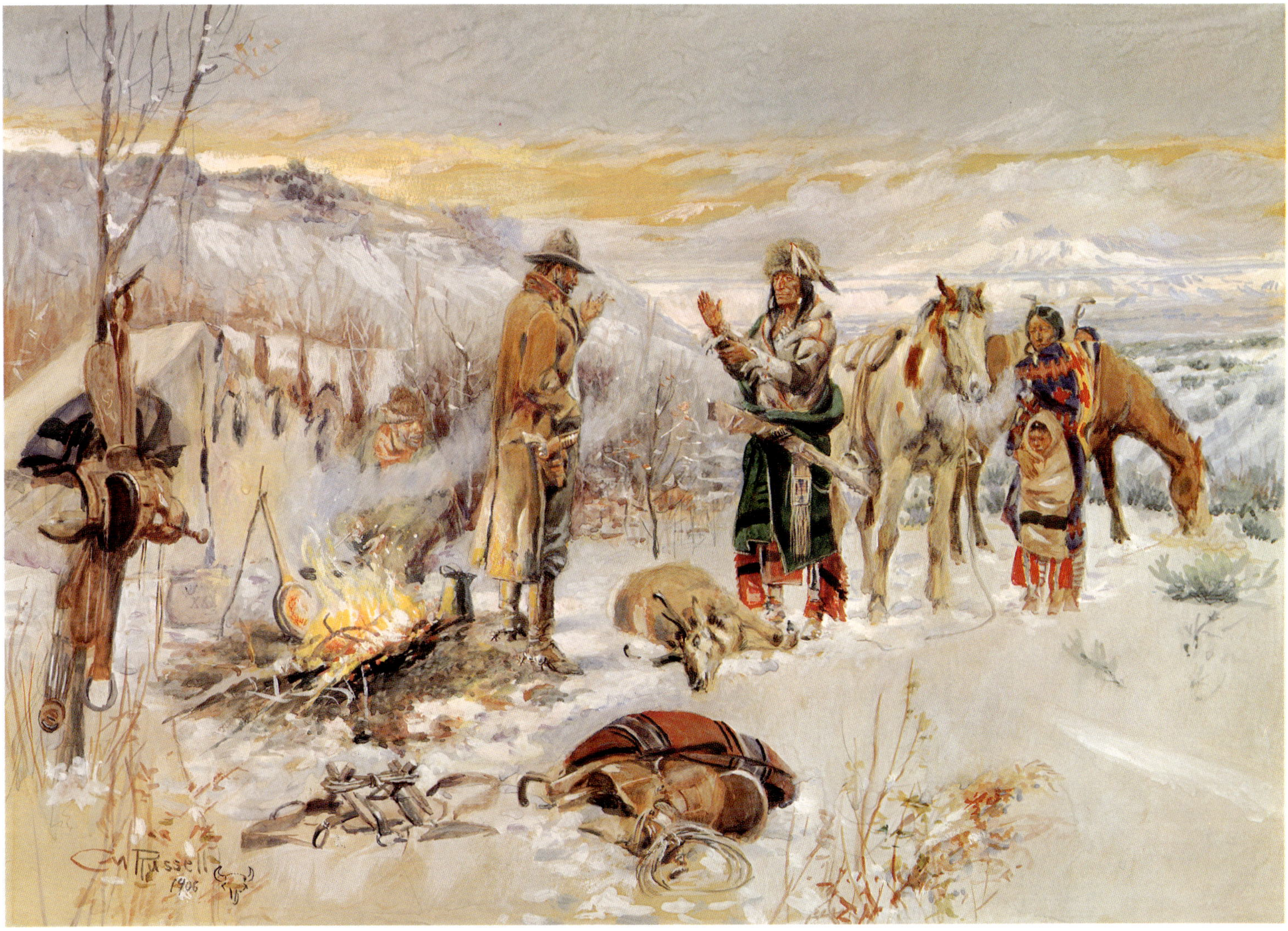
CM Russell
1906

Lost in a Snowstorm—We Are Friends

1888 • 24 × 43⅛ in. • Oil on canvas.

BLIZZARDS IN THE Montana territory could be swift and bewildering, soon blanketing over the few landmarks. "Nothing between us and the North Pole except bob-wire fence," the old-timers used to warn, perhaps on a deceptively mild Indian-summer morning.

It was into just such a day, on January 12, 1888, that the storm came crashing which could well have prompted this gifted early painting, and which has been known ever since as the "schoolchildren's storm." At midday it was still warm; and when in mid-afternoon the blizzard struck over much of the upper plains, its toll took in dozens of children on their way home from school across the prairie.

Although cowboys were better fitted to outwit these extremes of weather, Russell's painting dramatizes how crucially dependent even they could be on those with still deeper knowledge of the land. Fortunate enough to come across a few friendly Indians, these two are being told through the Indian leader's sign language that the friends from whom they have been separated are "on the other side of the mountain."

The story told on this wide canvas—with buzzards circling ominously overhead and the North Pole seeming close indeed—is well reflected in the two-part title. And the word "friends" reaches warmly two ways: across the mountain, and between both these small parties.

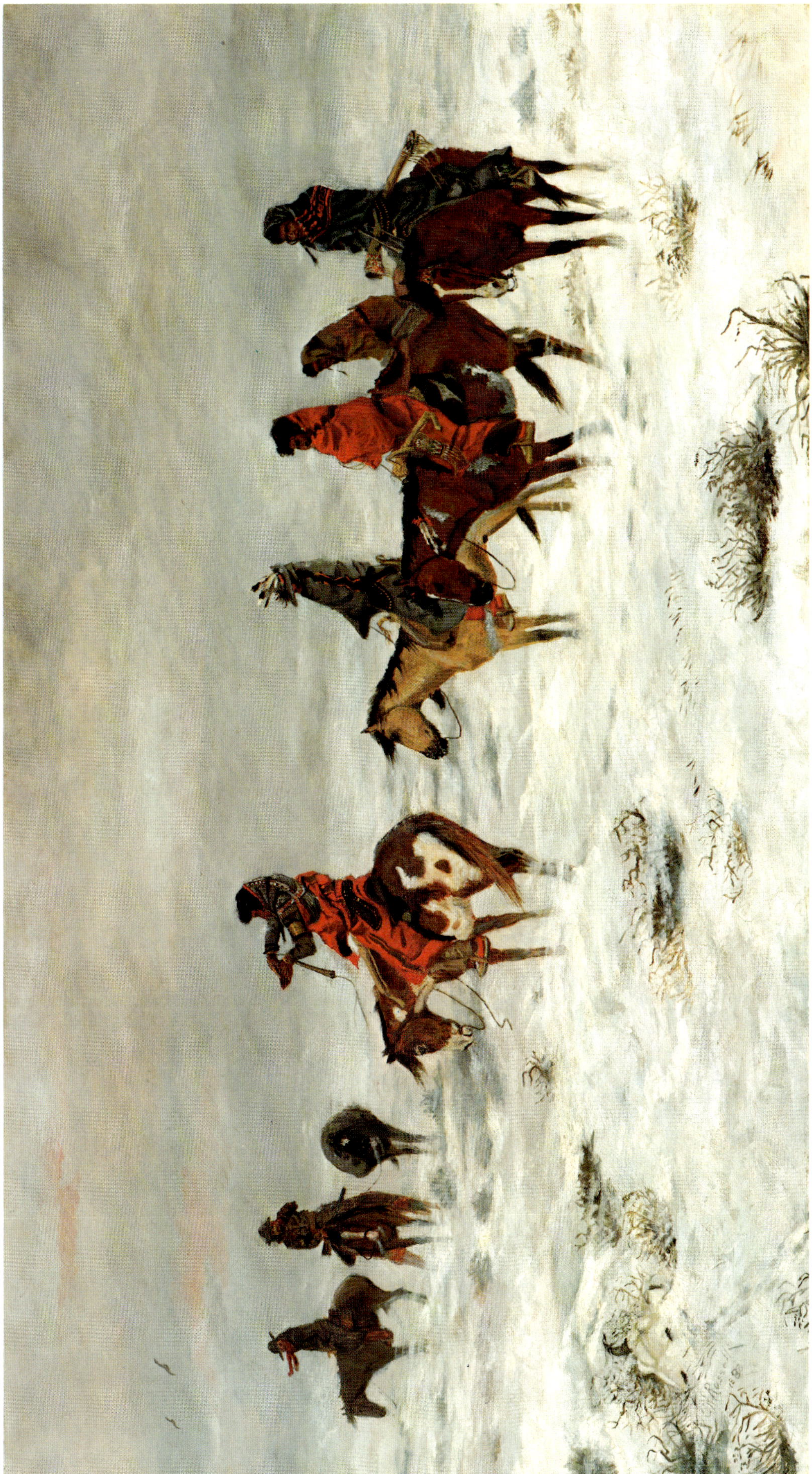